Twenty-Eight Pounds Ten Shillings
A WINDRUSH STORY

by

Tony Fairweather

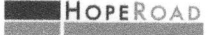

HopeRoad Publishing
PO Box 55544
Exhibition Road
London SW7 2DB

www.hoperoadpublishing.com
@hoperoadpublish

First published in Great Britain by HopeRoad 2022
This special edition published 2023
Copyright © 2022 Tony Fairweather

The right of Tony Fairweather to be identified as the author of this work has been asserted by him in accordance with the Copyright, Designs and Patents Act 1988.

All rights reserved. No part of this book may be reproduced, stored in a retrieval system or transmitted in any form or by any means, electronic, mechanical, photocopying, recording or otherwise, without the prior permission of the publishers.
This book is sold subject to the condition that it shall not, by way of trade or otherwise, be lent, re-sold, hired out or otherwise circulated without the publisher's prior consent in any form of binding or cover other than that in which it is published and without a similar condition including this condition being imposed on the subsequent purchaser.

A CIP catalogue record for this book is available from the British Library

ISBN: 978-1-913109-19-6
e-ISBN: 978-1-913109-28-8

'Those weeks on the Empire Windrush ultimately gave life and hope for future generations to build and achieve their dreams. On behalf of us all we thank them for being the original trailblazers'
Orin Lewis OBE and Beverley De-Gale OBE, Co-Founders, African Caribbean Leukaemia Trust

'A wonderfully written story of a generation and the happy and sad times spent together on their journey to England'
Junior Giscombe, Singer, Songwriter and Producer

'A book telling the stories of the Windrush generation is vital not only for this generation but for generations to come'
Rudolph Walker CBE OBE, Actor

'From the docks in the Caribbean to Tilbury docks in the UK, that journey is yet another chapter in the untold stories of a Windrush generation. GREAT READ!'
Daddy Ernie, Radio Superjam

'What a wonderful story of a generation who brought an exuberant and pioneering spirit to the British shores'
Carroll Thompson, Singer, Songwriter and Producer

'An essential addition to the history of those who made the post-war journey from the Caribbean to 'the mother country', to those that followed, and their descendants. It is maybe through Fiction that we can get the fullest understanding of the motivations, lives, loves and betrayal felt by so many. For those that faced and still face hostility and continuing institutionalised racism'
Tim O'Dell, Brixton Library

Tony Fairweather was born in Clapham South, South London, the son of Jamaican parents. He opened one of the first Black bookshops in the UK, with an art gallery and artifacts, located beneath the new Brixton Recreation Centre. He then went on to work for the *Voice* newspaper heading up its bookclub. In 1989 he founded 'The Write Thing', an events company established to promote Black authors, which led to his working with a veritable Who's Who of the Black literary world while producing events in the UK, USA and Africa. Tony is the founder and curator of the Windrush Collection and the Windrush Exhibition of artifacts associated with the Windrush Generation. He lives in South London.

Names, characters, places and incidents are the products of the author's imagination or are used fictitiously to build a believable historical world. Any resemblance to actual events, locales or persons, living or dead, is entirely coincidental.

All songs' names and words in this novel (unless stated below) are the sole rights of the author.

The language used in this book is of its time. Some people may find it offensive ... and so did the people at whom it was directed.

A Glossary at the end of the book may help those readers unfamiliar with some of the terms used.

FOREWORD

It is no surprise to me that Tony, the founder of the Windrush Collection and Exhibition, has written such a fantastic novel about the people who were passengers, soldiers, staff and personnel on board the HMT *Empire Windrush* on their epic journey from the Caribbean, arriving in Tilbury docks, Great Britain, on 21 June 1948.

They did not realise they were making history, but they certainly were.

The action-packed novel tells the stories of over ten characters whose lives were intertwined over the two-week voyage that changed their lives. It pulls no punches as it covers love, friendship, jealousy, racism – even murder. It is, of course, a work of fiction – Tony has used full creative licence to give a vivid description not only of the journey but also of his main characters – but as you read it, many of you will realise that you can identify with some of the characters and individuals portrayed. Maybe they will remind you of a family member, a work colleague or a neighbour? Perhaps one of the Windrush Pioneers featured in the campaign and book, *100 Great Black Britons*?

The book also highlights issues connected with the Empire, the aftermath of the Second World War and the expectations of that Windrush Generation coming to Britain. In many ways the novel challenges the narrow perceptions or misconceptions of the Windrush passengers and therefore the Windrush Generation who settled in Britain in the 50s to the 70s. Often we think of these first passengers disembarking at Tilbury as God-fearing, starry-eyed, grateful, passive colonial subjects, but on reading this novel you can see that it was often the complete opposite! You can also see the antecedents of future generations of Black Britons through the passengers' pride, food, dress, fashion, resilience and community solidarity, as well as both the machismo and the sisterhood.

What I found particularly interesting and fascinating was how Tony has imaginatively interplayed the very personal – the stories of his individual characters – with the background in 1948 in Britain: the social and political aspects of race, such as the colour bar, the fragility of the Attlee government and the ongoing issue of fascism with Oswald Mosley and his Blackshirts supporters, who basically wanted to make sure that the Windrush ship (and other ships) would not dock in England.

Other important issues are raised too – including the frustration of the West Indian soldiers and aircrew who were coming to Britain after serving in the Second World War but still felt angry and traumatised by the lack of respect afforded them or recognition of their war effort. In a powerful reflection by one of Tony's characters, Garfield, who had served in the war: '*I meet some nice people on the ship, mi and de man from Brazil is talking about an import business and we hear two other people will be opening a shop in the Midlands, we don't come to Inglan to beg, we are proud people … we come to better ourselves, we come to help the*

Mother Country like we did in the war ... why, oh why do some bad-minded Inglish people don't want we here? Five years, just five years then mi gwan back-a-yard.'

This passage in the book – Garfield's expectation that he would return to Jamaica after just a few years – reflected the sentiment of a lot of people who came not just on the *Empire Windrush*, but on other ships and planes during what was known as the golden age of Black migration from the Caribbean and Africa between the 1940s to the 1970s. That was my parents' expectations as well, but as we now know the majority who came stayed, and have contributed immensely to post-war Britain.

As we approach the 75th anniversary of the docking of the HMT *Empire Windrush* in 2023, I think a novel like this, together with other publications, plays, memorials and television programmes, will be a fantastic and fitting tribute to this moment in our collective history.

Patrick Vernon OBE, co-author of 100 Great Black Britons, *Windrush campaigner and founding member of the HMT Empire Windrush Memorial Anchor Project*

This book is dedicated to my mother, Olga Fairweather, and my late father, Ivoral Fairweather, who came to the Mother Country as young people and raised their family against the odds. They taught me the lesson that you should always give back to your community.

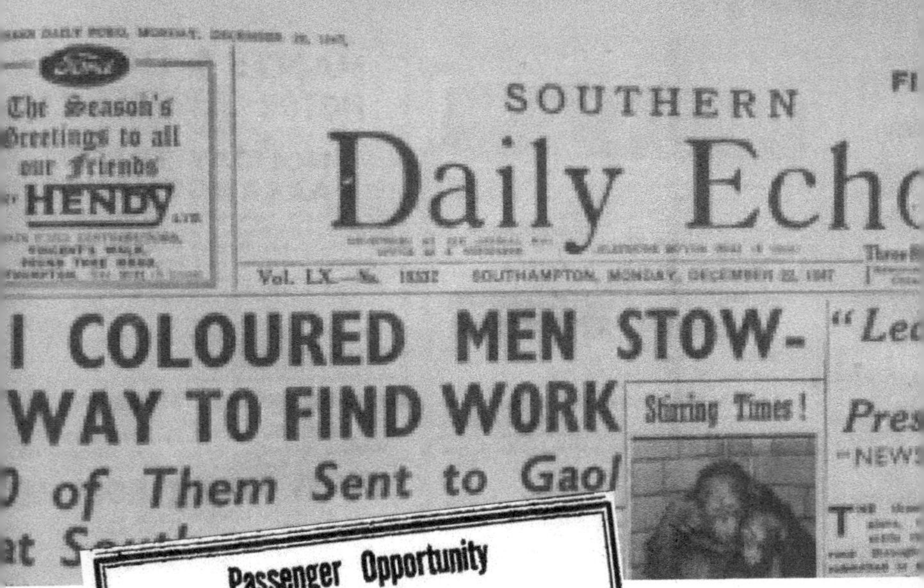
The Season's Greetings to all our Friends
HENDY
SOUTHERN
Daily Echo
Vol. LX.—No. 18332 SOUTHAMPTON, MONDAY, DECEMBER 22, 1947
I COLOURED MEN STOW-WAY TO FIND WORK
0 of Them Sent to Gaol
Stirring Times!
"Lea
Pres
NEWS

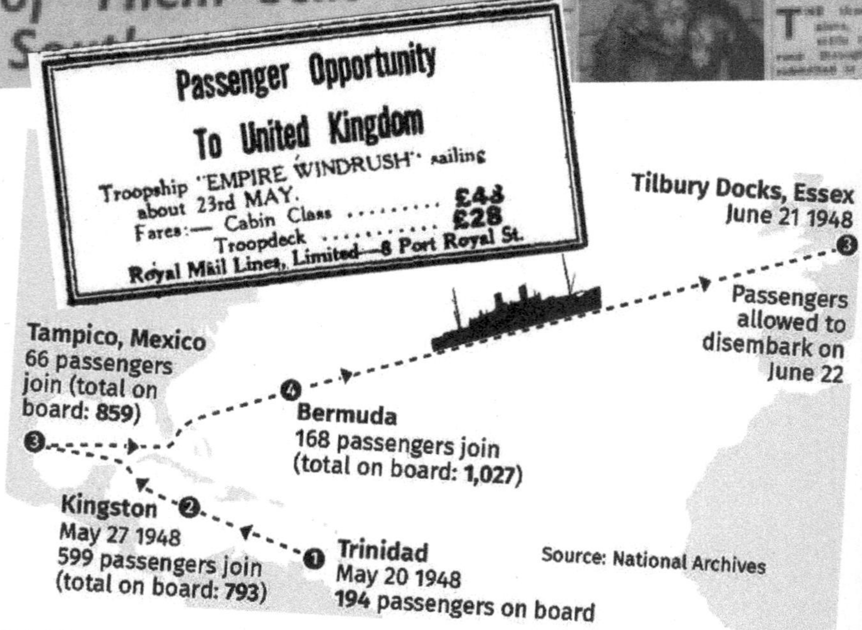
Passenger Opportunity
To United Kingdom
Troopship "EMPIRE WINDRUSH" sailing about 23rd MAY.
Fares:— Cabin Class £48
Troopdeck £28
Royal Mail Lines, Limited—8 Port Royal St.
Tilbury Docks, Essex
June 21 1948
5
Passengers allowed to disembark on June 22
Tampico, Mexico
66 passengers join (total on board: 859)
3
4
Bermuda
168 passengers join (total on board: 1,027)
Kingston
May 27 1948
599 passengers join (total on board: 793)
2
1
Trinidad
May 20 1948
194 passengers on board
Source: National Archives

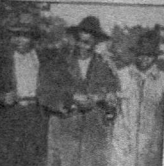

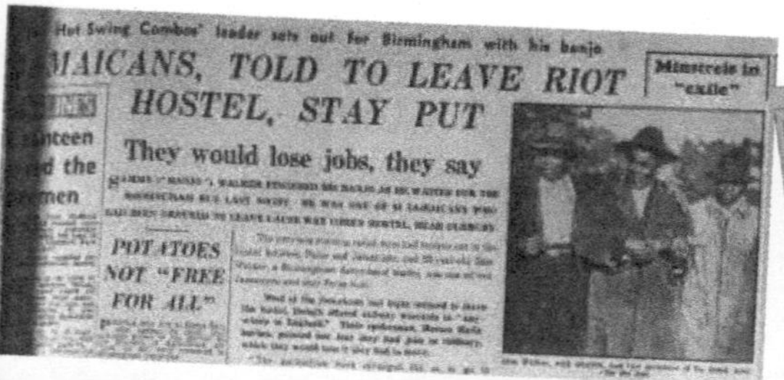
'Hot Swing Combo' leader sets out for Birmingham with his banjo
JAMAICANS, TOLD TO LEAVE RIOT HOSTEL, STAY PUT
They would lose jobs, they say
Minstrels in "exile"
POTATOES NOT "FREE FOR ALL"

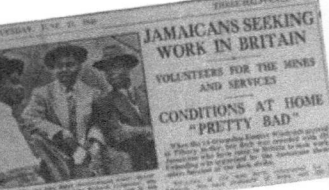

JAMAICANS SEEKING WORK IN BRITAIN
VOLUNTEERS FOR THE MINES AND SERVICES
CONDITIONS AT HOME "PRETTY BAD"

AUTHOR'S NOTE

After the Second World War England was on her knees. The call went out to the British Empire for men and women to help rebuild the 'Mother Country'.

Young men and women from different Caribbean islands responded. They boarded HMT *Empire Windrush* – the 'ship of dreams' that would take them to the Motherland.

Why did they come? The motives and back-stories of these West Indian people is a key part of the Windrush story that has never been fully told.

This novel fills that gap with a powerfully told narrative that reveals what happened on board that ship, which was packed with young, excited people who had never before left their parents, their parishes – let alone their island – in the course of a journey that took two weeks ... parties, friendships made and broken, fights, gambling, racism, sex and discussions of God and love.

PART I
Island Hopping

CHAPTER 1

TRINIDAD, PORT OF SPAIN

The first stop of HMT *Empire Windrush*

... Miss Mavis Walker ...
'Mavis, get up and fetch some fresh water from the well,' Daddy said loudly.

I jumped up, rubbing my eyes and looking around the bedroom. My two younger sisters were on the other bed and my young brother was in the next-door bedroom.

My little sister Debbie starts singing: 'You're going to get it, you're going to get it, Dad will t'ump you in yur head, go get the water ...' I lunged across the bed to lick my sister in her head but she was too small and too fast.

This was country life in Trinidad ... you had to milk the cows, get the water and feed the chickens before you went to work or school, which was a one-mile walk in the hot sun.

As I was getting dressed I looked at myself in the mirror – at my twenty-two-year-old body, not bad ... but I could lose some weight. My wavy, jet-black hair that showed the

Caribbean Indian side of my family was always fighting me, but I got my mother's bottom.

Many people say: 'You have your mother's natural beauty.'

I don't see it.

I am now the mother and the big sister after Mother died, one year ago. Dad did the best he could, but he never got over Mother's death. He drank too much rum, every day, and it took its toll.

Things got so bad that Dad's sister, Aunty Bee, came to live with us after a year of hardship for our family.

Sometimes I daydream of life in another country, away from my job as a junior nurse. Every day I'm doing more work than I should be, and I know I will only move up the ladder in the hospital when someone around here drops dead or is moved on.

The hospital is just too small.

But every night I listen to the BBC World Service on my wireless radio ... as I read my medical books by candlelight. One night the radio announcer started talking about the *Windrush* ship that was stopping in Trinidad in two weeks, how the Mother Country needs our help ... if you're a nurse you can get a special free ticket to England ... but you must stay for five years and work for the new National Health Service.

I put down my pencil and started to think about working in the National Health Service, England and ships.

From when I was a child once a month Mother would take all the family down to the harbour to see the big ships coming in from all over the world. She would fill our heads with stories from around the world even though she had never left the island. She was well read and passed this on to us. I knew there and then I was going to see the big world out there.

Tomorrow, I thought, I will apply for the free ticket through my hospital. I thought, I bet I don't get the ticket. Things like that never happen to me.

But it did.

Then my first concern was: how do I tell Dad that I have been accepted to go to England in seven days? I just knew it would not go down well because Dad depended on me to keep the kids in line.

As I sat on the bench in the yard with the sun shining down, the goats and chickens running around, Dad was sitting on a piece of wood across the yard drinking the strong local rum and smoking a cigarette. For the first time in a long time, I took a good look at him ... a brown-skin man, very tall, with powerful arms and a fit body, strong legs with rough hands from working on the family land every day of his life, and he seemed to have aged more since Mother died.

'Dad, I need to tell you something ...'

He looked up from his glass of rum: 'Na-bather tell mi you is pregnant,' he said in his heavy Trinidad accent.

'No, Dad, I am not pregnant. I am going to England in seven days.'

It just jumped out my mouth. I put my hand over my mouth but the words had got out.

Dad looked at me and erupted. 'Come out! Tek your tings and come out mi yard!'

His big voice made the chickens and goats scatter to the corner of the yard; the glass of rum in his hand went flying. I just started to cry and ran into the house.

Moments later Dad's sister Aunty Bee come out and shouted, 'Man, how you're so bad. You lose your one wife now you going to lose your first-born. Man, fix-up.'

Dad looked at the ground, looked up to the sky. As if he was waiting for an answer from his dead wife. He sat on the log, swallowed all the rum left in the bottle then walked into the house and looked at me: 'When is it you a go to Inglan? How you did pay?' he said.

I answered though my tears, without looking at Dad, 'I go in seven days ... I get a special free tickets for nurses, but I must stay for five years, Daddy.'

Seven days later Dad took me to Trinidad Harbour in his buggy with all my brothers and sisters holding onto the buggy and me holding my one grip. All the neighbours had heard that I was going to 'forin'. As the buggy was coming down the hill from the countryside where my family land was, all the neighbours young and old came out to say goodbye as we passed by. Local boys started running behind the buggy waving and shouting 'send for mi' and 'mi a come'.

For the first time in my short life I really took notice of the bountiful red and yellow flowers, the vast palm trees, lizards crawling down the rocks, chickens running everywhere, goats eating the grass, the wonderful, wonderful colours of the Caribbean plants, green bananas, the blue of the sky; feeling the heat of the tropical sun on my face, the fragrance of the mint. Just as the buggy came around the bend, I saw lovely old Miss Wilson, Grandma's best friend when she was alive, waving goodbye from her porch. My eyes were now wet, remembering the many Sunday mornings we went to church with Miss Wilson and Grandma. Miss Wilson in her church hat, with her white gloves and a Bible which had been handed down to her from her mother. Dressed in my Sunday best as a child and later as a young woman. After Grandma died I continued helping Miss Wilson up the hill to the church as the years took their toll on her ninety-three-year-old body. All the old stories she told me about the brutality of slavery that her mother had told her, she now passed on to me. 'This is why I look the way I do and have a name like Wilson ... Master's blood was passed down from my mother to me; she was one of Master Wilson's favourite toys.'

Plantation owner Mr R. Wilson from England owned you and could walk down to the slave quarters and pick who he wanted.

As we walked up the hill to church Miss Wilson would tell me how the slaves fought back on the slave estates throughout the Caribbean. 'You must never forget where you came from and be proud of your brave ancestors.' I will never forget those stories. As beautiful as the Caribbean looks to the eye, it has a dark history of brutality. Of genocide, slavery and colonialism.

I hope 'eff God spar mi life' I will see Miss Wilson when I come back home from England.

Dad was driving the buggy as if he was vex with the donkeys; we were bounced from side to side. As we got nearer to the docks I could see the outline of the big *Windrush* ship. My eyes could not believe how big it was. I had never been on a ship, I had never been off the island, I had never been away from my family.

The family just kept pointing at the big ship saying: 'How it floats?'

I looked at Dad looking up at the ship; he had stopped drinking as much as he did. From that day in the yard he was a bit nicer than he normally was.

There were many, many people moving around the docks, different-colour people, white English soldiers, dockworkers and Trinidad police. The Governor of Trinidad was talking to the white official men sweating in their uniforms, soldiers checking people's paperwork before boarding the ship. Boxes of rum and food flying through the air onto the ship, man unpacking boxes. Trinidad people were lining up to board the ship, people were crying, waving, hugging.

I took all this in as we got down from the buggy.

Dad handed the grip to me and wished me well. 'Mind them white men, don't get pregnant and come back safe.' This was the old Dad I knew and loved. He did not mix his words.

I turned to hug all my family, one by one, telling them to behave and not to get Aunty Bee and Dad vex. I then turned to give an awkward hug to Dad, who looked at the big ship over my shoulder as he hugged me. 'Send back some money for the pickney dem,' Dad said as I started to walk away towards the ship in my best white hat and gloves, a cream cotton dress with my mother's twin-set pearl necklace and earrings she gave to me before she died. Holding my one grip, and with tearful eyes, I looked back at the family, smiling, waving and Dad standing by the buggy as if he was frozen to the spot ... Dad looked like a little boy who just lost his best friend. I stopped walking, put down my grip and ran back into Daddy's arms: he held me like it was the first and last time. Coming from a hard country life he was not a man to show his emotions, but he had lost the love of his life, Pearl, my mother, and his best friend ... he will not lose his first-born.

'Mavis, walk good, my little gal. U-madda spirit a walk with you,' were the last words Dad said to me.

I returned to the big ship with tears in my eyes and a lot of hope in my heart. 'I will be back in five years,' I said to myself. 'I will be back.'

CHAPTER 2

TAMPICO, MEXICO

The second stop of HMT *Empire Windrush*

... Pele ... with Anton and Verndo
'Keep running, don't look back!' Anton shouted.
We were three young boys running through the backstreets of Mexico in the middle of the hot night with four men in pursuit.

'Quick, get under the rubbish bins, pull over the cardboards on top of us.'

We lay perfectly still. We could see the feet of the men who were looking for us.

'They must have come this way,' said the biggest man. He was unfit, taking deep breaths. I imagined sweat running down his round face in the heat of the night and onto his multi-coloured shirt. 'Look in the bins,' he said to a short man carrying a gun.

'I not going in any dirty bin in my new suit – to hell with that! This cost mi more than six dollars.'

'You were rob,' the big man said. 'Now look in the damn bins.'

'Over there – that looks like one of them crossing the street!'

All three men ran over the road.

Under the pieces of cardboard, beside the stinking bins, I watched the men running away across the street. We lay still.

'No one move,' Anton said.

'It smell, I am getting up,' Verndo declared.

'Don't you move if you want to live,' Anton growled.

We lay there for the next ten minutes, then very slowly got up and came out, looking left and right.

'They have gwan,' Verndo said.

'For now,' I replied. I felt worried.

Aged nineteen, twenty and twenty-one, wearing old T-shirts and shorts, we walked back down the alley. We knew we had to get out of the city: you don't rip off the local drug dealers and live to tell the tale.

Walking down the backstreets, out of sight of the bad men looking for us, I thought about how the hell we got into this mess ...

This was meant to be a robbery that no one got hurt. The drugs and money were in the gang's office; our job was to stack the boxes with cigarettes they used to move the drugs around town. We had left the back window just a little open. We waited till the drug runners went for their nightly drinks in the bar next door ... we were going to get in through the window, take the money – then go. But Verndo had to go back for the drugs and ran right into one of the dealers' women.

'What the hell you doing in here?' she said. The world stood still. She turned on the bright light. We were caught like a deer in the headlamps of a car. She knew every one of us.

SHIT... Verndo shoved the woman, who fell backwards on the floor by the door. As she landed Anton was trying to keep her from shouting by pushing his shirt into her mouth. The drug dealers were next door.

'Let's get the hell out!' We all ran to the half-open window, but got stuck in the window space trying to get out. The woman was shouting out loud and we knew the drugs men with the big guns would be in the room any minute. We were stuck in that bloody window ... no way we could all get out the window at the same time.

'Pull back,' I said.

'NO – you pull back.' We all pulled back, but shit – the men were coming. It was like a scene from a Marx Bros film, but we would get a real bullet in the ass if they caught us.

BANG! The door was trying to open but the woman lay behind it; we knew that four very big men with very big guns were trying to get in. We were still stuck in the window, with our legs in the office and our heads and bodies outside the window in the car park.

'We are going to get shot in the ass, then they will slowly pull our eyes out,' Anton said. Don't ask me how I took note of this when so much was going on, but Anton was wetting his pants. Piss was running down his leg. The door was moving but the big woman was lying in front of the door blocking their entrance.

The first shot went over our heads as all the men fell over the woman on the floor – they did not see her laying there. Somehow we got through that window and ran through the car park, dodging bullets, jumping like antelopes. How the hell we did not get shot I do not know.

'We can't go home,' I said. 'They will be waiting for us.'

'Shit, let's give them back the drugs and money. We can say it was a joke?'

'Have you lost your damn mind? They will kill us.'

Then as we sat on the wall in the alleyway (Anton in his wet pants) thinking about what we had just done and what to do next, Verndo peeled off a piece of newspaper that had got stuck to his feet. He was about to throw away the newspaper but the headline got his eye: 'One-way tickets to London on the HMT *Empire Windrush*. Docking in four days.' We all looked at each other, and then at the newspaper.

'Can we stay alive for four days?'

CHAPTER 3

KINGSTON HARBOUR

The third stop of HMT *Empire Windrush*

... Miss Norma Bell ... with Miss Lucretia Grey
Kingston Harbour was full of boxes with *London/England* stamped on them. Men were shouting, boxes coming off the back of people's vans and buggies, ropes being lowered from the side of the ship. Plenty of local food, water, rum and other provisions were going on board the ship.

The ship was so big it blocked out the sun. Seeing all that steel and the guns made it feel real.

As I stood on the docks, taking in the size of the ship, I thought about Mother and Father, my brothers and sisters all combining their savings to pay the cost of the cabin ticket and putting together the living money to survive in the 'Motherland', England. The family knew I would make more money in England than in Jamaica.

So there I was, standing on the docks in my yellow cotton dress and red head wrap. I always liked to be neat and tidy and have everything in place.

I had it all worked out. I would be sending back money every month to repay my family, but would save the rest – 'so when I comes back in five years' time I can marry a man and will have my vex money so he can't mess with me,' I thought.

I loved teaching and had just turned twenty-five years old. I had been teaching for two years. But the money was bad in Jamaica and there were more teachers than schools. Country life was good, with its green palm trees, lovely flowers and sweet ackee and mango trees. Once a week my family would go down to the beach and enjoy the baptisms and church services – there is nothing like a West Indian church with its Sunday hats, dresses, handheld Jesus fans, good food and white gloves, and 'when the spirit take them' God is in the house, with the pastor banging the Bible, the handclapping, the choir of older women very slightly out of tune but no one cares, people 'talking in tongues' and rolling on the floor, dancing like the world will end if they stop, and the deacons helping them back to their seats ... this was the life I knew.

My school was set on top of the hill, with a wonderful view of the countryside and a cool breeze that helped to keep the school building cool. It was one big room for everything – teaching, playing, sleeping. My family was not poor, but not rich either; they had done well farming the plantation land that my great-great-grandfather Mr U.N. Bell was born on. About 300 acres. Originally Caribbean Arawak Indian land.

My great-great-grandfather purchased a small piece of land from the estate that was cut up into smallholdings once emancipation came to Jamaica. The plantation owners went back to England fully compensated. The slaves received nothing, not one English penny. They were just abandoned on the plantation.

He squatted on the land until he could afford to buy it from the Jamaican government. My family, the Bells, supplied the local market and some small hotels and hospitals with fresh fruit, herbs, hot scotch bonnet peppers and some handiwork.

Many nights I sat on the porch of my wooden house listening to the night orchestra of sounds in the Caribbean air mixed with the heat and mosquitoes. I knew there was more to my life than teaching in the countryside.

All my life I had read about England at school, the King and the Motherland, and I now needed to see what was out there. 'This island can't be it ... it just can't be all my life will add up to,' I thought. 'I am a good teacher and I will teach in England.'

One day I was taking a lunchbreak at school, sitting in the shade of the palm tree reading the Jamaica *Gleaner* when I saw the ad: 'The King of England invites the peoples of the Empire to live and work in England ... Help to rebuild the Mother Country ... special-priced one-way ticket to England ...' I read on, learning that there were many jobs in the Mother Country that paid well, and so much overtime. I sat the paper on my lap and thought about England, the end of the war, living with white people, cold weather in England, finding a job, being away from my family ... I was never a person to rush into anything, and thought about it all day.

On the way home from school I stopped off at my best friend Lucretia's farm, just down the lane from our house, and showed her the newspaper.

We read the advert together. Then we stopped, looked at each other, then read it again. We screamed out loud, our voices filled with joy: 'We are go to Inglan.'

There was a buzz in the air on Kingston Harbour. The sun was shining as Mr Brown, my neighbour and a good friend of the family, pulled into the harbour in his pick-up truck. Lucretia and I had said our goodbyes at home; in the truck there was room only for our bags and grips. Otherwise, the vehicle was filled with supplies Mr Brown was planning on selling to the ship.

He placed our bags beside us on the docks and wished us a happy trip: 'You're going on the adventure of your life, my children, enjoy the good days and na bother about the bad ones.'

As he drove off we had to pinch ourselves – we were here in Kingston Harbour, going to the Motherland. We looked up to see wooden cargo with **London** stamped on the side being placed onto the big ship, boxes flying through the air, supplies of meat, rum, food, water, fruit being loaded. Jamaican people were boarding in their Sunday-best outfits.

The ship was so big. I had never seen anything like it. Everywhere there were people moving, in no particular direction, just moving. Then I saw my first white soldier in uniform and it all became very real. I was going to England to be a teacher, make lots of money and come back to Jamaica in five years.

'Bwoy, the ship big, how it will float? Why it called *Windrush*? We all a drown in the sea,' Lucretia said in her broad Jamaican accent.

'Stop it,' I said.

But Lucretia kept talking, paying me no mind. 'The soldier-man look good in dem uniform anyway. Mi a watch them white men, mi hear that the white man love to beat women on the bottom! I just don't want any of them white men trying to get them bony tings next to mi. I will lick them with my coo-coo-maker stick,' she said.

I just shook my head from left to right.

Lucretia Grey was my oldest friend. Stout in build, velvet dark in complexion, she was very proud of her breasts, which defied the laws of gravity, and of her ample backside. She was very pretty, very funny: every word that came out of her mouth was true Jamaican, or just funny. She'd been a country girl all her life, living with cows, pigs, goats – and horny men she had to fight off as her young girl's body developed into that of an ample woman.

Lucretia still believed that London's streets were paved with gold. That's what everyone in Jamaica was saying. Her grandma had to sell two cows, a pig and the old goat to pay for the *Windrush* ticket and give her living money. Lucretia's grandma had a little land in the hills that had good mango trees and green bananas that they sold at the market. Her grandma raised Lucretia from the day that her daughter just got up and left Lucretia in Grandma's care, when Lucretia was five years old. Grandma knew Lucretia needed to see the world and get that country life out of her or she would end up barefoot and pregnant.

'Gweh,' said Grandma. 'Gwan and see the world. Na bader end up like mi, old and alone,' she said.

Lucretia kissed her on the cheek and held Grandma's old hands, with veins that pushed against her old black skin. She looked at Grandma's worn face, which had seen hardship, the loss of her husband and her no-good daughter, and old age that time can't stop ... 'I love you, Mother,' she said.

Grandma looked at her through her moist, hazy blue eyes in a way she never had before: it was the first time Lucretia had used the word 'Mother' in all the years she had been raised by her. Grandma was certain that 'if God spare mi life' she would live to see her come back to Jamaica in five years to bury her in the family plot.

People who didn't really know my best friend Lucretia thought she was funny, a bit 'country' and rough around the edges, but she used this persona to cover up her insecurities about not being that well educated and feeling abandoned as a child. The only family she knew was her grandmother, me and the church. She told me she dreamed about the mother and father she never knew:

'Why did they leave mi? Why didn't they come back and take mi home?' She pined for affection. 'Just a hug from mi mother, just a hug ... What does mi father look like? Do I have brothers and sisters?' These thoughts played in Lucretia's head too many times. I would comfort her with a sisterly hug and tell her that she was loved.

Saying goodbye to her grandmother was the hardest thing Lucretia ever did: she was not sure the old woman would be alive when she got back but she knew Grandma wanted her to go to England and 'better herself'.

Lucretia and I had gone to our first school and big-people dance together and had our first kiss with boyfriends on the same night. Now we were going to England, standing together in our Sunday best, with white gloves, ankle socks, colourful dresses with red, blue and orange, pretty little bags and one each of Grandma's hats that she used to wear to church: 'When you wear the hats you will know I am with you always,' she told both of us as we said our goodbyes.

As we walked towards the ship, I looked at Lucretia fussing and carrying on and I just knew this was going to be a long, long two-week journey to England – but I would not have made this journey without my best friend and sister.

When we were about to board the ship a tall man said to me, 'Sister, let mi help you on board with you grips and tings. They look so heavy.' He was in a brown double-breasted suit with a brilliant white open-neck shirt and a nice cream trilby hat with a feather.

The bags were indeed heavy, so I let him hold some of them; I kept looking back at the strong, good-looking man carrying the bags, and there was something about him – mmmm ... Lucretia was ahead of me with her one grip and one bag.

Some of the crew members were on the docks, checking boarding papers. Soldiers on the ship were leaning over the guard rail, checking out the women and rubbing their hands.

'My name is Miss Norma Bell and my friend is Miss Lucretia Grey?' I said to the big white man in a British dark blue uniform with many medals on his chest. He was sweating profusely as he held an old clipboard checking the names on the list. He did not look the women in the eyes: he just looked at the long list of names; he had a smell of tobacco about him and something else I could not identify ...

'Yes, Miss Bell and Miss Grey. I have you on the list. Who is this man?' the soldier asked, looking behind us.

'Sir, he just helping me with my big bags and things.'

'OK, drop them off at the top of the walkway, then get off the ship,' the soldier said.

'Yes sir, master, yes sir,' the bag man said as he picked up the bags.

As we walked up the stairwell to the ship I could feel the eyes on us. On one side was a group of white soldiers – they were pointing and laughing as the women got to the top of the stairs. We also noted a group of well-dressed black men, some in suits and ties with nice white shirts and some in military uniforms – they must have been the demobbed West Indian soldiers people had been talking about. Most of them were looking at the women and smiling with those white teeth that look so good on a dark-skin man. I must say one of them man really caught my eye.

I kept looking behind me because the men must be looking at the other women following us up the stairs. I don't believe they would be looking at me in my Sunday-best outfit and glasses.

There was another crew member in a different white uniform at the top of the stairwell. 'Go that way, follow the rest of them.'

I did not like the way the soldier spoke to us – it had a nasty tone to it. We all made our way down the corridor to the main hall and were told to wait there.

There were many people there, just waiting around, and now and again you would hear 'Man a-you-dat? Mi never know you is coming to Inglan.' People were getting to know each other on the ship.

There were little children sitting with their mothers, groups of West Indian men with bags and boxes, lots of bags and boxes everywhere. People were just looking around, getting used to this big ship.

The man helping me with my bags dropped them in the hall and said, 'Have a nice trip.'

Just before he turned to leave I said, 'Thank you for your help. What's your name?'

'Roy,' he said as he walked away.

Mr Winsell Glen Benjamin ... aka Chef

'The hard food ready?'

'Yes, man, you have the snapper fish. Yes, man, it season up and grilled,' said Junior.

'Good. Go and put out the rice and peas.'

'Yes, Chef.'

I looked around the kitchen that mi had been working in for too many damn years and thought I did need to get to forin but don't have all the money. Mi head full, thinking about mi one son fighting in the white-man war in France, him go get him left leg blown off, the boy just nineteen years old, him all alone in some hospital in Inglan.

Mi is a smart man – mi take bread, water and flour and make a meal. Mi grandma always said to mi, 'If you learn to cook you will never starve. God give us food free, so learn to cook.' Mi is the best cook inna the parish ... cha-man pan de hole island. When there is a wedding or funeral it's mi dem a call, mi the chef, mi know how to make food taste soooo good.

Mi did hear about the big ship coming to Kingston and mi know this was a chance to see mi son in Inglan. Mi know people had to eat ... them Inglish cooks don't have a clue how to feed West Indians people.

I did take the day off to go to Kingston Town to the docks. It was four days before the big ship was docking. Mi put on mi best white shirt and pants. I did went to the booking office and asked to see the dock manager. A white man about six feet tall in a blue navy uniform came out.

'How can I help you, sir?'

'Yes boss, you have de ship going to Inglan next week? I need to be on that ship.'

'The booking office is right this way,' the soldier-man said inna him Inglish accent.

'No, no, no soldier-man ... I come to make a deal with you.'

The soldier-man looked curious but him did listens to what mi had to say about the war, mi son and how I can work on the ship. I did tell him I is the best cook in Spanish Town. When mi stopped talking the soldier-man just looked pan mi and said, 'Sorry, you have to pay to go on that ship.'

Mi head went down. I was about to turn and walk away when it hit me.

'Soldier-man, mi have something for you. I will cook for you and some soldiers a meal later today. Let mi go to Coronation Market down the road. I will pay for the food. If you like mi food then I will pay you half the money in cash and work off the rest inner de ship kitchen.'

The soldier-man looked at me. 'I like your fighting spirit,' he said. 'How can I turn down a Caribbean meal from you when you claim to be the best chef on the island?' Mi heart did feel he had no intention of honouring the deal ... maybe him just a tak mi for a fool? But him did say the British cooks were running out of ideas when it came to food, and they just would not cook 'that foreign muck', as him call it.

I did go to Coronation Market in Kingston and see mi good friend Mr Narada Sinclair the food supplier. He gave mi the food 'on trust'. Then mi went back on the docks to meet the soldier-man, him took mi into a small building on the docks where there were about four white English cooks sorting out supplies for the incoming ships. 'This man said he is the best cook on the island of Jamaica. Let's see what he's got!' the soldier-man said to the Inglish cooks who looked on has I cook up a storm using the small army kitchen and utensils.

The Inglish chefs just look pan mi bemused and laughing, mi did sure them did think mi is a mad West Indian man as I cut, boiled, stewed, seasoned and cooked de rass out the kitchen. The smell of the food made every soldier-man walk over to the army kitchen. Dem just kept looking at mi, mi know them was talking behind mi back. By the time mi was ready to serve the food there were about fifteen soldiers waiting, licking dem lips. Mi could not feed them all, so mi laid it out as a tasting table.

Then by the time the soldiers and cooks walked around the table, tasting mi food I was been patted on the back by the soldiers and told: 'You can bloody well cook!' The other Inglish cooks just looked pan mi with a vex look pan them face. As the soldiers were eating the food in walked a man that made them all jump.

He must be important in his all-white uniform with gold buttons and yellow and blue trimming. All the soldiers stood to attention and saluted him. He said, 'What's going on in here? I can smell this food from my ship.'

The soldier-man went red in him face and said, 'I'm trying out new cooks for the *Windrush* ship that will be docking in a day or two ... as they have West Indians travelling to London, we will need to provide their kind of food. Plus two of the ship's chefs are ill.'

I did look pan the soldier-man and think this man is a bear-face liad. But mi nar do nothing has it get mi pan the ship.

'Good idea, Sergeant.'

'Yes, Admiral.'

As the big man was speaking he looked pan all mi food on the table then he pulled out a chair, sat down, took off his hat and said, 'Who cooked this wonderful-smelling food?'

'It mi, sir,' I said, looking him in the eye.

He called mi over with a wave of the hand: 'What's this yellow stuff?'

'That's ackee with salt fish.'

The admiral took a mouthful. 'Mmmm,' he said, '*very* tasty. Is that a banana you cooked over there?'

'Yes, sir,' I said. Right now mi is thinking if I get this important man on my side mi gweh a Inglan ... 'It called a plantain, it from the banana family but you have to fry or boil it in hot oil.'

'That's right, sir, it's not the yellow banana you have been eating,' the sergeant interjected.

The admiral just gave him one dirty look. 'I am aware it is from the banana family, thank you, Sergeant,' he said in a vex way.

As I was talking to the admiral I did notice that all the soldiers in the building did not move. They just stood there, waiting for the admiral to finish his food.

After some time, after tasting most of the food and giving mi many questions about how mi did cook it, he did get up from the chair with him belly full of food. The admiral shook mi hand and said, 'That was the best food I have had in a long time. Welcome aboard. What's your name?' 'Winsell,' I said, 'but everyone calls mi Chef.' The admiral looked at the sergeant. 'This man will sort out your paperwork,' he said. 'You'd better get some more West Indian cooks for the *Windrush* ship as there will be over eight hundred people on board. Good thinking, Sergeant.'

'Yes, sir,' the sergeant said in a nervous tone.

With that, the admiral left the building, with all the soldiers saluting him while looking at the near-empty table of food. I did look at the red-faced sergeant who now had to honour the deal because the food was so good and the admiral and rest of the soldiers would have bust his backside if he did not take mi with them.

'You can pick three more chefs to go with you on the same deal,' the sergeant said with a vex voice. 'You've got a lot of people to feed, you will all work off the ticket money,' he said. 'Now give that officer over there the list of foods and stocks you will need for the journey.'

On the day the *Windrush* docked I did kiss mi son-mother goodbye and said, 'I will send for you.'

She sucked her teeth. 'Winsell Glen Benjamin, mi na wait five years for you to come back? Just let mi know how mi son stay. Inna de morrows.' My relationship with her was more convenience than love. We had been young when the baby came. I did know mi had to help to raise mi boy, mi did love him from the day him born ... As mi left the small wooden house mi had a feeling this was the last time mi would see her.

As I made my way into town, mi only thought was mi son.

On the docks mi did meet my three-man kitchen crew. Mi did put out the word about Inglan and a hol-eep of chefs wanted to go forin on that good deal. I was talking to mi crew of men in front of the *Windrush* ship docked in the harbour. They all were looking up at the big ship.

'It what-happen,' I said. 'You not listen to me.'

'Cool, man,' said one of the team.

'Man, what a big ship. You sure we will make it to Inglan?'

'Boy, stop your noise. You know how many people did want to make this trip for the little money we are pay? We going to show them Inglish boys how to cook.'

'Yes, Chef. We na rump,' the crew said.

CHAPTER 4

BERMUDA, HAMILTON HARBOUR

The fourth and last stop of HMT *Empire Windrush*

Precious Friedman – with Betty Burton and Doris Goodmen
'This water is too warm, get me another cup.'

'Yes, Miss Precious. I will get it now.'

The young man walked as fast as he could to the kitchen.

'This is what happens when you're too nice to these people. I told Daddy we needed new help.'

I was sitting on my wooden veranda with a jug of cool lemonade on the table. My family's white-painted plantation house sat comfortably in the shade of the palm trees, with their green coconuts, ginger plants, colourful curcuma twister, red tree ... and the green, green grass. I was talking to my friends, Doris and Betty, whose dads worked with my daddy.

I liked sitting with my girls because we are all from the upper classes of Bermuda. We were three light-skinned girls whom everyone looked up to. Some say we are full of self-importance.

What do they know ... we knew we were privileged, but we didn't care. And please don't call us West Indians or Caribbean – just Bermudan.

We all go to the young ladies' private school with white English teachers. My house was one of the old white slave plantation houses with dark wood everywhere, plantation shutters, highly polished floors and servants – lots of servants in the house and workers in the fields of the old plantation.

My family, the Friedmans, have done very well and we like to show it. In 1834 my great-great-grandmother was a slave on this very plantation. My family were the direct descendants of the plantation owner, an Englishman named Mr S Frasier Friedman. His blood ran in my veins. The white Friedman men had the run of the slave women and whenever they wanted a woman they just walked down to the slave huts and picked one out ... and sometimes young boys as well.

The wives and women of the slave plantation owner looked the other way when it came to their husbands, sons and partners. But then some of these wives and daughters were known to dip into the slave-man pit when their husbands were away for a long period of time.

This sometimes would show itself nine months later, with a mixed-race baby born to the white woman. Once the baby was delivered and the secret was out, the husband would just take the baby to the river or the yard and kill it in cold blood. No white man in the West Indies could or would live with that shame. And if the husband found out who the slave man was who had slept with his wife, the man would be tortured, castrated and sometimes male-raped in front of his wife, his family and the rest of the slaves. This was the bloodline of my Friedman family and of many Caribbean families.

Come freedom day, the freed slaves worked on the same land. It was called an apprenticeship ... the term applied to the stage between slavery and freedom. To add insult to injury the plantation owners were compensated the equivalent of millions of pounds by the British government for the ending of slavery.

As the years moved on a new Governor came to power on the island. By 1948 my daddy had done very well by working his way up to become the CEO of the Bermuda Port Authority, overseeing all the boats in and out of the docks, all the cargo and duty payments, which brought financial kickbacks that made him and his group of friends very, very wealthy. He bought the old plantation that my family worked on all their life for cash, when it was in a run-down condition and no one wanted it. It was Daddy's way of saying he was the master of his life.

Daddy overindulged me and gave my brother a hard time because all he wanted to do was have women, drinks, drugs and parties. I went to the best school on the island and all my friends were the sons and daughters of Daddy's group of workmates. They were as rich as me and liked to show off.

All this changed the day the police raided the old plantation and Daddy's group of friends' houses, all at the same time, looking for Daddy's paperwork and money.

The shame of the police at my door. I couldn't look my friends in the face – *they will think I am a crook!*

Where was my mother when I needed her? Mother was in France attending the funeral of her only aunty, who was part-French and part-Bermudan and who died fighting in the French Resistance. She left Mother a house and land in the South of France.

When Daddy was arrested I knew things were going to change dramatically for my family. The government had launched a crackdown on corruption on the island and the Friedman family and Daddy's group of businessmen were the number one target. Daddy had a bad time in the police cells, where he met many of the men he had mistreated or sacked in his management of the docks. His friends were also included in the scandal; they were looking for a way out.

When he finally got police bail Daddy telegrammed Mother in France with the bad news. As he sat at home reading the island newspapers to see what they were saying about him, looking down from the old plantation veranda at the wonderful view of palm trees, he saw an advertisement from the King of England inviting West Indians from the British Empire to the Mother Country with tickets to London on the HMT *Empire Windrush* from £28. 10s each.

He stared at the advertisement. He drank a full glass of brandy. And as he placed the glass back on the table he knew what he had to do – get his daughter and his friends' families off the island. 'My son will stay with me,' he thought.

The next day Daddy held a meeting at the old plantation with his business partners and decided there and then that me, Betty and Doris and three of Daddy's business partners' children aged eight to eleven would go to London and meet Mother who would look after us all until things blew over on the island. The rest of the families of his friends would go to the Americas.

We were not happy about going to England. So we made up a story that we were going to an English finishing school in London.

Most of the people we told did not believe us.

The HMT *Empire Windrush* was docking in three days, so there was a mad rush to pack and get on the boat with our belongings. Daddy put plenty of money in my grips and booked the biggest and best cabin on the ship he could buy; he also gave me heaps of paperwork to give my mother.

Daddy said goodbye to me at the house because he knew there were newspapermen at the docks taking photos of people getting on board the ship and he didn't want them to see him.

'Precious, I am depending on you to look after the group and yourself. Don't let anyone, I mean anyone, see the box of papers I have given you. I will need them to get me out of this mess.'

'Yes, Daddy, I will give them to Mother in London.'

I gave him a long hug, and as I did this I could feel how much weight he had lost over the last month. I had never seen his eyes look so sad. He was a proud man who now had sorrow and fear in his eyes.

The Governor of Bermuda was at the docks with the First Lady, who knew Daddy very well; the press and local people were saying their goodbyes. This was a big deal for the island, with the war ending and many soldiers from my island having died in the long conflict.

'We need to look after what's left of the Bermudan people,' the Governor said from a stage, flanked by rows of councillors in their best outfits and with the press taking non-stop photographs of the ship and the people getting on board.

After my group was dropped off at the docks we walked towards the big ship with our heads held high. We saw the group of white soldiers standing by the ship's entryway. We showed all the paperwork to the soldier standing by the ship with his many medals on his chest and looking very hot in his uniform. As he was looking at the list of names the children kept looking up at the big ship and said to Aunty Doris, 'Where are the sails? Where are the oars and paddles, Aunty Doris?'

Betty and Doris smiled and were about to tell them when the soldier asked to see their papers.

'All the children's names are in my passport,' I said.

'Yes, I have all your names here. Please move on board the ship.'

He waved us on with a condescending gesture.

Keeping my head high, I walked towards the ship. The young children were trying to keep up with me, Betty and Doris.

Doris was holding two of them by the hand, and the children were dawdling, gazing up at the bulk of the ship and not looking where they were going. As we were walking I saw many people at the other end of the docks, where the dignitaries were making speeches and taking press photos.

Just as we were going up the gangway to board the ship one of the newspapermen said, 'Hey, that looks like Friedman's daughter, the dock manager.'

I saw the reporters moving towards us as we were going up the gangway. Two of the pressmen ran over towards us. Doris pulled the children closer, while one of the men tried to board the ship to take photos. The white soldier who was standing guard shouted, 'Hey, where are you going?'

'I want a photo of that family!' the man yelled.

I looked at the soldier with an 'I don't want my photo taken' expression.

'No way!' said the soldier and prevented the reporters from following us up the gangway. 'Once they are on that ship they are on British soil ... now piss off! Bloody press!'

The soldier gave me a smile as our group made our way on board the ship.

PART II
Settling In

CHAPTER 5

GRIPS, BAGS AND CABINS

A group of West Indian soldiers on deck were talking about the women coming on board. Some of the soldiers had not seen a woman for a long time.

'Man, that is a fine-looking bunch of women!' All eyes focused on the women coming up the gangway. As the women looked up all they could see were Caribbean men looking and smiling.

'I have to meet that woman in the blue hat. I hope she don't have some man back home,' Willard said.

'No, man, I did see her first,' Ivan said. 'You is just a boy and them women need a man.'

All the members of the group were laughing out loud, so loud that the white soldiers at the other end of the ship, who were also looking at the women boarding, stopped talking and looked over at the Caribbean men.

'What the hell them coons laughing at? They better not be laughing at us. Let's go over there and deal with them wogs!'

'Davis, cool down. Can't they just laugh? It's not always about you!' a fellow soldier replied, looking at Davis.

Davis sneered back at him. 'Don't be a fool Edward, you wog lover.'

The group of soldiers stared at Davis and Edward. 'Come on, lads, let's not get into this,' one called over. 'We were enjoying watching the women coming on board, let's just have a cigarette and take in the view.'

'Garfield, is when we can take off the uniform?' Willard asked.

Garfield took a long drag on his cigarette as he leant on the ship's guard rail. 'The government man say when we reach Inglan then we is demobbed,' he said.

He flicked his cigarette into the water, turned to his mates and said, 'We all know the deal the Inglish government give we. Free passage to Inglan and work if we stay on the ship. So why you are asks mi what the deal is? You agreed to it so huss-up, man. We is all on the same deal.'

Garfield took out another cigarette and was about to light it when Willard looked him right in the eye. 'Mi did know the deal, Garfield, mi is not stupid. Mi just a ask why we have fi wear this itchy hot uniform when the war don.'

Garfield moved his well-built, 5ft 8in frame away from the guard rail and as he started to walk past Willard he said, 'Me is not your madda.'

Willard give him a 'cut-eye' look, then suck-him-teeth. 'Him think him is a big man,' he said as he watched Garfield walk away along the deck with his cigarette smoke swirling around him.

'Him eaise haad,' Garfield thought. 'If you don't hear you will feel...'

... *Norma* ...

I was sitting below deck in the big hall getting used to the movement of the ship. Waiting to be put in a cabin. The hall looked like a ballroom ... I gazed around at the mirrors, fancy red walls, multi-coloured carpet, padded chairs, two drinks bars, oval booths on the side and a big wooden dance floor with a wonderful crystal chandelier in the middle that had children and adults mesmerised.

There were people everywhere — families with small children who were just so excited to be on the big ship going to forin, men with grips, boxes and bags. On the other side of the hall were West Indian soldiers in full uniforms looking over the crowd ... as if they were surveying their prey. Everyone was talking at the same time, everyone doing what I was doing — taking in the whole atmosphere. There was a large pile of bags and boxes in the corner.

'Is when them is going to put us in our room?' Lucretia asked.

'It's a cabin,' I replied. 'I'm sure one of the soldiers will be letting us know.'

'You think the boat will hold all the people?'

'It's a ship and the captain would not take on more than they could handle.'

Lucretia gave me one of her 'you tink you know it all' looks. 'I'm sure that is Mr Porter from Portland over there,' she said. Lucretia was looking across through the crowd of people. 'He did sell us some good pigs and goats ... Mr Porter! Mr Porter!' she called so loudly that everyone looked over.

'Miss Grey, is you dat?' he said as he eased his older body out of the chair. 'Me did not know you a go forin?'

Lucretia moved quickly out of her chair and gave Mr Porter a warm hug. 'Mr Porter, you na too old to be going to Inglan? It what make you want to go, sir? You never did tell mi grandma, as she would have tell mi?'

'Miss Grey, you know mi wife some years pass now, mi pickney dem gan about them business so it just mi and the big land and house. Mi brother and him wife a live on the land so mi can go to the Mother Country and see mi sick sister before God take mi to the Promise Land.'

Lucretia took a good look at him as he talked. She had known this man all her life, baby to young woman. He was an old friend of Grandma and was the best breeder of pigs and goats, which he sold to many people in the parish. 'I did never see how old him a get,' she thought.

'She ha meet mi in London with mi nieces and nephews so I can know them,' Mr Porter said.

'Mr Porter, when we settle in this boat – sorry, ship – I will look in on you?'

'Thank you, Miss Grey, that would be nice.'

'Where is mi manners?' she said then. 'You remember mi good friend Norma?'

I rose from my chair and shook his hand.

'Yes, I remember you and your family,' he said. 'I did do some business with your father.'

I looked at this well-dressed man in a light-blue suit with a V-neck jumper underneath and a yellow-and-blue kipper tie. He reminded me of my own daddy. 'Yes,' I said, 'I remember the goats. We still have a family of them.'

Just then a loud voice came out of nowhere. 'Will all the passengers remain in the hall till the duty sergeant addresses you. You will be moving to your cabins very soon.'

Everyone was looking around to discover where the voice was coming from. 'It coming from a Tannoy, mi children, 1 remember them from when I served on a ship in the old days,' Mr Porter said as he laughed at us.

'We best go back to our seats ... I will talk with you later, Mr Porter.'

As the ship slowly moved out of the harbour its movement made people hold onto tables and chairs.

In walked four soldiers with a white woman in uniform. They made their way to the stage at the back of the hall. Every eye in the hall was on them as they pushed through the crowd. The people parted like the waters of the Red Sea did for Moses.

'This should be good,' Lucretia said.

'Ladies and gentlemen, I am Duty Officer Sergeant Dionne Adam. You will refer to me as Sergeant Adam. To my left are Private Wilcock, Private Mitchell, Private Cooper and Private Bailey. They will be helping me to place you in cabins. We will call out your names. Once you hear this, make your way over to them. Some of you will be sharing your cabins with other people – but only married people or families can share. The rest of you will be in same-sex cabins.'

I looked at the sergeant woman and said to Lucretia, 'That's a woman you don't want to mess with.'

'Mm, mm,' Lucretia said. 'Mm, mm.'

One by one the names were called out and groups of people left the hall.

One woman caught my eye sitting by herself, looking a bit lost. 'You have your people with you, sister?' I asked her.

The young woman looked over at me with a 'you talking to me?' look on her face. 'No,' she said, 'I is travelling alone.'

'Well, I am Norma, and this is Lucretia,' I said.

'I am Mavis Walker. Are you two sisters?'

This made us laugh. 'No, we are very good friends.'

'I wish I had mi good friend with mi. You is lucky.'

'Well, sister, you just made some new friends,' Norma said, with a big smile on her face.

'Miss Norma Bell, Miss Lucretia Grey, please make your way over to me,' a soldier shouted. We got up, picking up our bags and grips.

'Stay here,' I said to Mavis. 'I will be back.'

'Sir, I am Miss Bell and my friend here is Miss Grey,' I said to the soldier. He looked at the list.

'Yes, I got you here. Please stand over there. We will be moving out real soon.'

'Private Edward Wilcock,' I said, looking at his name tag. 'My cousin is all by herself – can she stay with us?' I spoke in my very warmest and sweetest voice.

The soldier looked up at me. He smiled and said, 'Does she have a cabin ticket? What's her name?'

'Miss Mavis Walker,' I said, looking him right in the eye.

The soldier checked the list, looked back at me smiling at him. 'Miss Mavis Walker, please report over here,' he shouted. Holding her one grip Mavis made her way through the crowd over towards us. 'Miss Walker, I have added you to my list. You will be staying with your cousin.' Mavis was about to say, 'What cousin? And I don't have a cabin ticket,' when Lucretia cut in.

'Soldier-man, will we have toilets in the room?'

He turned to look at Lucretia. As he did this, I looked at Mavis and laid a finger across my lips to say, 'be quiet'.

'Yes,' he said, 'there will be toilets in most of the cabins.' He turned back to Mavis and for a moment took in her good looks. 'Please follow me,' he said, with a smile.

Mavis moved over to me and Lucretia. 'Thank you, thank you,' she said.

'You is with us now,' Lucretia said as we made our way out of the hall.

Precious, Doris and Betty had to hold onto the children as all they wanted to do was run around like some of the other young ones were doing.

'You just sit down here and behave yourself. Don't embarrass me inna here.'

'The German people did live a very, very good life,' Betty said, out of nowhere. 'Look at the wallpaper and the nice chairs and tables ...'

'Yes, this is luxury living, Doris,' said Betty.

Little George asked: 'Why is the windows round?'

Betty looked at Precious, who looked at Doris with a blank expression. 'It round to keep the water out,' she said.

Little George came back: 'Aunty, how that work?'

'Miss Friedman, Miss Burton, Miss Goodmen and family, please make your way over to me,' said Private Bailey.

'Selwyn man, a you dat?'

'Yes, man, it mi.'

'Delroy, man, you did make it?'

'Yes, man, mi is here – with Evans.'

'Selwyn, you is looking good. Is where you get that sharp suit from?'

'Portland, man. Mi have a bad tailor there.'

'We a make some business in Inglan,' Evans said.

'Yes, man. I don't want to stay no more than four years. Mi have mi land and things to do,' said Selwyn.

'Talk to the soldier-man, so we can room together,' Delroy said.

Selwyn, never a man to back down from a challenge, stood up, adjusted his best grey suit, double-breasted with faint blue lines, white shirt and blue kipper tie, touched his trilby hat that always leant to the right. 'Soon come,' he said, as he walked over to the white soldier holding a list of names.

Delroy and Evans watched Selwyn talking to the soldier-man. They could not hear what he was saying but at the end of their conversation the soldier-man shook his hand, then shouted out all the names of Selwyn's group. The group looked at Selwyn as he bossily walked back to them with a big grin on his face.

'Man, is what you did say to the soldier-man?' Devon asked.

Selwyn looked at his friends and said, 'I made him an offer that he liked and we did a deal. Mi na tell you what because I may have to use it again.'

'Cha, man, you – a – joker.'

'No, man, him is "Mr Fix it",' Delroy said.

'A true dat. Now pick up your tings and follow me,' Selwyn said, as he walked off.

*

'I hope we don't have to share our room with any of them West Indians,' Anton said as he sat on the chair in the big hall with

Pele and Verndo. 'There not many Mexicans people I can see on board the ship.'

'Hey, dummy, many Mexicans look like West Indians. Where did you think some of us came from?'

'OK. OK. I was just saying … Anyway, the West Indian women look good.'

'Yeah, and you na get any woman on this ship,' Pele said laughingly.

'Piss off,' Anton replied. 'Hey, they're calling our names. Let's go.'

'Chef, do we get our own cabins?'

'I don't know. As we a work off our passage them may put we in a staff cabin.'

'No, man, I want mi own cabin.'

'Then you will pay the man him money.'

'Cha, you is never satisfied.'

As the Chef looked around, a soldier appeared.

'Mr Winsell Glen Benjamin?'

Chef looked up. 'Yes a me, dat.'

'Will you and your team follow me? You will be staying near the ship's kitchen.'

'Do we get our own cabin?'

'No, you sleep four to a cabin.'

'Rassclaat,' Glen said under his breath.

Chef heard him and gave him a 'cut-eye'.

'This way, gentlemen.'

The group walked along a corridor, down some stairs, into another hall.

'Wait here,' the soldier said. The group put down their boxes and grips and looked around the hall.

'Boy, this is a big ship. Mi never knew them have so many dancehall on one ship.'

'Look pan the wooden floors and the bar over there full of drinks.'

All the men were taking in their surroundings, looking left to right, up and down. They were trying not to appear overwhelmed.

At thirty-five years old, Chef was the oldest in the group. The other three men were between nineteen and twenty-three years old. All had worked in hotel kitchens or food shops. Every man had a reason to go forin.

'This way,' the soldier said. Very soon they came to a door. 'This is your cabin. You are in the staff quarters, so you can get to the kitchen quickly. You will receive your orders very soon.'

With that said, the soldier turned and left.

Chef pushed the door open. All the men were trying to get in the cabin at the same time. 'Easy na, man. Mek we work this out.' The cabin had four bunkbeds, no washroom and no toilet.

'Man, this is like a jail house,' Erskin said.

'If you had been to lock-up you would know this is clean compared that shit jail house.'

'Cha, man, is where we a piss?'

The vice-captain walked into the ballroom. 'At ease,' said the duty officer.

'Sergeant Adam, have all the passengers been placed in their cabins?'

'Yes, sir, we have some people who are not happy with sharing a cabin but we will deal with it, sir.'

'Carry on, Sergeant.'

'Yes, sir.'

The vice-captain made his way to the kitchen, where the head chef Neil has asked to see him or the captain.

'Why have we got four nigger chefs on board the ship? I am the head chef and I do the cooking and I should be notified if there is new staff!'

'Chef Neil, you were told we would be having West Indian chefs on board the ship in Jamaica. We have more than eight hundred West Indians on this ship. You should be glad that we have arranged more help for you.' The vice-captain knew this was about the chef's ego. He was always a handful.

'Well, I am not working with them wogs.'

'I would advise you to mind your language around me. This order has come from Admiral Wilkinson and Captain Stanley. I would advise you not to question this order.'

There was silence in the kitchen. The two white men were standing face to face. Chef Neil was getting redder and redder.

'If that's all, I need to report back to the captain,' the vice-captain said in a cool tone.

As the vice-captain was about to leave the kitchen, Chef Neil said in a fumbling way, 'There were obviously crossed wires. My kitchen team and I will follow the admiral's and captain's orders ... We can work the two teams on different days to the West Indians so my men can get some rest.'

'A wise decision, Chef Neil.'

With that, the vice-captain was out the door. As he walked down the corridor he could hear the angry banging of the tin-pots and pans.

CHAPTER 6

'GETTING TO KNOW YOU'

Norma was unpacking her things. There was not much room, so she kept most of her possessions in her grip.

Lucretia was putting her clothes in the wardrobe.

Mavis just put down her one grip and her Bible, then lay on the bed. 'When are they going to let us out?'

'De man say to stay in your yard till you hear the bell. I hear them a look for stowaways. I hope dem don't find any?'

Norma looked at Lucretia and said, 'We paid good money to be here. Why dem na pay?' When Norma got angry her Jamaican tones grew stronger.

'Did you see them fine men? Everywhere I looked it was fine men and them look damn-fine in the uniform.'

Norma just kept folding her clothes.

'Norma, you lose your sight? You never see them men in the nice suits and uniform?'

'Of course I did. Some of the white boys were very good-looking.'

'Cha, them is fit,' Lucretia said, 'them is damn fit.'

As Norma was sitting on the bed playing with her clothes she was thinking of Roy ... Why she was thinking about him she did not know. She kept thinking about his lips – he had full brown lips and chocolate skin with long fingers. She felt a little sad she would not see him again.

'Mi wouldn't mind one of them soldier-man showing mi how to use him gun,' Lucretia said, as she pretended to stroke up and down the nozzle of a big gun in her two hands and looked at Norma playfully. They just burst out laughing.

Mavis was lying on the bed laughing along with them. She just lay on the bed looking at the ceiling, not believing she was on a ship that was going to Inglan. 'Thank you, Jesus, I am going to Inglan,' she thought.

'Look in the back of the boiler room,' Sergeant Davis said. 'You two, look below. Anyone who is not in their cabin will have to show their papers or be put in the Brig.'

On all levels of the ship there were soldiers looking for stowaways. They knew that there were at least three stowaways, as the count of the people going on board was out and the captain was far from happy about that.

'Hey, you! Yes, you! Why aren't you in your cabin?'

'Mi a go to the toilet, sir.'

'What's your name?'

'Delroy Spencer,' he said.

'Well, hurry up, you should be in your cabin. No one should be out of their cabin.'

The soldiers slowly entered the boiler room and started to look around. When Private Ross moved a box, a man suddenly made a run for it like a rat out of a hole.

'Grab him!' Sergeant Davis said.

The soldiers ran after him, but he was fast and as he got through the door he bolted it so the soldiers had to go back and up to the next floor.

The stowaway was looking where to go next. The ship had just left the dock and people were in their cabins. Suddenly the door to the toilet opened and out stepped Delroy. He jumped, as the man was standing right outside the toilet door.

'Sorry, man, you need the toilet?'

'No, man.'

'The soldier said we have fe go to our cabin. Don't let soldier-man see you out here, man.'

Roy played it cool and said, 'Yes, man, mi was looking for your cabin. Mi will follow you.'

Delroy started to walk towards the cabin when he turned and said, 'What's your name?'

The man said, 'Roy.'

'Captain, we have found one stowaway who is in the Brig, and one who got away ... we are looking for him all over the ship, sir.'

The captain was not amused. 'How the hell did he get away?! You're in the King's army on board the King's ship and you let a little monkey get the better of you?!'

'Yes, sir,' Sergeant Davis replied.

'Take two more men down to the lower level, the boiler room and the engine room,' the captain said.

'We will find him, sir.'

'You'd better, Sergeant, you'd better. I will be making a Tannoy announcement to all the passengers.'

... *Captain Stanley* ...

There was a loud whining sound, then my voice came on the Tannoy.

'This is your captain, Captain Stanley. Welcome aboard the HMT *Windrush*. We have just left Bermuda, our last stop before London, England. The voyage will take fourteen days.

'There will be a safety drill later today. All passengers must stay in their cabins until you hear the bell. Once the bell has sounded will all West Indian chefs report to the kitchen on Deck Two Zone R.

'Decks One to Three meet in the Ballroom at 1300 hours, decks Four to Five meet in the Lower Mess Hall at 1400 hours.

'There will be a talk about the ship rules, which you must obey. Anyone not following the ship rules will be placed in the Brig. Anyone found outside their cabin before the bell will be sent to the Brig for the journey. At 1700 hours there will be a "Meet and Greet" in the Ballroom. We will be serving dinner, tea and drinks.

'This is Captain Stanley. Over and out.'

Precious and her group were one of the last to board the ship in Bermuda. They were still adjusting to the ship floor, which kept shifting with a gentle movement, and getting used to the very steep stairs everywhere. Having metal walls and round windows was strange.

'He sound like a captain I feel safe with.'

'He sound like a bully,' said Betty.

The kids were making noise about who was sleeping where and in which bed.

'Stop the noise!' Precious pointed at the kids, then at one of the beds. 'You all will sleep in that bed. Now take out your things and put them in the cupboard.'

She sat on her bed and looked out the porthole at the sea. She tried to see if her island was still in sight. It was not. She looked around the cabin, at the kids, at Betty and Doris, and felt suddenly, alone. And for the first time in her highly privileged life she was frightened.

'Nice room,' Verndo said.

'It called a cabin,' said Anton and Pele together.

The boys were still in a daze about the drug gang and how they got away.

Pele ran for the biggest bed.

'That mine!' Verndo said.

'To hell with you! I am having that bed,' said Pele. He just lay there and looked at Verndo.

Anton just gave Pele a bad look and moved over to the next bed.

'Do you think the soldiers got all the gang at the docks?'

The room went quiet.

'This is a two-person room; you two are in there.' Ada and Gabriela walked into the cabin and went to the porthole to see if they could see the land but all they saw was the blue sea. They looked at each other and then looked out the porthole as if they could not believe they were on a big ship. Everything was new, the English soldiers, the big ship, but most of all the sea.

'Feeling the sea beneath you is a weird sensation,' Ada said. 'You know the gang want us to help them?'

'I thought we were going to a new life, not taking the old ways with us?'

'You don't have to do anything ... I will get the job done before we get to England.'

... Roy ...

'Evans and Selwyn, this is Roy. Him a stay in a de cabin with us.'

'Cool, man,' Evans said. 'Teck de bed over there.'

'Roy, where your things at?'

Thinking on my feet, I said, 'Them get mix up with some group. All mi have is the clothes mi standing in.'

'Man, don't worry. We have things you can use till them find your things.'

'But you can't have my briefs,' Delroy laughingly said.

Selwyn was looking out the porthole. 'Man, we have fe take some of that soldier money.'

'Boy, we don't leave the Caribbean and already a work up a scheme,' Delroy said. 'Stop your noise, man, and pass mi the Park Royal cigarettes.'

Just as he said this, the captain's announcement was going all over the ship.

'I hear say them a look for stowaways pan de ship,' Evans said out loud.

I just kept looking out the porthole at the sea and the clouds touching the water. I knew there was no turning back, and I did not want to go back.

'I'll be damned if I don't find this stowaway,' Sergeant Davis thought. 'The captain's on my case, and I don't like it. Keep looking in the boiler room and in the very bowels of this ship, he said. Where the hell can they hide?' The soldiers were moving everything that was not nailed down.

'Sir?'

'Yes?'

'Maybe the stowaway is hiding in someone's cabin, sir. He did not get past us, sir.'

'We will get the bastard.'

'Yes, sir.'

CHAPTER 7
HELLO (ARGY-BARGY)

The bell sounded, then a voice came over the Tannoy.

'Will all the Caribbean chefs report to the kitchen. At 1700 hours there will be a "Meet and Greet" in the main ballroom and the mess hall. You are free to move around the ship. Over and out.'

'Lord, about time,' said Norma. 'Let's see what's on this ship. Best put on mi gloves. Hold on, Lucretia. Let mi put on some lipstick.' By the time Norma had said this Lucretia was halfway out the door talking to some man.

Norma got to the door to hear: 'Yes, me and my friend Norma will meet you on the deck in ten minutes.' As Lucretia turned around, Norma was standing right behind her.

'Meet man in ten minutes? Woman, you just got out the cabin and already you find a man.'

'A very nice man,' said Lucretia.

'Relax na.'

'You have two week to relax, Norma,' Lucretia said as she moved past her on her way to the upper decks.

The stairs were very steep and you had to hold onto the guard rail all the time; the ship was just a rocking and a rolling.

*

When Norma and Lucretia entered the ballroom there were about three hundred people standing around talking. At one end of the ballroom was the bar, with drinks and water. Around the edges were round tables and chairs, with men sitting in them – and dominoes players. There was a glitter ball, velvet wallpaper and a wooden dance floor in the middle of the room. Norma and Lucretia had never been in a ballroom on a ship or on land.

'Hi,' said a well-dressed, dark-skinned man. 'Hi, my name is Evans and I'm from Jamaica.' He looked around to introduce his roommate, but Roy had disappeared in the crowd.

Roy was looking from the other side of the room, as Evans was walking towards the women. Roy thought, 'I don't believe it, of all the women on this ship, it had to be her. I can't take the chance that she may tell the soldier-man that I am the stowaway.' So he started to talk to a man he did not know to get away from them.

'There one more man in our cabin but he somewhere in this ballroom,' said Evans. As he was saying this to Norma, Lucretia was eyeing him up and made her move.

'You buying me a drink?' she said, looking very deep into his eyes.

'Of course, what do you ladies want?'

'I will have an orange,' Norma said. 'It too early to drink.'

'I will have a rum with water,' Lucretia said. As Evans walked away Norma said to Lucretia: 'Take your time. There are more men on this ship than women. Take your time, Lucretia.'

But she sucked her teeth and keep looking around the room.

'Ladies and gentlemen,' came over the speakers. There was a lady soldier standing on stage. 'May I have your attention?' The people just kept on talking over her, then with one move the soldier took out her gun and shouted: 'The next person who disobeys my orders will be shot!'

The room went quiet, very quiet, as she put the gun back in her holster. She said, 'Now, that's better. My name is Sergeant Susan Hastings. You are on a government ship. Any officers or soldiers tell you to do something, you do it. Now I will go through the safety drill that you need to know in case of any emergency at sea.'

After the safety demonstration the soldier said, 'There will be dinner served and then there will be free time to play cards and have drinks. The rum is all free, courtesy of your islands. The beer is one English bob a pint.'

Evans and his group had been talking to the other men around them.

'Who's got the dominoes? Take that table as the dominoes table.'

'Who has the cards? Then move over there.'

'Tonight,' Evans announced to the hall, 'there will be an Inter-islands Competition. Jamaicans play Trinidad, Mexico play Bermuda and the rest is open play.'

Pele looked on at what was happening, then said, 'I know this game?'

Evans said, 'Take a look at how they play this game. It not the Mexico way.'

As the evening wore on, and the rum started to flow, everyone was getting relaxed. The women were talking by the tables and some of the men were by the bar. Suddenly the white soldiers entered the ballroom and went to the bar. Sergeants Edward Wilcock and Andy Davis – the other men always called him by his second name, 'Davis' – were ordering a round of beers with two other soldiers. As the drinks arrived, Davis said, 'A toast to the King!' very loudly. The rest of the room looked over, but said nothing.

Edward was leaning against the bar, but kept looking at Mavis. Mavis saw him gazing at her and thought he looked kind and nice. Norma said something to Mavis, but soon realised she was not listening to her.

'Me just going to the bathroom.' As Mavis stood up she fixed her dress then laid on the best Caribbean woman's walk you had ever seen, the hips moving side to side, the bottom flicking to the right and the shoulders square with the head. She had on her blue cotton dress with a white border that always fitted her just right. Looking forward at all times. She knew Edward and a lot of the men were watching as she walked past them and she felt the electricity coming off their bodies. She just kept walking, they kept looking, then Edward heard the voice of doom …

'If you keep looking at that woman like that you will get her pregnant!' Davis said. Edward just glanced at him, then looked at her again leaving the ballroom.

'Let's have some fun with the men,' said Davis. 'Hey, mister,' Davis said as Verndo was walking past, 'where you going to stay in London?'

Verndo looked at him and said, 'At your mother's house,' then kept walking. He did not like the way that soldier talked to him. Davis was about to move over to him in a threatening way, but Edward stopped him.

'You asked for that, mate, just drink your beer.'

'Bloody coon,' Davis said. This was heard by a group of West Indian men standing at the bar, and by the dominoes and cards players. They all stopped dead.

'Who you calling a coon?' Selwyn said.

Davis looked around and snapped, 'Am I talking to you?'

The air in the ballroom turned heavy; everyone was now looking at a possible fight, five white soldiers and a room full of West Indians ...

'All right, all right,' said the military police (MPs) who were standing by the doors. They moved so fast no one saw them coming across the ballroom. 'Let's just cool down,' said the head of the MPs. 'You men, go and stand over on that side of the room. I will be watching you tonight.'

The group of Caribbean men by the bar were cussing the white soldiers at the other side of the bar. All you could hear from the West Indians was 'rassclaat' and 'bumboclaat' and many other raw words.

As this was happening, Mavis walked back into the ballroom, saw that something had gone down and said in a loud voice, 'It what is going on here? You men must not fight over us beautiful West Indians women.' This made all the men laugh and the air went clear again.

Selwyn turned to his group and said, 'Don't get mad, get even. Let's beat them rass in dominoes and cards, and by the time them get to London them will be bruk.'

Precious was sitting with Betty and Doris looking on and said, 'Why dem people can't behave themselves? We just left for London and already them ready to fight.'

'It was not their fault, the white soldier should not have said that nasty word.' Doris liked the fact that her West Indian men stood their ground. 'By the way, what does "coon" mean?'

Roy was on the other side of the room staying by his table. He saw Norma and was trying to work out if he could trust her: would she sell him out to the white man? Like some slaves did on the plantations ...

'There you are,' said Evans. 'I was looking for you.'

'Yes, man, I went downstairs to the next ballroom. I never knew there was a room below ...'

'Yes, man,' Evans said, 'the ship is big. Come and have a drink and play some cards.'

Roy got up and followed Evans to the card table.

'Look at her she feel say she nice,' Lucretia said.

'Why you saying that?' Norma asked. 'She a gwan like them "up town", gal. See how she a "lic-up" to the white soldiers.'

'You just jealous.'

'A jealous you jealous, so,' Norma replied, looking her dead in the eye.

'Mi going to the toilet.'

'I will come with you,' Norma said. As they made their way past the bar Norma looked around the room, then thought, 'That man looked just like the man who help mi with mi bags.'

'Harry up, mi want to wee-wee.'

'Deuces,' the man said as he slammed down the winning domino.

'Your backside,' said his opponent. This made the white soldiers jump and look around; they thought there was a fight.

Selwyn leant over and said, 'You get used to the sound of dominoes players. Wait till his playing partner drop the game.'

The white MP just looked on. He then moved over to the stage to announce that it was 2300 hours and that all the passengers and soldiers must return to their cabins. The dominoes players just sucked their teeth. The cards players did the same. The MPs walked into the middle of the ballroom and simply looked at all the people in the room, black and white, and everyone got the message. Mavis, Lucretia, Norma and Doris all got up at once. The rest just followed; you don't mess with the MPs. They were mean to everyone.

'Well, that was fun,' said Pele as he took off his shirt.

'Did you see the way the West Indians stood up to the white men?' said Verndo.

'If that was me I would have kicked him in the nuts, then punched him in the mouth –'

'Someone needs to punch you in that big mouth of yours,' said Pele as he lay on top of the bed.

'That white boy keep looking you up and down,' Norma said.

'I didn't notice,' said Mavis.

'I did like that Selwyn man,' Lucretia interrupted. 'He had good hair.'

'PLEASE,' said Norma in a fed-up tone.

'Bloody coons, I was going to knock his block off,' Davis said as he sat on the edge of his bed. 'Next time I see that coon I will let him have it.'

'You do that and the MPs will have you,' Edward Wilcock said as he took off his shirt and shoes. 'Let's just get some sleep.'

'Everywhere we West Indians go there has to be a fight ... they must learn to behave themselves,' Lucretia said to anyone ... No one was listening.

'Selwyn, you is a bad man, you just get on the ship and you are fight the white boys. All the men in the room were saying ... yes man, bad man.'

'Tomorrow night we will tek them money.'

'Captain, sir, the evening was quiet,' said the MP. 'We had a little argy-bargy with Davis and some coloured men at the bar, but nothing we could not handle.'

'Keep an eye on that Davis. Dismissed.'

PART III
Adventures

CHAPTER 8

SALT WATER ON YOUR LIPS
(WHO IS YOU?)

5 a.m.
'Ah-ten-shun, all soldiers! Report to the deck at 0600 hours.'

'Get the shit up, you Hackney peasants,' said the overnight sergeant, who was happy to hand over to this drunken set of soldiers.

'Oh, my aching head,' came the response from one man.

'Morning, morning. That rum was bad.'

'Just because it free don't mean you have to drink it out,' Norma said.

'Gal, that was bad. Wow, my head feels like a coconut falling from a tree.'

Norma just sucked her teeth.

'Morning, Roy, you mashup,' said Evans.

'Na, man, mi cool, I can manage the rum. It the women give mi problems.'

'Good morning, my Bermuda family.'

'Aaahhhh,' came from the other side of the room. Doris had drunk too much, she was always a lightweight. 'I feel sick, I'm going to be sick.' She was running to the toilet, then came the 'Oooaaaa!' into the toilet bowl. Precious just sat there in her bed looking at all the drama and was amused.

'From now on, no one comes back to this bedroom drunk.'

Doris just did not give a damn. Her head was over the toilet, and she was violently vomiting. It was the combination of the rocking of the ship and the rum.

'Where the hell am I?'

'Wake up, you damn fool. I told you not to drink so much,' Verndo said. He himself did not drink. He just did not like it.

So Pele and Anton were wasted.

'I need some water,' Pele said.

'Really? We need some sleep. You kept us up all night with you damn snoring.'

'What happened last night?' Pele asked.

'You got pissed,' said Verndo, 'and we had to take you back to the cabin.'

'Aaahh, what was in that rum?'

'This is not Mexican rum. This is the hot Jamaican rum. So you need to go easy or you will not make the two weeks on this ship.'

'Attention!'

'All soldiers. We have two stowaways on board. The soldier who finds the stowaways will receive two weeks' leave and a barrel of beer.'

The hunt was on.

'Captain, the sea is calm, but there will be a storm tonight. So we will need to be ready for a lot of seasick passengers.'

'We will have that barrel of beer,' Davis said. 'We work as a team. Let's show them that London soldiers are the best.'

Edward was thinking about Mavis ... why, he did not know. But come tonight, he was making a move.

'Last night was good,' said Hyacinth. 'It was fun watching the men showing their tail feathers ... just a bunch of boys with guns.'

'You going to breakfast?'

'No, I need to sleep.'

'Well, we must all be on deck at 11 a.m. So, get up.'

*

The kids from Bermuda were standing on deck looking out to sea. For the first time in their whole life they could not see land – just sea, miles and miles of sea. There was a collective silence on the deck. Scattered around were groups of families, couples, well-dressed men ... everyone was just looking out to sea and into their own thoughts.

Not a word was said for about ten minutes as everyone gazed out over the waves. Feeling the breeze and the taste of salt water on their lips. Many had never left their parish, many had never left their island, all were thinking about home, family and friends.

'There are so many people on the ship, you just don't understand how many people there is.'

'You do know there are four levels?' someone said out of the blue. People were getting to know one other. Some were finding old friends on board the ship. The passengers on the ship were a young group, mainly, ranging from eighteen to thirty-five years old.

The sea breezes were blowing hard and you had to hold onto your hat. Women had to hold down their skirts as they kept flapping up, much to the delight and amusement of the men.

... Mavis ...
'Mum, if you could see me now ... Look what your little girl has done, going to Inglan on a big ship with white people. Oh, Mum, I wish you were here ...' I leant over the ship's guard rail. I could not have dreamt this would happen to a little girl from Trinidad who had never left the parish or island. 'I wonder if the streets *are* paved with gold,' I thought. 'I wonder if I can make it through the five years I have to stay. I do feel alone on this big ship.' My eyes were watering. I couldn't decide whether it was the beating of the sea breezes or the swirling of my emotions.

'Sister, you is from Portland. I know you is from Portland.'

'No,' said Norma, 'I'm from Runaway Bay.'

'Country gal.'

'Mmmm,' was the look from Norma. 'Your face does look familiar. Did you used to deliver the kerosene to my neighbour's farm?'

'A me that, yes, you is up the hill from Mr Porter.'

'Yes, that my family land. What is your name?'

'Ivor Thompson. From Runaway Bay. I am very pleased to meet you, Miss Norma from Runaway Bay.'

Norma looked at him as if to say, 'Why do you feel the need to give out long sentences?' As this was happening on the windy decks of the ship a big shout came from nowhere, then this well-dressed man came walking up to Norma and Ivor.

'Man, it you! Man, mi never know you was coming to Inglan!'

'Jerry, boyo a-you-dat!'

As the men hugged, Norma looked at Jerry and recognised him as one of the men who had been eyeing up her and the other women as they came on board the ship.

'Jerry, this is Norma.'

'Hello, Norma,' said Jerry. As he put out his hand to meet hers he looked deep into her eyes, and he held onto her hand just that little bit longer than was needed. Norma had a bad feeling about him.

'Where the land?' the young ten-year-old said to Precious as he looked out the round window.

'George, I told you, we are on a ship and going to see England. And Buckingham Palace.'

'But where is the land? There is always land.'

'We will see the land in two weeks,' said Doris. 'Till then, let's see how many birds and fish we can see. The winner get a sweetie ...'

'Look, look, I just saw a bird over there – over there.'

'Well done, that's one to you.' Precious was never good with children. She just saw them as a noisy problem. Or was it because they took away the attention from her?

'How is your cabin?' said Private Edward Wilcock to Lucretia.

'What is happening on the ship today?' she said, paying no mind to what she thought was a chat-up line.

'There will be a further safety drill, then there will be lunchtime food. Your Caribbean chefs will be cooking tonight.'

'So it's English food today?'

'Yes,' he said. Lucretia just sucked her teeth and slowly walked off, knowing he was gazing at her.

The ship's Tannoy was telling everyone who was listening about the lifeboats and how they work. Most of the people were on the decks just looking at the big open sea, lost in their own thoughts.

'Who is that white man with the pen and paper? From we come on this ship the man non-stop writing,' Mavis said.

'Well, he not a soldier so he must be a spy.'

'Don't be so silly. Why would you put a white-man spy on a ship full of West Indians? Better them send one dat looks like us,' Norma said.

Before the words had left her mouth Lucretia was walking over to the white man and was talking to him. 'Lord, that woman will be the death of me,' Norma thought as she started to walk over to them. Suddenly the white man took out a camera and began to take photos of Lucretia ... 'My Lord, what has that woman done now?'

'Norma, come here!'

As Norma approached she took a good look at the white man. He was dressed in a brown suit with a natty trilby hat, a long mac with brown shoes, and carried a camera and a notepad. He was about the same height as Norma.

'The man is from an Inglish newspaper,' Lucretia said.

'What it called?' Norma asked.

'The *Daily Express*,' he said.

Lucretia jumped in again. 'Him a do a story for the people in London about West Indians coming to Inglan and him want my story. Him said he sending it back to London every four days,' she said, in a very excited voice. 'How you a do that, sir? By the wire? How the story go down the wire?' Lucretia thought about that for a second, couldn't understand, then turned and fixed herself for the photo that the man was still trying to take.

'What type of story will you be writing?' Norma asked in a stern tone.

The reporter approached Norma and said, 'Such bad manners on my part. Let me introduce myself. The name is William Johnson, from the *Daily Express* ...'

'I'm Norma, and my friend is Lucretia. From Jamaica.'

'There has been a lot of interest about this ship and West Indians coming to work in England. My paper wanted to give you a voice, hear your side of the story, get to know you and your people.'

'I see,' said Norma, in a non-committal tone. 'We would be happy to take a photo and have a talk with you once we have settled into the voyage.'

Then she just turned on her heel, grabbing Lucretia by the arm. And off they went. By this time a lot of people on the deck were looking at them and the white man with a camera.

'Come on,' Norma said.

'Let go of mi arm. You think you is mi madda,' Lucretia said.

'Still tongue keep good head,' Norma said. 'You don't know what he is doing with the photo. You don't know what him a do with your story. I told you about the rumours on the ship that a lot of English people don't want us to come to England. He could just be using you?'

'Why is everyone bad in your world? How are we going to get on with the white people if we don't talk to them?'

'Cha, Q ...' Norma only used Q when she knew she had really upset her. 'Q, I got your back. We will go and talk to the paper man later today, when we pretty-up ourselves. We can't let the world see two ruff-nick women from the ghetto ...' The two women looked at each other and smiled.

'Well, I will be wearing my hot blue dress. That will knock dem Inglish men out,' Lucretia said, as the arm hold became a sister hug.

Standing by were some white soldiers.

'No one told me we had the press on board,' said Davis. 'Did you know, Edward?'

'No, mate.'

'Right, I will take this up with the captain at lunchtime.'

... William ...

Bloody woman, If she had not butted in, I would have had a nice photo of that coloured woman with the big tits.

I sat in my cabin and looked at my messy desk. It was covered with notes for the *Daily Express* story. I put down my pen, looked out the porthole and thought, 'How the hell did I get on this ship?'

I was working in the Fleet Street office of the *Daily Express* when the war broke out, a young reporter hungry to get some good stories ... I was a good reporter, but my bully of a manager knew different. He didn't like me because I come from Dulwich and he said I had 'airs' about me.

The bastard manager sent me to report on the ending of the war and what life was like for the English soldiers in Europe. After six months of bombed cities, bad food and dead bodies I was ready to go home. Then that bloody telegram came to go on to Trinidad to write a front-page story about how the war had affected the British Empire.

I was to visit three islands in the West Indies and interview the British governors in charge. I was ready to go back to London, but this was a front-page story and I would get some sunshine.

As my ship moored in the Port of Spain, on Trinidad's northwest coast, I was met by the British Governor-General who took me to the British residence in the capital, Port of Spain. This was an opulent building, with servants and lots of land; it was part of the 'Magnificent Seven' near Queen's Park, a row of extravagant mansions from around 1900.

'I could get used to this,' I thought, as I sat on the veranda overlooking the land, drinking brandy. This was the life … privileged living for the past masters of the Trinidad slave plantations who were replaced with British masters.

After my interview with the Governor I was sitting with a group of white English people discussing how the people of Trinidad were lazy and slow when I was handed the phone.

'Sir,' the young West Indian boy said. 'Sir, you have a long-distance phone call from London.'

I looked at the boy, then the phone. 'Boy,' I shouted, 'I will take the phone call over there,' pointing to a room on the left.

'William?' A very crackly voice came down the wire. 'This is Bill, from the London office. It's a bad line.'

Before I could say hello, Bill just carried on talking. 'The King has invited people from the British Empire to live and work in England. A ship, called HMT *Empire Windrush*, will be docking in Trinidad in five days. The boss wants you to travel on the ship all the way back to London, collecting stories from the West Indians on board, which you can send back to London by telegram. We have got you a ticket on the ship and paid for ten minutes every night on the telegram for you to send the copy to London. Don't you mess this up. We'll be getting a scoop over all the other papers.'

I didn't say a word against the idea. There was nothing to say. This had come from the top, from the boss himself.

'Yes, Bill,' I said. 'I will be on the ship. What about the story you sent me here for?'

'To hell with that. This will be bigger because we got Mosley Blackshirt supporters ready to go to civil war over here about having West Indian and Pakistani people working and living in England. William,' Bill said, 'this is a powder keg and our paper will be the leading paper, with the exclusive stories from our man on the ship. You're the right man in the right place at the right time. The boss wants some juicy stories. I will call you back in five days. Goodbye.' The phone went dead.

I looked at the receiver. I could not believe what I had just heard. They were giving me a big story. B-L-O-O-D-Y-H-E-L-L, this was the kind of story that would make me a lead reporter and get me awards. I took a big gulp of brandy and shouted out, 'Yes! Bloody hell!'

My family were middle-class people on the way up. Granddad owned a bead shop and property in Dulwich that he left to my dad when he died from cancer. I was just fourteen years old when my granddad died. I loved him so much, he always took me fishing ... Granddad was the first person to die that I knew.

Gran had died when I was a young boy and I did not understand that she was in heaven and not coming back.

My father did not get on with his dad because years before, he used to beat Gran when he'd had too many drinks. Dad never talked about Granddad. I remember the few times we went to Granddad's Dulwich house Dad never talked much to him, he just sat in the front room listening to the radio.

So when Granddad died, Dad did not talk about him and never went to his grave.

He was the only child. Everything went to him, including the shop and a big house in Dulwich.

My parents could not afford to send me to a boarding school. So I went to Dulwich College, which I hated from day one. But the college did give me a love of writing and of taking photographs.

I felt happier with my friends from the state schools in Brixton and Clapham, who took me to clubs and pubs around South London. At one of the basement clubs me and my mates got into a big fight with a group of West Indian men over a white woman who was dancing too closely with a West Indian man.

It did not end well for us ... we got a good beating outside the club. From that day I have felt a loathing for any West Indian man.

I got the order from my manager that I was being posted to Europe to cover the end of the war at twenty-six years old. This was a dream come true. Now I could be a real reporter – 'no more county fairs and society weddings for me,' I thought. On the day I was leaving for France I said goodbye to my dad and mum in the front room of the family house. I took one last look around my bedroom with its unmade bed, wardrobe, green carpet, sideboard and a big pile of newspapers in the corner – papers that held all the stories I had written over the years as a reporter ... Not much to show for twenty-six years, no girlfriend and still living at home. I was glad to get out and see the world, to be honest.

I caught sight of myself as I walked past the mirror, standing 5ft 4in tall in my double-breasted brown suit, with cream shirt, brown tie and grey trenchcoat. I paused, took a good look at myself – my pointed nose, inherited from Granddad's side of the family, a thin moustache and brown hair from my Scottish mother, with a side parting. I placed my favourite trilby hat on my head, picked up my suitcase, took one last look at myself in the mirror, then walked out the door ...

'Captain. The lunch will be served at 1300 hours. Will you be saying Grace today?'

'No, I will let the pastor do his job. I want to meet our guests on the ship. Let's have a walkabout, as my Australian friend calls it.'

'Yes, sir. Right away, sir.'

At lunchtime the children were queuing up for the food in the big mess hall. Behind them were Precious, Doris and Betty looking around the room.

'I hope the Caribbean chef cook the food.'

'No, mi did hear it the English-man food today.'

'Aunty Precious, what is this?' Pointing at pie and mash.

'Aunty Doris, what is that brown round thing?'

Precious looked over and said, 'That is pie and mash. It made from meat and flour – and they boil the potatoes, then they mash them.'

'Why them mash it up?' the kids all said at the same time.

'To make it taste better,' Doris said, looking at Precious. The kids laughed under their hands.

'There's a table over there.' Everyone followed Precious to the table. As they got there Evans and his fellow cabin-mates arrived at the same time.

'You don't mind if we share the table?' said Evans.

'Please feel free to join us.'

As they sat down Roy said, 'This English food look nasty.'

'Stop your noise and try de food,' Evans said. Roy took a mouthful of the mashed potato and pie. It tasted undercooked. The kids followed the example of the big people and tried the food. It did taste undercooked, but they would never say that as you would get a box around the head for being rude.

'Where you from?' Evans asked.

'We are from Bermuda – and you?'

'We are all from Jamaica and Trinidad. Have you been there?' he asked as he looked at Doris.

She was in mid-chew, slowly replied, 'Yes, I have been to Trinidad when I was a kid. My people are from Montego Bay.'

Evans said, 'That's nice. Tell me, do you have somewhere to stay in London?'

'Yes, our people will be meeting us in London.'

'If you have or know anyone with a room let mi know.'

'We are looking for a room.'

'You hear that there will be music and dancing tonight as a welcoming party?'

'No, I didn't hear that.'

'Well, I hope you save one dance for me' – looking directly into Doris's blushing face.

'We will see,' she said, 'we will see.'

*

The captain entered the hall as the food was being served.

'Hello – and what do we have here?' All eyes on the table looked up to see the captain in his full white uniform with gold buttons, white hat with gold-leaf embroidery, holding a black wooden stick, with his two MPs behind him. 'And what's your name?' he said in a soft voice as he bent down to greet the children on the table.

'I am George, sir, and she is Carmel.'

'And I am Rosemarie.'

'I hope you all have a wonderful time on my ship. Tomorrow I will take you up to the captain's cockpit for a tour.'

The children got so excited. He tipped his hat at the rest of the table, then moved on.

'The captain's coming this way,' said Pele.

'Hello, you are …?'

'I am Pele – and this is Verndo and Anton. We are from Mexico.'

'Tonight we have a welcoming party – please bring your group to this event,' the captain said. 'Please take a walk around the ship.'

The captain met the eyes of most of the people in the mess hall. Everyone was impressed with his authority, his uniform and the very fact that the captain was in the same room as them.

He was moving towards the door when a well-endowed West Indian woman stood up and said, 'You not coming to our table?'

The captain looked to see where the voice was coming from. He stopped, moved to his left and walked over to the lady standing by her table. 'I am Captain Stanley,' he said. 'You are?'

'I am Lucretia, and this is Norma – and Mavis. We are from Jamaica and Trinidad.'

'I am very pleased to meet you. I hope you have had a wander around the ship. How was your lunch?'

That was the wrong person to ask this question of.

'Well ...' began Lucretia.

'It was very nice,' said Norma, interrupting the conversation. She knew this was not the time to tell the captain that the ship's food stinks.

'Very good,' he answered.

'We have never eaten English food,' Lucretia said.

Everyone just looked at her, but said nothing.

'I hope to see you at the welcoming party tonight.' He tipped his hat, then turned and walked away, followed by the MPs.

'Why you interrupt mi when mi a talk to the captain?'

'I know you were going to run down the English food. This is the captain – you don't tell him the food is bad.'

'We all know it not good, cha,' said Lucretia, pushing out her lips.

'There he is, the facety soldier-man. Let's us have some fun with him and make some money,' Selwyn said. 'Mr soldier-man, tonight we having a card and domino game with a little wager on the side. You soldier-boys want in?'

CHAPTER 9
DEUCE! ... PARTY NIGHT

'Mi hear there a big game on tonight in the boiler room.'
'Sssshhhhh, na say nothing, mek the soldier-man hear you.'
'Come, man, over here.'
'Big thing a gwan. You have to have five Caribbean dollars to sit in the game.'
'What? That's big money.'
'You can be one of the lookouts. You get twenty cent.'
'What? Mi in.'

'Evans, where you going?'
'I'm going to see a man about a nice shirt and pants that I will wear at tonight party. I want to look hot, so hot all the foxy ladies will be rushing me.'
The men just looked at him and said, 'Them have a shop on the ship?'
'No, there a tailor-man who has clothes.'

'Let us go with you,' they all said.

'How does this look?' said Hyacinth. 'I want to look good tonight.'

Maria said, 'You're looking good, gal. Maybe the red dress is better?'

'Well, if I wear that red dress all the soldiers will be running after mi. But don't worry, I will leave some man for you ...'

'That's sooo nice of you,' Maria laughingly said.

Hyacinth was about 5ft 8in tall, slim but not mawga, had a good head of hair and full breasts that would make any man hold a conversation with them first before moving on to her very attractive face. Hyacinth had two men in her sights, and she was not the type of woman to lose a man to any woman again.

'It the red dress. Let mi be the Jezebel tonight ...'

'Kids, I want you on your best behaviour at the party tonight. We have your best outfit on the bed. Go and baide. We leave at six p.m. You can stay up till seven thirty. Then it bed,' Precious said.

Doris was going through her outfits. She did not feel happy with what she had.

She wanted sexy, but not sultry ... city gal, not country gal ... godly, but not church.

'We will take turns on checking up on the kids when we put them to bed.'

All the ladies said, 'Mmmm.'

'Evans, how you a play tonight?'

'Well, at eight thirty the games begin in the back of the boiler room. No one goes in there.'

'The white soldiers who are in the game tonight is some of the guard; all you have fe do is watch out for the MP guards who may come down to the boiler room. You is the lookout man so look out ... you will be at the top of the stairs. Any soldier-mans come, run down the stairs and bang on de metal wall.'

'Got it. Bang on the metal wall.'

'Set up your tin-pans or whatever you call it over there,' said the white soldier who was the stage manager for the evening event. He gave the musicians no eye contact and had no time for the 'coloured entertainment'. As far as he was concerned, an English singalong would do just fine.

'Soldier-man,' the pan player said, 'you have a mike we can use?'

'No,' said the stage manager. 'You don't need one.'

As he said this they both looked at three microphones sitting on the back stage table. This was the dark side of the English way, the in-your-face racism.

'OK, boss. We will make do with what we have.'

The musicians, led by the famous Lord Pan & the Pan Players set up on stage with no PA but a determination to make the party a full-on Caribbean jam-down.

As the stage manager walked out of earshot Lord Pan told them, 'Na warry about the soldier-man, he don't know us. We will blow up the place tonight, but we must play fool fi ketch wise.'

The ballroom was looking good, ready for the big Welcome Party. The bars were full, with free rum from every island the ship had docked at, beer for the English soldiers and wine from

Mexico. The tables each had a low light on them – and the atmosphere was all set.

The captain's voice came over the Tannoy. 'All persons attending the Welcome Party, please assemble in the main ballroom at 1900 hours.'

As the captain was saying this Ada was pacing up and down the cabin. Gabriela said, 'You don't have to do it. We will be in London. They can't get you there.'

'They can get my family, my little sister. They are bastards, bloody bastards,' she said, looking out the window at the churning sea. 'I got to do it, I got to get them off my back.'

The children were sitting on the bed, excited to be going to the big-people party.

'Mi look pretty?' Doris asked, standing in her yellow and blue dress with her white gloves and slingback shoes.

'You look hot, sister. That dress looks better on you than me,' said Precious.

'But Miss Precious, you is looking good yourself. Mind I don't send a telegram back to your father about how hot his daughter is looking?'

Precious was looking in the mirror as Doris said this. She looked herself up and down and said, 'Yes sir, I'm sure hot.' This was greeted with a wail of laughter.

'Anyone see mi red and blue tie?' Selwyn was looking for his lucky tie; every time he wore it, he had good luck.

'I can't find mi cufflinks. Is who pick them up?'

The men were falling over each other trying to get dressed and trying not to look too excited about the party.

'I know I put mi tie on the bed. Where it could go?'

'Here, wear one of mi ties,' said Evans.

'No, man, I need mi lucky tie. It must be in here somewhere.'

As Roy adjusted his blue suit with white shirt that Selwyn had lent him, he looked in the mirror and combed back his hair, which had a touch of a wave in it. 'I gan mush up the dance tonight. Hey, na bother with anything, because when them gal see mi you have fe go home, go you yard.'

Evans and Selwyn just gave each other the man-look and smiled.

'Now remember the MPs will be watching the dance tonight. We will be patrolling the lower decks, so we got control of the boiler room.'

'The first game is at 2130 hours. The West Indians will have lookouts at the top of the stairs. If anything goes pear-shaped then we blame the West Indians. Admit to nothing.'

'I'm going to samba across the dance floor tonight,' Anton said.

'You've got two left feet, you will just step on the women's shoes.'

'You like my new shirt and pants?' Anton asked as he spun around on the spot.

'You're a joker?'

'If I get lucky you guys can sleep in the ballroom ...'

'Like hell,' said Pele.

'Mavis, where you going in the short dress?' Lucretia said.

'This is not short. It the new fashion that all the Europeans women are wearing.'

'Well, it looks short to me.'

'Mmm,' thought Mavis. 'You just don't want anyone looking at me.'

'Bob, you're on stage first, then a few records, then the coloured players after the Intermission. Lads, let's show them that we British know how to have a good old knees-up.'

More and more people were coming in. The ballroom started to fill up. The barmen wore short blue jackets, the lighting was soft and the mood was good. The top ballroom was live music, the hall below was playing records. Both had bars, and dance floors.

As the room filled up the stage manager shouted, 'Bob, you're on!' Bob was in his soldier's white shirt and trousers with braces. As he jumped up on the stage he sat down behind the piano and gave a big shout, 'God save the King!'

'From who?' said Lord Pan quietly to his friend.

Bob began by playing the song 'Buttons and Bows', then went straight in to 'The Old Bull and Bush'. As he played, the white soldiers started to sing along, each with a pint in one hand and the other over the shoulder of his neighbour. The West Indian people just stood and watched the English boys singing their hearts out.

'You know this song?'

'Me? You must be joking.'

'Why them a sing about a bull?' Evans said.

Bob was buzzing off the crowd. 'Here's one for all you cockney boys.' He hit the piano keys, then burst into song. 'On Mother Kelly's Doorstep Down Paradise Row ...' All the soldiers were singing at the top of their voices.

Bob was on fire. The cockney boys were on the dance floor, dancing arm in arm with a beer in the free hand.

'Hey, Roy, them must be singing about you bein' flung out of some woman house onto the doorstep.' Evans and the boys were busting with laughter. The whole group of men were on their knees.

'Cha, man,' Roy said, 'a you who a go home holding your manhood.'

'The tables are in place. The drinks we nicked from the bar are down there. Forty-five minutes for the first game. We will clean them out.'

'Look, I don't want to dance right now. Maybe later,' Lucretia said. 'The man just a rush me.'

'Really, Lucretia, really?' Norma remarked.

She fixed her eyes on a man in the crowd that she thought she knew. She moved forward through the crowd towards him. He had his back to her and just as she was about to tap him on his shoulder a hand pulled her around and there she was, standing in front of Evans. 'I think this is my dance,' he said.

'What, who?' she said.

'Come, woman, mek us dance.'

'You coloured women are very sexy,' the drunk white soldier said to Hyacinth. 'And you smell great.'

'I am not some animal and I have a name, Cha!' she said as she walked away. 'Chaaa!'

Mavis was sitting at the table talking to some women when a drink was placed in front of her. 'I took the liberty of buying you a drink.'

She looked up at a very nervous soldier-man, and said, 'Thank you, Edward, that was sweet of you.' Mavis moved away from the table, where all the women were now looking directly at the white man who had the balls to walk over and make his move.

As they stood there looking at people dancing he said, 'You enjoying tonight?'

'Your English songs are new to me.'

'Maybe when your West Indian music comes on it will get you in the mood?'

'Mood for what?' Mavis said.

'No, no. I mean happy mood. No, I mean dancing mood. No, I mean ...'

Mavis stopped him. 'I know what you mean, Edward.'

'You bloody fool,' Edward thought to himself.

He could not keep his eyes off Mavis; as she was talking he was observing the colour of her eyes, the smoothness in her neck, the shape of her lips, the natural curls in her hair ...

'So who's Mother Kelly?' Mavis asked.

Edward emerged from his dreamworld to say, 'It's an old English song about any English mother. It's just a good singalong song. Let me teach you the words: "On Mother Kelly's Door ..."'

'Mickey, they will be coming down in about ten minutes. Keep a look out.'

'Yes, sir.'

Sergeant Davis had his money and three other soldiers as back-up.

Evans and Selwyn were in the hall having a drink when Roy came over and said, 'It time.'

'Cool, man.'

'Just leave one at a time, so the soldier-man don't notice.'

As you entered the boiler room by the heavy door you saw two tables, four chairs per table. There were boxes against the metal wall, pipelines and valves, boxes of beer and two cases of rum. The lighting was dim; there were no windows. All you could hear was the regular throbbing of the ship's engine.

Evans and the boys pushed the metal door open. Davis and three other soldiers were sitting at the tables.

Evans said, 'You boys ready for a beating?'

He has a strong hand and for a white boy he can dance, Betty thought. She did not know the song, but the soldier had asked her for the dance politely. Betty and the soldier danced with his left hand holding her right hand covered by her white glove; his right hand was placed in the centre of her back, not too hard and you did not move that hand till the end of the dance. Nothing was said till the end of the song, when the soldier said, 'My name is Peter Green. And you are?'

'Betty,' she said. 'Thank you for the dance,' she added as he walked away.

Betty walked back to the table where Precious and the kids had been watching her every move with the soldier.

'Mmmm, you looked good with the soldier-man.'

'I did, didn't I?'

'Bedtime, kids.'

'Aaaahhhh,' came the reply.

'The pot is one pound per game blackjack.'

There was a light mood in the room. But some tension, as well: £1 was big money, and no one wanted to lose. Evans shuffled the cards, then dealt them out. He looked at his hand, then across the table to Winston, who raised his left eyebrow.

Game on, Evans thought.

The next table was dominoes. Selwyn had a good hand, his partner Roy across the table did not look happy with his. But you style it out.

'One more round of applause for Bob!' He was bowing on stage. 'That's how you have a good old cockney knees-up. Lord Pan will be playing in fifteen minutes,' the stage manager said over the PA. The DJ, next on the stage, put on a record – Glenn Miller's 'In the Mood'.

'O Lord, when we going to hear some good music?' Hyacinth said as she walked out of the ballroom.

'I like your dress,' said a voice from behind her. Hyacinth turned to see a blond-haired, 6ft-tall white-looking but not English-looking man in a very nice dark suit, with a cravat in place of a tie and very shiny shoes. And what appeared to be a glass of champagne in his hand. He said it again, 'I like your dress.' This time it felt like he was saying, 'I would like to take you away …'

Hyacinth looked him dead in the eye and said, 'Thank you for your compliment.'

The man took two steps towards Hyacinth, who took two steps backwards. 'May I introduce myself? Mr Franceway Dangle,' he said, as he bowed from the waist.

Hyacinth found this very amusing, and a big smile spread across her face. 'Well, well, well, a gentleman. My name is Hyacinth,' she said as she curtsied.

'May I buy you a drink?'

'You may.'

Dangle extended his hand in the direction of the ballroom. 'Ladies first.' Hyacinth flung back her head, then walked back into the ballroom.

'DEUCE!' Selwyn said as he slammed down the winning domino on the table in the boiler room.

'How the bloody hell did you win that?'

Selwyn looked at the soldier, then put his hand around the money in the middle of the table and pulled it towards him. The soldier jumped up, knocking over his chair. Selwyn stood up very slowly. It was eye-to-eye. The soldier's red face said he was a bad loser. Selwyn was ready for any sudden movement he made.

'What's going on here?' Davis said. 'You're screwing up my game, so sit down or go and have a beer.'

The soldier said something under his breath that sounded like 'bloody nigger' as he walked towards the beers. Selwyn and Roy exchanged a look that said, 'We will deal with this later.'

Norma was looking around the ballroom. She thought, 'That can't be Roy, it just can't be?'

Lord Pan was setting up the steel pans in a V shape. The musicians had their red, yellow and black colours, with straw hats. They looked good and they knew it. Then Lord Pan raised one hand in the air, held it a moment and dropped it – and a wave of steel-pan music stopped everyone in the ballroom: the barmen, the drinkers, the people sitting at the tables. The sound of the Caribbean was alive and beating on the ship. The musicians were playing an old West Indian folk song about a woman who goes to the well and comes back with a goat.

As the sound washed through the ballroom all the West Indian heads went up. Then they stood up.

'I love this old song,' Lucretia said. 'Mi grandma used to sing it all the time.'

Norma was coming back from the other side of the room when the music started. She took one look at who was in the middle of the floor and thought, 'Gal, you is looking good, let mi join you.' Norma put her hands on her hips and wiggled up to Lucretia, who was dancing with herself till Norma came on the dance floor – followed by many of the men. The white boys were trying to keep up with the pan music. All the women were dancing with the Caribbean men, who were grooving in front and behind the women. The whole room was rocking.

The Pan Players went into the next song without missing a beat; everyone kept dancing, the group of Englishmen and some women by the bar were standing at the side of the dance floor, moving their hips out of time but loving the sound of the Caribbean. Norma, Lucretia and all the women were being danced with by different Caribbean and white men – everyone was smiling, everyone was happy. The chef and the team came out of the kitchen and got on the dance floor in their cooking uniforms. Chef pulled the white woman soldier onto the dance floor. She tried to follow what he was doing. He said to her, 'This is the calypso dance – move your arms up-down and left-to-right.'

The woman soldier just kept on laughing.

There was an unspoken feeling that all the people in that ballroom needed this release.

The stage manager stood by the stage and said to his colleague, 'Bloody noise.'

The soldier replied, 'I think it's nice.'

The sound of the pans made its way down to the boiler room. The game was in earnest. Davis had won two, Evans had won two, with two more games to play. The players at the domino table were sitting down to the next game in an uneasy atmosphere. Selwyn was not smiling, nor was the soldier; as the game went on, BANG went the domino.

'Yes, we have the game!'

'Hold on a minute,' said the soldier as he calmly played his hand.

'What the backside?' said Selwyn.

'I think this is mine,' the soldier said as he slowly pulled the money towards him. He looked Selwyn dead in the eye.

'Cha, cha, man, mi done. The game na work for mi tonight. Next time soldier-man, next time.' Selwyn got up and walked over to Evans who was on his last game.

'You get washed out?' Evans said, without looking up. 'You let them wash you, man?'

Davis was holding the game. Evans just looked at it — a six and four. Selwyn had a grin on his face. Evans was not amused.

'Well, my West Indian friends. Looks like you boys got what they call in England a "good flogging",' said Davis, putting on a very posh voice.

'Bumboclatt, Cha.' Evans got up and poured a big rum and sucked his teeth. 'We will see you guys in two days.'

'Don't forget to bring lots of your money,' Davis said mockingly.

'You're not a soldier, you're not a reporter. So what are you?' Hyacinth asked.

'Let's say I work for the government.'

'The English government?' Hyacinth asked.

'You could say that,' Dangle said. 'Tell me about your island. Are all the women on the island as pretty as you?'

'Your mouth is sweet,' she said.

'I will take that as a compliment. Would you like to dance, as the party is coming to an end?'

'You having the last dance does not mean we're going home together,' Hyacinth said.

They laughed and moved to the dance floor. The announcement came over the Tannoy: 'Last dance of the night. Please return to your cabins after the dance.'

'Don't lose him, he just went down the stairs.'

'OK, let's just follow him to his cabin so we know where he staying,' Ada said.

Pele, Verndo and Anton were making their drunken way back to their cabin. Pele looked around but there was only two women talking. He did not know why but his blood ran cold.

CHAPTER 10

DAMP KNICKERS

'How much did you guys win last night?'

'About eight pounds,' Davis said, 'but tomorrow we will go for the kill.'

'Colin will be playing.'

'Colin?'

'Yes, the army dominoes champion. Colin Matthews. He will be glad of the games. No one wants to play him in my squad, he just keeps winning.'

'That's going to be big money.' Davis put his finger to his lips. 'Don't tell anyone. I don't want them to find out. I want them to feel they can beat us dim English boys ...'

'Hyacinth, you got a big smile on your face.'

'Have I really?'

'Come on now, what happened last night? When I got back, you were not here. You must have come in twenty minutes later. So – who is he?'

'I don't know what you're saying. I am a lady and I don't play with the wolves. I have a man who's in my head all the time. He will be in London with a warm coat and hat,' Hyacinth said. Then she let out a big roar of laughter. 'He called Dangle. He a bit cool, you know that type? But, gal, he look GOOD. If mi never have a man in London, well …'

*

'You see, you can't get up, that's what happens when you stay up late,' Precious told the kids.

Doris said to the cabin, 'That white man can dance.'

Everyone looked at her. Doris was still dancing in her head with the English soldier.

'Captain,' said the vice-captain, 'the MP guards have heard rumours of a big game the night of the next dance.'

'Really? And I bet that Sergeant Davis is in the middle of it? Let's not say anything right now. Let's just let them think we don't know.'

'Yes, sir.'

'Whas happ'ing today?'

'Nothing. You're not on a cruise ship. This is not a holiday.'

'OK, Pele, you don't have to talk to me like that.'

'Well, get up.'

Verndo was not happy with Pele and the way he talked to him.

'Ada, are you really going to do it?' said Gabriela.

'Don't ask me that again.' Ada's voice was tense. 'You don't need to be involved. Just watch my back – that's all I need you to do.'

Pan Players was talking to his steel-pan players.

'Man, we mash it up last night. But we could do better, man ... Today we is rehearsing at two p.m.'

'Man, mi is meeting a hottie women at two today,' Elroy the pan player said.

'Well, you better make it three p.m. – or tonight.'

Elroy suck him teeth and walked off.

'You ready to tell mi what happened with you and the slick-rick of a man mi see you dancing up all night, eh?'

'First,' said Doris, 'I was not dancing "UP" all night with anyone. Second, nothing happened. He was very "fresh". That man could ...' Doris stopped in mid-sentence when she noticed that the kids were sitting on the bed, taking a keen interest in the 'big people' conversation. 'That man "charm Eve to eat the apple".'

Betty got the message. 'We'll talk later,' she said.

'Hyacinth, why you putting on make-up at this time in the morning? The sea air is messing with your skin? Or are you going to meet a man?' Maria said.

Hyacinth looked at her and looked back at the mirror. 'You're not mi madda,' she thought.

After breakfast people were just walking around getting to know the ship and meeting people. Pele, Anton and Verndo were sitting on the deck, smoking and talking. As Pele said something to Anton, he looked over his shoulder at a woman that was walking by.

'She looked just like Ada,' he said.

'Who?'

'You know, Ada. She used to run with the gangs back in the day?'

'I thought she was dead?'

'Shit, he nearly saw me. I got to be more careful ...' Ada thought. 'Anyway, it been a long time. Maybe he forgot what I look like.'

'Knock, knock.' The door slowly opened. 'So very nice to see you, please come in.'

'We don't want people to gossip, do we?' Hyacinth said as she walked quickly into Dangle's cabin with a swagger in her hips. She wore a close-fitting cotton-white dress that highlighted her curves and ample bosom. As he closed the door she saw it was not a normal cabin. There were two rooms – a bedroom and living area with a bar, sofa and comfy chairs. The walls were wood-panelled and in the open-plan bedroom the bed looked like it had silk sheets. 'A drink?'

'Stop your running around. I told you not to run on the ship!'

'Yes, Aunty Precious. Come and look at the dolphins at the front of the ship!' the children said excitedly.

'Over here!'

'Wow!'

'Can they breathe underwater?'

'No. They are mammals. But they can hold their breath for a long time ... Now listen to me. If you don't behave today you will not go to Captain Stanley's cockpit,' Precious said, holding onto her hat. It was very windy on the decks. With her other hand she was trying to keep her dress from flying up over her head.

'Yes, Aunty Precious.'

'Champagne in the morning? I thought this was war times?'

'Working for the government has its benefits,' he said, smiling. He was dressed in a dark-red quilted smoking jacket with a yellow cravat and held a smouldering cigar in his hand.

'Exactly what do you do for the government?' Hyacinth asked.

'If I told you, I would have to kill you,' he said, looking deep into Hyacinth's brown eyes.

'What's that the English say? "Loose lips sink ships"?' she said.

'Absolutely. Now tell me more about you. I have some breakfast for you.' As they sat down on the sofa he asked, 'Do you mind if I touch your hair? I have never touched a coloured woman's hair before.'

'Well, I have never touched a white man's hair before.'

'Let's do it at the same time,' he said. Hyacinth felt comfortable about this; she felt at ease ... she had never been so strongly attracted to a man so quickly. And a white man, 'me-dear'?

She slowly touched the back of his neatly cut hair. It was blond, but not light blond – kind of a dirty blond. It felt like a cat's fur. As she did this, Dangle gently touched her short but neat natural hair. 'What is it you put in your hair? It smells wonderful — and so soft.' His stroking became more intense. She closed her eyes and it felt pleasant ... she was not sure if it was him or the champagne? Whatever it was it felt damn good.

'May I say for a man you smell good?'

'Mmmm, thank you. You feel good.'

Her head went slowly back as if she were anticipating something. And she was not disappointed — all of a sudden she felt a warm pair of lips on her mouth. She still had her eyes closed and it was feeling and tasting a white man for the first time that made her wet.

Most people were sitting in the ballroom, just talking. Everyone had heard that tomorrow would be the big island cook-up ... all the 'yard' chefs would be cooking native dishes.

'Thank the Lord we are getting yard food.'

'Yes man, mi a eat some real food.'

'Mi a take back some food to mi cabin.'

'Selwyn, come here,' Davis said. 'We got to be careful not to let too many people know about the card game tomorrow. I could get in a lot of trouble if it gets out.'

'Cool, man, mi and the bred-rin na say a thin.'

... *Hyacinth* ...

Dangle's hand was rubbing the back of my dress. The kissing became very intense, which was a new feeling to me. Suddenly it was too much.

I pulled away. 'Hold on, just hold on. You're good, you're really good. Any woman in your hands will have a hard time saying no ... I like you and you kiss nice, but mi not ready for that.'

'I respect you and would not do anything to hurt you,' he said with that broken-English foreign accent. 'But you turned mi head the minute I saw you. My head started spinning.'

I felt embarrassed; he just kept kissing my neck, which I really did like ... I was feeling high, so high.

But I was now losing control of myself. 'No, no, stop, PLEASE stop!' I said.

He drew back. 'What's wrong?'

'If you respect me like you say you do, then you will understand.'

He stood up and said, 'Let's have a glass of champagne. Just enjoy the moment.'

I got up and I took the glass of champagne and stood looking out the porthole, thinking, 'I have a man waiting for me in London. He will be at the docks there, with a warm coat and a hat for me.' I kept looking out the porthole.

'Will I have the pleasure of buying you a drink tonight?'

'Of course you can. See you in the bar later.' I opened the door, and made my exit.

'I do like the way you keep the pickney dem in line.' Precious looked around and standing behind her was a tall, dark man in a double-breasted blue jacket and yellow shirt, with a loud tie and wonderful trilby hat. She was taking all this in when his face broke into a full smile. 'It holds you, disarms you, flatters you,' she thought.

'My name is Lloyd Fredrick Carter.' He extended his hand for a handshake. Precious was not expecting this. She stood there with her mouth open, but no words were coming out. She was almost in a dream state, then she snapped back to life. 'These little creatures are my cousins George, Rosemarie and Carmel.'

'Hello, sir,' they said.

Lloyd took off his hat as a mark of respect. Out of nowhere in flew Doris, who held out her hand. 'My name is Doris, a friend of Precious.'

'My, what a good-looking group of people you are,' Lloyd said, looking deep into Precious's eyes. 'Ladies, may I invite you both to a drink tonight?'

'That would be lovely,' Doris said without looking at Precious. The two women watched as the man walked away with that West Indian movement that was more a skip than a walk. They looked at each other and let out a 'Mmmmm ...'

CHAPTER 11

'THINGS A GWAAN'

'Where is Pele?'

'He on the deck looking at the dolphins. I'm going for a walk,' Anton said.

'OK. See you here later.'

It was a sunny day and the sea was calm. 'I hope my family don't get worked over by the drugs gang. I can't think that way … I have really put them in the shits, how can I make this right? Aaahhh! I just want this nightmare to go away.' Ada's mind was going round and round.

Pele was looking out to sea – the dolphins were following the ship; the air was fresh … 'Life has got to get better in England, it's got to get better,' he thought. 'When I get to England I am going it alone. I can't be with them boys any more. Look where it's got me …'

'Hi! I notice you've got a Mexican accent?'

Pele turned his head in the direction the voice was coming from and saw a tall, dark-haired South American-looking woman who had all the curves, beauty – and backside – of a Mexican señorita.

'My name is Ada Mae,' she said.

Pele responded with one word, 'Nobility. The meaning of your name. Pele, my name is Pele.'

There was a pause as Ada extended her soft golden hand in greeting, Pele held onto it before finally giving it back. 'I'm honoured you know the meaning of my name,' she said. 'So where are you from in Mexico?'

'Chimalhuac,' he said.

'I am from Barrio San Hipolite,' Ada replied.

'Did you get on the ship at Mexico?'

'Yes, I did. I saw you and your friends getting on board.'

'Really?'

'Yes, really ... did you not see the soldiers taking down the drug men at the docks?'

'Yes, I saw that.'

'I am so glad. That bastard has been running south Mexico for years ... putting kids on the street, forcing pregnant women and children to go on the game.'

'You seem to know a lot about the drugs gang?'

She turned her head and said, 'Where did you say you came from? There's no way you lived there and did not know or see them nasty men who work for that gang.'

'Yeah, you're right. He is a bastard ... Who you travelling with?'

'No one. I'm meeting my family in London. My dad was in the war and was demobbed in London ... Did you try the English food?'

'Jesus, that was nasty,' Pele said, laughing. 'I will eat the food tomorrow the West Indian chefs are cooking.'

Pele was feeling very comfortable with Ada – the way she laughed, the way she moved her very long, jet-black curly hair to one side and her lovely curvy finger, her thin lips and the deep brown eyes with very black eyebrows.

'You going to the bar tonight for drinks?' she asked.

'Yes, me and my friends will be there.'

'Great, I would love to meet more Mexicans. We have to help each other on this ship and when we get to England.'

Pele moved his head up and down in agreement.

... Private Mickey ...

'Doctor, I can't sleep. I try to get to sleep but I keep on getting bad dreams.'

'What are you dreaming about?'

'Dead bodies, lots of dead bodies.'

'That's normal for a soldier who has seen action on the front line ... I want you to take these tablets. They will help you to sleep. If you keep having the dreams, come back to see me again.'

'Yes, doctor,' I said.

'Sergeant Davis, any news on the stowaways?'

'No, sir,' Davis said to his captain.

'Well, you'd better get your finger out of your hole and find them. When your team is patrolling tonight tell them to look in every place someone could hide out. And look in all the lifeboats.'

'Yes, sir, right away, sir.'

'Would you like to play cards?' a lady said to Mavis as she sat at the table alone, shuffling the cards in the half-empty hall.

'Yes, let's play a game.'

The woman sat down. 'My name is Betty. From Bermuda.'

'I am Mavis, from Trinidad.'

'How you find the ship?'

'I get a bit seasick, but feeling better now. But the English food keeps repeating on me...'

'You, too, gal? Mi never pass so much wind in mi life!'

The women laughed out loud.

'What we playing?'

'Gin,' Mavis said.

'I think I know this.'

'OK.' Mavis dealt the cards. 'You see them nice West Indians soldiers?'

'Yes, they are a fine-looking bunch of men. You get one yet?' Betty asked.

'Please. I just get on board the ship.'

'The best thing about this ship is there are more men than women on board, so I will take mi time to find a good man.'

'Every bench has a batty.'

'Mm-mm,' they both said.

*

'No, man, that's where you're going wrong. It-go-so, pin-pin don ...'

Lord Pan was playing the steel pans to the band in a side room.

'If you just think about the song and not that woman, we will soon be done here.'

'This man a get under mi skin. Mi a play pan since mi was a pickney, mi know what mi a do,' Elroy thought.

Two West Indian soldiers were leaning over the guard rail of the ship looking out to sea.

'Have you noticed that ship?'

'Where?'

'Right over there. Way, way in the distance?'

'There must be many ships in the ocean?'

'Yes, but that ship left the same time as us in Bermuda. No one got on and no one got off. It just sat there in the bay as if it was watching us, man.'

'You're letting the war get in your head.'

'You feel it a German ship?'

'Cha, man a mad, you mad.'

'Will the coloured chefs be cooking tonight?'

'No. It's our bloody chef.'

'I thought the coloured chefs were cooking all the time?'

'No, every other day they cook and on the special party night.'

'Oh shit, I should have taken more of the coloured chefs' food. I'm sick of that muck our chef is giving us.'

'You on patrol tonight?'

'No. Tomorrow.'

'I hear there is a big card game happening on the ship.'

'Me, too.'

'But who's behind it?' the soldier said.

In a small cabin just below deck two people sat either side of a table. One, in a lightweight cream suit with a very white shirt, was smoking a cigarette; the other man had a brown suit, camera, notepad and pen.

'And where in the West Indies are you from?'

'Trinidad, sir.'

'Why are you going to England?'

'Mi a look work. The Mother Country need our help so mi a go.'

'Do you have a job in London?'

'No, mi will find work in England.'

'Do you feel there will be more people from the West Indies coming to England?'

'Yes, sir. Hol-eep of people want to come.'

'Do you feel the English people will welcome you and your people to London?'

'Mi hope so. We is nice people.'

'Do you smoke drugs?'

'No, man. Mi is a rum man.'

'Will you be dating white women?'

'Well, sir, I have not met many Englishwomen, but I will keep mi eyes open.'

'But if white women wanted to take you dancing, holding you close on the dance floor, how would you feel about that?'

'I would hold her if we were dancing. I would show her how to move the West Indies way.'

'Show me how you do that.'

The West Indian man stood up and moved his hips in a circular motion, waggling his hand and smiling from ear to ear. All you could hear was the clicking of the reporter's camera.

'One last thing. Will you be marrying and having babies with the Englishwomen?'

'Sir, I am a man. A single man. Who knows what women I will meet and when the babies will come?'

'Thank you, Mr Aston Lindford Isaac,' said the *Daily Express* reporter.

CHAPTER 12

DEAR DIARY ...

... Norma ...
The people on board the ship are mostly nice, there are lots of soldiers and island people. I'm in a cabin with Lucretia who is very messy, she already put herself in problems with the newspaperman. 'Her ears too haad.' The English food taste bad and she was about to tell the captain. A what wrong with that gal? Thank the Lord there are some of our people cooking some good yard food. I watched the white soldiers eat the yard food then go back for more before we had a chance to eat! I can't get used to the rocking of the ship all day and night. When there a storm you feel really seasick. So many people have been seasick. The ship is so nice. I can see how well the rich German people lived. Most nights we all meet in the hall, playing some records, talking and dancing, playing dominoes and cards.

Them dominoes people need to behave themselves, they are so loud.

I can't wait to start work in London. I'm going to work so hard that they will make me the headmistress in three years. I feel I will teach them English people new ways of teaching. I have had some nice West Indian men talking to me and some of the white soldiers are not that bad-looking.

Some of the soldiers talk to you as if you are a fool, though. I'm missing my home and my family. At the time of writing this I'm three days over the Atlantic Sea.

I will add more when the ship is days away from England.

... Hyacinth ...

Day 3, I'm well on my way to England on a big ship that has guns and a ballroom. The ship was a luxury liner, now it a warship. With big guns and velvet walls, bars and a dance floor, it a strange mix. There must be about 700–800 people on this ship from all over the place; they are nice people just looking for a better life.

I can't wait to get to England to see you. I dream about you, I feel you in my dreams, I smell you. When that ship gets into London I will be looking for you standing there with my coat and hat. I just want to hug you. Love H xxxx

... Sergeant Davis ...

To hell with this diary shit…

... Rosemarie ...

Mi did see dolphins today. I don't see any land. Aunty Precious said we will see land in about a week or so. Carmel and George are feeling seasick a lot of the time, it's so funny seeing them running to the toilet. I miss Sandy, I bet she misses me. Has she been howling for me? The Jamaican food is good, but the white-people food looks funny and it smells. Mummy, the English people boil their potatoes then they hit them till them mush up and they cook a 'toad in the hole'. Why would you eat a toad and why cook it in a hole? White people are funny. Love, Rosemarie xxxx

... *Captain Stanley* ...

0600 hours Day 3: the new crew over the Atlantic are a mixed group of soldiers. There's a lot going on with the London soldiers. They are trying to pull the wool over my eyes, but I am on to them. The going is fair to good; the West Indians are giving us no problems at the moment, but we are watching them. The undercover spies are keeping me informed about any activity that they may be up to. There is gambling going on, but I am keeping an eye on that. I know I have to allow the soldiers to let off some steam. The reporter from the *Daily Express* gives me a bad feeling. He is asking too many questions. This is not needed, but I will follow my orders.

There have been 'interactions' between the soldiers and the coloured women. I understand the needs of the men, so I will not intervene unless it becomes a problem.

... *Betty* ...

I wish I was not here. Precious is Miss Bossy Bossy and I am not taking any more of it. She too hard on the pickney dem and keeps telling us what we can and can't do. Dad, why did you have to send mi to England? I got no family there, just Precious's mother – who is nice but not mi mother. I am meeting some nice people and making some friends. They looking for stowaways on the ship. The poor men will be locked up till we get to England. As soon as we get to London I will be sending you some letters. Doris is coming out of her shell (at last). I think the time away from Bermuda will help all of us to be better people. Missing you, Mum and Dad ...

... *Edward* ...

I am really missing home! I can see my sisters and you at the docks. I am never going back into the army after this. I hate the uniform that bloody well itches all the time. I hate the war, the food is bollocks and the beer is weak. The coloured chefs are good, though, and the West Indian women look and smell so nice. I must say I have an eye on one of them ... what would my mother say?

... *Selwyn* ...

The ship big, so big mi never know there was two ballrooms. The rooms we have are nice, and them have carpet on the floors and some kind of wallpaper. Mi room has three good men that are working with mi to teach the white boys a lesson. The women are nice ... the Mexican women look hot, there is about ten white women mi see on board the ship. Mi have never kissed a white woman. Do I want to?

The talk on the ship is that the Inglish people don't want us in London. If them a deal with us the way the soldiers on this ship have, then all of us West Indians people will be having a bloodclaat hard time in forin. Us men will be setting up our own business in London but we need to make some money before mi reach Inglan. Mi have somewhere to live in Notting Hill. The white soldier boys don't like our people. 'Cha', after all we have done for Inglan in the war. They is full of shit.

... *Mavis* ...

The rocking of the ship night and day reminds me I'm on a ship. Not seeing land is very scary; the ship is so big you wonder how it floats. I'm meeting some nice men and women and some nice white men ... I have never lived this close to white people. They smell different to us and they sweat a lot. And their food! Well, it is wartime so I will see with them, yet the more I talk to them the more I see we are all alike.

My room-mates are OK, a bit bossy, but OK. I must say that one or two of the soldiers have caught my eye. That Edward is handsome, but that's my secret. Missing you all ...

... *Precious* ...

The kids are behaving themselves, getting seasick, but behaving. Doris and Betty are helping out, but not that much. I read the letter Daddy gave me to read when I got on the boat. I will do as it says. The ship is nice but I thought we were getting bigger cabins? The men on board the ship are fresh – you have to keep an eye on them as they outnumber us about four to one.

But there are some nice-looking men. Sometimes I do feel alone and just want to go back home and sit on our veranda. I hope Daddy has sorted out that bad business back home and Mother is back in London waiting for us.

... *Private Mickey* ...

I'm not sure about this: I feel that they are coming to get me. I see them in my dreams ... I see them in the day. The doctor said it will go away – what what does he know? I can't keep going like this ... no one is taking any notice of me – no one cares. I can't look in mirrors.

*

... Lucretia ...
I'M SICK OF THIS SHIP… I'M SICK OF THE FOOD … I'M SICK OF THE RULES … I'M SICK OF THE SMALL CABIN … I'M SICK OF MISS MADAM TELLING ME WHAT TO DO … I'M SICK OF THE SHIP ROCKING ALL THE TIME … I'M SICK OF BEING SEASICK … AND I AM SICK OF PASSING WIND, LOTS OF WIND … AND IT DON'T SMELL NICE.

PART IV
Lockdown

CHAPTER 13

'BLOODY HELL!'

'After lunch you're all going to meet the captain, so I want you all to be on your best behaviour. No running on deck.'

'Yes, Aunty Precious.'

'You can take a walk around the ship, but you can't go near the ship guard rail when you're not with one of the adults.'

As the kids happily put on their coats and hats and made their way out of the cabin, glad to be getting away from the aunties, Precious sat looking in the mirror. Doris was stretched out on her bed, looking up at the ceiling. Betty was sorting out her outfits.

'What did that man say to you last night?'

Precious kept looking into the mirror at her nose, lips and lipstick.

'He sounded very nice, maybe a bit too nice.'

'What the hell does that mean?' Betty said.

There was a pause … 'You know, the sweet-mouth man.'

Betty looked at Precious, then at Doris, who sat up on her bed. 'Gal, you really did notice him?'

'Stop your noise!' Precious said. 'You're just looking to faas wid mi.'

'Are you seeing him tonight?' Doris said.

'It a ship, I can't not see him! Sometimes, Precious, you can be a real pain in the ...'

'We just a talk,' Betty said. 'Maybe we did hit a nerve. Mmmmm?'

... *Hyacinth* ...

I can't believe I let that man kiss me like that! The drink went right to my head. I was feeling drunk, yes, I was drunk. No need to tell mi man about this, it will not happen again, anyway. I moved over on my side as I lay on the bed in the empty cabin. I can still feel his kiss, it feel so nice, but wrong. But nice . . . wrong? But?

'This is the location for the controls and dashboard, we control the ship from here, and this is my vice-captain, Mr Trevor Hobbes.'

All the children looked at him. He was holding the big ship's wheel, which was made of wood with a metal rim; the cockpit was filled with knobs, lights, switches and buttons with a wraparound window giving you the best view of the sea from the top of the ship. You felt as if you were in the air. Precious was standing back in the control room watching the kids. They were mesmerised by the ship's captain wearing his white uniform standing next to the ship's controls in his white captain's hat with gold leaf on the black peak, the different coloured medals on his chest, with the short black stick he always had in his hand.

The children could not take their eyes off the gold buttons on his white jacket. In the children's eyes they were dazzling, he was a god.

'Can all the people fit in the lifeboats?'

'Yes, but it's always women and children first.'

'What about the men?'

'Are we drinking the sea water?' Another question came out of nowhere.

'No, we take on fresh water at every port.'

'How does the metal ship float on the sea?'

The children were firing questions at the captain, who took it all in good humour. Some of the crew put their hats on the children's heads and let them hold the big wheel, steering the ship. 'They look so happy,' Doris thought.

Standing at the back watching the children were groups of parents and family members.

'Hello, my name is Doretha. From Tobago. Are they your pickney dem?' one lady asked standing next to Precious, who was looking at all the children enjoying themselves.

'No, they are my cousins and family.'

'Look at them. Who would have thought they would be on a ship taking them all the way to London? When we were that age we was milking the cows and taking in the water.'

'Well, some of us did,' Precious interjected.

Doretha turned her head and said nothing.

Doris just looked at Precious. Betty thought, 'What the hell is wrong with her?'

'What you wearing tonight?'

'It's just drinks at the bar. You look good the way you are.'

'Yes, I do.' Norma looked in the mirror. 'But my hair is playing up. All this sea air is messing with it.' She tried to get the comb through her hair.

'Try this in your nappy hair.'

'Who you a call nappy hair?' Norma said, as she threw the comb at Lucretia. 'Cha, gal, you too bad ...'

'I got to get some clothes. I can't keep up the story about my things being missing. Let mi go and see de man who is selling things to people,' Roy thought.

As some of the men were leaving the cabin, Roy moved off the bed and said, 'Mi soon come.'

'The ship is not rocking so much as it did when we left Bermuda,' Doris thought. 'I don't feel as sick as yesterday.' She looked hard and long at Precious. 'She always gets the good-looking boys from when we were kids; when I told her in school I liked Mikey Jameson she start talking to him. She never looked at him till I said mi like him. She can't stand anyone looking better than her. Her daddy looked down on my family: mi overhear them talking late at night 'bout how her daddy feel him is the BIG-MAN on the docks. My daddy said, if her daddy was not so greedy the government would not have come down on Daddy and the rest of the men so hard, and mi would not be on this ship. Well, Miss Precious needs to look out! Doris is grown up and I is not playing this time,' she thought as she looked at Precious putting on her make-up.

'Come on. It seven p.m. I want to get a drink from the bar before the English boys get there and drink out the drinks.'

Anton and Verndo put on their jackets and followed Pele out the cabin.

Walking along the corridors, Anton looked at the carpet and the patterns on them.

'We never had carpet in our house,' he said.

'What would you need carpet for in a hot country like ours? Yah thinking of taking the carpet back to Mexico?'

Anton looked at them with that 'why you messing with me?' look.

'Hi again. Are they your friends you were telling me about?' Pele looked around and Ada Mae was standing there by the bar looking so, so good.

'Hi,' he nervously said. 'Yes, this is Anton and Verndo. Everyone, this is Ada Mae – she from Mexico.'

'What you drinking?' Pele said. 'I don't think they have tequila. Let me find out.'

They all gazed at the people standing around in the ballroom.

'There a lot of different people on the ship,' Verndo said.

'Not a lot of us, though,' Ada said.

Pele came back. 'They don't have tequila, but there a drink from Trinidad that the barman said you will like.'

She took a sip. 'Mmmmm, yes this is good. What is it?'

'Trinidad ten-year-old rum, with a touch of lime.'

'Yes, this will be my drink till we get to London.'

'Cha-man, I need to go over to her tonight and let her know that I'm a good man just trying to get to Inglan. *What the hell you saying? She will turn you into the MP on the ship. You will go to jail and then be deported back home.* Bumboclaat, I can't go on this way.' Roy had this argument going on in his head all the time.

'Can I trust her? Is she working for the Englishmen?' He began beating his head with his hands as he was about to go to the ballroom.

... *Pele* ...

'Can we meet for a drink on deck at the back of the ship?' she said quietly in my ear. 'Just me and you?'

I looked at her and said, 'Yes, yes. What time?'

'In about ten minutes.'

I was knocking back the drinks and was talking through my rum drink. The boys already had had one too many and were unsteady on their feet.

The ballroom was rocking, with people talking, drinking, playing cards and dominoes.

Ada Mae sent me a look indicating that I should follow her outside onto the deck.

'It dark out here,' she said.

'It not that bad,' I said, looking up at white stars in a black sky and around at the black ocean. We were leaning on the guard rail, feeling the warm air on our skin.

There were two other couples on deck who were locking lips. In their own world on the other side of the ship.

'What you going to do in England?' she said.

'I will do whatever they have. I hear they need people to work on the buses, hospitals and building sites.'

... *Ada*...

The ship hit a wave. I held onto Pele as I was tossed forward. I looked deep into his eyes. He held me on my lower back; I moved my mouth closer to his, kissed him on the cheek then rubbed his back. The boy was half drunk and half turned on.

As he leant back against the railing I saw my opportunity, and suddenly I pushed forward hard on his chest. As I did this I pulled out his feet. In one move I sent Pele flying over the guard rail, somersaulting over the side of the ship into the black of the sea.

My heart was thumping. But on the outside I was calm. I looked down as he disappeared beneath the restless waves. Checked all around to make sure no one had seen what happened, then adjusted my clothes and walked back to the bar.

I picked up my drink, turned to Anton and said, 'When is Pele coming back from the toilet?'

Anton drunkenly said, 'As soon as he finds his little dick.'

I forced a smile. They all burst out laughing.

'Your round.'

'No, I got the last round, you mean bastard.'

'OK, this is my round,' Private Mickey said as he walked over to the bar.

Edward turned to Davis and said, 'How's he doing? He still seeing the doctor and having them bad bloody dreams?'

'We all get them.'

'Yeah. But we don't wake up screaming and going for our gun, do we?'

'You're kidding!'

'Do I look like I'm kidding?'

'Bloody hell.'

CHAPTER 14

'OVER AND OUT'

Roy was running out of money. He stayed away from the ballroom so he did not have to buy drinks. In the morning he went back to the tailor-man cabin.

'What's you real name?' he asked the tailor-man.

'Me is Nicky Nicolson from Trinidad. Most people call me "Sharp" cos you look sharp in mi clothes.'

'A true that,' Roy said. 'How much is the jacket and shirt?'

'One pound, six shillin'. Inglish money.'

Roy knew he did not have the money, but he had a plan. 'Nicky, how many people know you is here giving this service? I mean, I just hears about you by accident. I is a salesman – I can get you a hol-eep of customers. Soon you will be looking for a bigger place to work from.'

'Is how you a do that? Mi just a keep this thing undercover. Soldier-man don't know about me or if him do he don't care.'

'Nicky, I will wear your clothes so the men can see what you have and I will send you new customers. You just give me a commission. You a do women things?'

'No, man, mi don't, but I can repair things.'

'Now you're thinking,' Roy said. 'You see already mi give you a new line of businesses.'

Nicky put out his hand. 'You has a deal, man.'

Roy put out his hand and said, 'So do you.'

'What time is it?' Anton said. Verndo was out cold. Anton rolled back over and fell asleep.

'The breakfast was English,' Mavis said.

'Very English,' said Lucretia. 'I want to know why them don't cook them meat.'

'The food was moving on my plate,' Norma said. The women laughed out loud, then a soldier walked past and they went quiet till he was down the deck. Then they fell about laughing.

Mavis sat on the deckchairs someone had put out.

'Look! Them have chairs. They were not here when we got on the ship.' As she said this a very manly voice came from behind them.

'We did find them in the bottom of the ship.' They all looked around to see the Chef.

'You is the Chef,' said Lucretia.

'Yes, dat mi – and mi never cook the breakfast.'

'Man we did know that! When you a cook again?'

'Tonight at the dance in the ballroom.'

'Praise the Lord,' Norma said.

'My name is Winsell Glen Benjamin. People call mi Chef from Spanish Town. And you are ...?'

'Pele must be hitting that gal hard. It three p.m. and him still not come back.'

'If you got lucky, would you come back to see us bastards?'

'You're right, lucky bastard.'

'I don't want any screw-ups tonight. There's a lot of money in the pot and we are going to win it. The MPs tonight are my friends so they will be staying in the ballroom and upper decks. You and the team will be patrolling the lower decks.'

'We can play most of the night, and no fighting or we are all done for.'

'Mickey, you get the booze from the back of the bar. Edward, make sure you have the two bottles of scotch for the MP guards tonight. OK, let's get Colin and get them wogs.'

'Thanks, Mr Benjamin, we'll see you later tonight.' As he walked off Norma said, 'What a nice man and what a way him tick to you, Lucretia.'

'Cha, him too small and too dark for me.'

'Sister, you never said that,' Mavis said. 'If you don't like him then say you don't like him, but don't run-down him colour.'

'Mi never say mi no like him. Him is very nice and funny, but the short man thing, no. Mi need to look up to mi man. Plus him is a chef.'

Norma and Mavis rolled their eyes and laid into Lucretia. 'What the hell you saying? Some of the best-looking men are some of the most wutless you can find.'

'Cyann buy puss inna bag. I na say you can't have a good-looking man, but sometime average looks is better ... them man are happy that you is looking at them because all the women are looking at the pretty boys.'

As the women were talking loudly about men, two men in soldiers' uniform were walking past and one said, 'Yes, sister, you tell them. We man a just trying to better ourselves.'

The women looked at them and the discussion picked up between all of them. By the time the discussion moved on to Inglan and what white people thought about West Indians coming to the Motherland about fifteen people had gathered around, all talking about what them hear, what them a do, what and where there were places to rent and the bad food from the Inglish chefs.

Norma and the women had made new friends. They agreed before everyone left that 'we must talk together and we must do this more often.'

'Yes,' Norma said, 'same time tomorrow?'

'Yes,' said one of the group members, 'tomorrow. Right here.'

'He must be coming back for a change of clothes,' Anton said.

'What's he need clothes for? He sexing her all day and night. You need to find a woman yourself.'

Anton was thinking, 'I'm not feeling this. Something not right.'

'That's how we are playing the game tonight. I need my partner to read the game, give mi the sign when you can't play ... them English boys can play dominoes better than we thought.'

'Yes, you're right. We need to be more tactical how we play. Man, get out the dominoes, we are going to practise the sign. Look at my eyebrows – when I rise mi left eyebrow then mi have some pears. When mi can't follow through then I will wipe mi nose.'

'Cha, man, I can't raise mi left eyebrow. What kind of foolishness a gwan?'

'OK,' said Selwyn, 'you come up with a better way?'

'Tonight we are playing two songs from all the people-dem island on the ship.'

'What song we a play from Bermuda?' Fitzroy said.

'The Coo Coo song,' Lord Pan said. 'You don't know that song?' He began to play it, the rest of the Pan Players joined in. Before long they were playing the hell out of the song. Lord Pan put up his hand. 'That's it – you got it. We will also be playing on the decks in the daytime tomorrow.'

'What?' Fitzroy said, in a fed-up way. 'Man, we need a rest, man.'

Lord Pan looked at him and said, 'You a pay all the fare to England? No, all of us know we is working off our fare to Inglan. So stop complain. We have a good deal and you're not going to mess it up for all of us.'

The pan group looked at Fitzroy. There was silence, then Lord Pan said, 'Let's take it from the top. One, two, three ...'

... *Private Mickey* ...

'Ahhhh ...' I was half awake.

I was working nights, so was sleeping in the day, waking up sweating and talking to myself.

The other soldiers were still asleep.

I lay back down and as I closed my eyes and drifted back into sleep I could see the battlefield, the guns, the face of the German soldier running towards me. I pointed my gun with the bayonet on the end at him, but the German kept coming, I kept shouting in my sleep, 'Stop! Go back! Stop! Go back! Stop!' The kind of dream-shouting where you can't make people hear you. The German soldier ran right onto the end of my bayonet and stopped. I could hear the last of the air leaving his body. I could feel my own body getting heavy: my hands and face felt like they were awash with blood. My heart was pulling hard, I felt as if I was having a heart attack, then as I looked at the German soldier I saw he had my face. I was looking back at myself with the bayonet inside me, pushing hard against my own heart, then there was a popping sound and lights, lots of lights ...

I opened my eyes and wiped the sweat off my forehead, sat up rocking on my bed, mumbling words, looking around the room, not blinking, just staring ... staring ...

'Do you know what cabin that woman Pele was with last night is staying in?'

'No, I think she left the bar with us ...'

'Man, I was out of it.'

'Did you see if she was with him?'

Verndo said, 'Stop being a mother. The man having a good time, he will let us know where he is when he good and ready. I bet we see him tonight in the bar.'

'Yeah, you're right. We'll see him tonight in the bar with that hot woman he been sexing. What time we going to the bar?'

Captain Stanley was speaking in an angry tone. 'I have called this meeting because we still have two stowaways walking around this ship. All the patrols say they cannot find them. This country has fought two world wars and won, so why the hell can't we find these stowaways on this ship? Gentlemen, it has been more than three days. This is embarrassing for you, and for me, and for the good name of this ship.

'Because of your failures I am suspending all entertainment and any activity for the passengers and all soldiers as from today.

'As from 1900 hours all passengers must be in their cabin till 0700 hours and all soldiers on this ship whether you're on nights or days will go from cabin to cabin checking all paperwork and searching throughout the ship from top to bottom, from bow to stern.

'I want the stowaways and I want them NOW! Dismissed.'

A room full of voices said, 'Yes, sir.'

The Tannoy came on: 'This is your captain speaking. All entertainment and any activities will be suspended till tomorrow at 0700 hours. You must be in your cabins by 1900 hours tonight; anyone found outside their cabins will be placed in the Brig. Have all your paperwork ready for inspection tonight. If we all cooperate we will be free to resume normal activity as soon as possible. Captain Stanley, over and out.'

CHAPTER 15

DUPPY IN THE DAY, DUPPY IN THE NIGHT

'What the bloodclaat them a say no dancing tonight?'

'No drinks ... Cha, man.'

Evans' cabin was not happy. They were ready for the soldier boys tonight.

Roy was standing by the porthole, looking out to sea, not saying a word.

'Look under the bed, there is a bottle of rum there for emergency like this,' Selwyn said.

'Man, that's why you're the boss-man,' Evans said.

'You heard the captain. We are serving food at four p.m. today, so we can get back to our cabin before seven,' Chef said to his team, 'so move, move, move.'

'Cha, mi was looking forward to playing the roof off tonight. Let's pack up the pans and have one last drink before them lockdown everyone tonight.'

'Shit, I never saw that coming. No games tonight,' Davis said to his team. 'We have to step it up. The captain's not messing around and we are not taking the shame of not finding two stowaway coons on our ship.'

*

'Kids, we can go and have a walk then some food. Then we must stay inside the cabin till tomorrow. No one must come out, you understand? No one.'

Precious looked at Doris and Betty, who had sad faces.

Doris said, 'The soldier-man danced sooo nice,' in a dreamy way. Betty just looked at her.

'Come on, it nearly five, let's go and get some food. The West Indians are cooking today, so the food will be good and it will run out once them soldier-boys get in the line. You coming, Anton?'

'Yes, I'm coming. I hope we see Pele in the food hall ...?'

... Roy ...

'Let's go and eat,' Selwyn said. 'You not coming, Roy?'

'Yes, I will catch you up.' Sitting in the empty cabin I thought about how I was going to play this lockdown the captain had ordered. I went to my jacket and pulled out some papers. I opened them slowly, looking at the words on the two papers.

Gladstone Vincent Carman, twenty-five years old, Hill Lane, Montego Bay, Jamaica.

I looked at the papers and thought about how I got them ...
Jamaica, nine days ago ...

'... You have the money, Roy?'

'Yes, man.'

'Then meet mi in the Q bar in fifteen minutes.'

I made my way down the backstreets of Trench Town deep in Kingston, Jamaica, with the big women selling everything and anything you needed from hot peppers to clothes ... music was bubbling out of every bar and every shop mi passed, mi see the Rasta man selling ital food, local boys selling ice scrapings from their wooded-cart, the good smell of jerk cooking in the air, moving out of the way of the goats and dogs running around the streets ... this was all part of the tapestry of life in Trench Town.

Mi heard the bar before mi see it. Music was blasting out, two bad-looking men were sitting at the side of the bar drinking and smoking. Them was the lookout.

Mi take a good look. The infamous Q Bar. If you could call it a bar, it was more of a shack with bits of wood for the bar and boxes to sit on. Them only sold beers, rum, water and weed. There were four big speaker boxes outside that would knock you off your feet if you walked in front of them, the sound was that loud.

Mi did hear that the owner was a well-known bad man who controlled drugs and women from the bar. It was him front so the police didn't bother him.

'One beer, man,' mi say in mi best bad-man tone. Don't let them see you as soft inna this bad-man bar.

One 6ft-tall, powerfully built man with a scar across his face took one from a bowl filled with water. 'Ten cents,' he growled, never taking his eyes off me.

Mi did sit on de box and wait about ten minutes. The men at the side of the bar never took them eyes off mi, weed filled the air and people kept coming and going very quietly. The man mi was waiting for, the man I only knew as 'V', was walking towards me as he called out to the barman, 'One beer', then sat down beside mi.

I handed him the money in a rolled-up piece of paper. He counted it, then gave me the papers.

'Remember,' V said, 'don't use it till you're on the ship. Don't use it to get on the ship, only when you're gwan from yard then them can't check up.'

'Then how mi must get on the ship?' I said.

'A what the rass you are ask mi for? Nof man get pon that ship ... use your rass head.'

The big man at the bar put down the beer on the box, then walked slowly away. V kept talking. 'If them stop you on the ship, just show them the paperwork. When you get to London you can use it to get a job.'

I had mi suspicions as to where it came from and how him get it, but mi wanted to go to Inglan and did not have all the dollars – and time was running out, so this was the only way mi could get pon the ship.

As V handed mi the papers a funeral card fell out. V coolly picked it up and put it in his pocket. 'Remember, you don't know me,' he said, with a searching look that said, 'Don't cross me.'

... I took a deep breath as mi come back to reality on the ship in the cabin, looking at the papers beside the cabin window. Mi know if mi got caught without the right papers mi would be locked up, if mi get caught with a dead man's paperwork mi would be locked up, then they send mi back home – so what choice did mi have? Thank the Lord everyone give in their tickets when they boarded, so all I need is mi dead-man ID ...

I made mi way to the table in the ballroom, where mi boys were sitting.

'There you are,' Selwyn said. 'Pull up a chair. The food nice, the rice and peas taste good – no meat today, but fish and vegetables are good.'

I started to eat, not saying anything to the table of men.

Selwyn looked at Roy a bit longer than normal, then continued to eat his food.

'That's the last of the food. Everyone has eaten. Let's clear up,' Chef said.

'Hyacinth?'

She knew that voice. As she turned around, there was Dangle standing there, looking so dapper and fine. She was putting back her plates on the serving table.

'You want to have some drinks in my cabin? It's going to be a long night. I got a record player and food?'

Hyacinth looked at him and noticed that everyone at the table where she and Maria had been sitting was watching her and Dangle talking.

Dangle did stand out in any crowd in his fitted cream suit, white shirt, blue tie and cream pointed shoes.

'The captain said we must stay in our cabin.'

'Don't worry about that, just get your papers and come over to my cabin before seven. I will take care of everything.'

'How will I get back to my cabin?'

'I got this covered,' he said in a low voice.

'Let's mi think about that,' Hyacinth said.

... *Mavis* ...
I lay on my bed thinking about Edward.

What am I doing thinking of a white soldier? If Mother knew this, she would tell mi to marry him as quickly as possible. She always said to marry up, not down. No boy I took home passed her twenty questions ... You have a job? You at school? Where your people from? You have God in your life? ...

I looked at Mother's photo. 'Mum, you're so bad ... but so right to look out for me. I miss you so much.'

I realised tears were running down my face.

'I will be OK,' Hyacinth said. 'He said he got it covered, he will take mi back to the cabin later on tonight.'

Maria looked at her. 'You really sure about this? You know he going to want sex? What about your man waiting for you in London?'

'Do you really think that he has been a good boy over the last year?' Hyacinth said in a pissed-off voice. 'I can handle it. Anyway, have you thought that maybe I may want the loving? It's not always about the man.'

Maria just looked at her. Hyacinth stopped putting on her make-up, adjusted her all-in-one white and brown cotton dress in the mirror, picked up her handbag and papers and walked to the door. 'Mi gaan,' she said as she went out the door.

'Take out your books. I don't want to hear a word from you kids till you have read your two chapter, then we will be going through the books with you, then bed.'

'Aaaahhh,' the children said together. 'Must we?'

'Yes, you must.'

Betty was about to say something but thought, 'Not in front of the children.' She was getting fed up with Precious being so bossy. Doris looked at Betty in an agreeing way.

... *Roy* ...

'Roy.' It was Selwyn. 'Let's have a quick cigarette before the lockdown.'

'I don't really smoke,' I said.

'Then walk with mi while I have one. We got fifteen minutes. Come, man.'

I got up, leaving the rest of the boys playing cards.

As we walked onto the top deck, Selwyn lit his cigarette and leaned over the ship's guard rail, looking out to sea.

I was looking at my hands in a nervous way.

'It's you dem a look for?' he said.

How did he know?

I did not move or react; I just kept looking out to sea.

'Man, talk to me. It you dem a look for? Tell me, man.'

There was a pause, then I moved around and looked Selwyn in the face and said, 'Yes, it's me.'

Selwyn took a cool draw on his cigarette and said, 'How can I help you?'

'Man, I don't know. In fifteen minutes I could be locked up for the rest of the trip, then deported back home.'

'Man, you should have told mi before we get to this.'

I just kept on looking out to sea.

'You have any papers?'

I hesitated, then decided it was best to come clean. 'Yes, but it not mine. Dead-man papers.'

I felt a heavy burden had been lifted from my shoulders.

'OK, then all you need is the proof of your ticket.'

I was shocked.

'Yes, that's right. You must have a the other half of the ticket.'

'But I don't have one.'

Selwyn kept dragging on his cigarette, then flung it overboard. 'Come, make mi sort you out,' he coolly said.

I looked at him.

'Mi said, Come now. We don't have much time.' Selwyn walked towards the stairs that led back to the cabin.

As we were walking, I said, 'What you a do, man?'

'Just trust me. Keep your mouth shut and do as I say.'

6:45 p.m. and the ship was getting very quiet. The soldiers had started to stand at the top of all the stairs in the ship and were moving people off the top deck. The ship was beginning to feel like a ghost ship. No one out of uniform was moving around. The Tannoy came on ...

'This is the captain. It is now seven p.m., 1900 hours. All passengers must be in their cabins. Anyone found outside will be put in the Brig.'

*

Knock, knock. The door opened and Dangle was standing there in his black and red smoking jacket with a glass of champagne in his hand.

'This, my dear, is for you.'

Hyacinth slowly walked inside holding her handbag and papers.

'Sergeant, we have searched levels one and two. We are now moving down to level three.'

'Private, you and your team start at that end of the ship and we will start from the other end. Remember – cabin by cabin, hall by hall, stock room by stock room.'

'Yes, sir.'

Knock, knock.

'Papers!' the soldiers shouted.

Precious opened the door. Standing there were three armed soldiers. 'May I see papers for all the people in this cabin?'

'I have them ready for you.'

'I need everyone to hold up their papers, so we can verify them.'

Precious said, 'The kids' names are on my passport. Doris and Betty have theirs.'

The soldier took his time and read everyone's paperwork, now and again asking questions.

'How long have you lived in Bermuda?'

'All my life,' Doris said.

'Who got you the ticket?'

'My father.'

'All of you, please stand outside. We need to search your cabin.'

Precious's group followed the orders and stood outside. The soldiers pulled up the bed, looked in the cupboards, under the beds and in the toilets.

'Thank you, thank you, you may go back inside.'

The soldiers moved to the next cabin.

'All done here, sir.'

Davis looked at the group of soldiers, then checked in the storeroom. It was full of boxes.

'Have you moved that wall of boxes, soldier?'

'No, sir.'

'Why not?'

'Sir, the boxes are next to the wall, sir.'

'I don't give a damn what they are against. Move the boxes and bloody well look behind and inside the damned things!'

'Yes, sir.'

As Davis moved back outside to the corridor to see what the other group of soldiers was doing, there was a shout, 'Get him!' and the sound of a tussle. Davis and the other soldiers ran back into the storeroom. The soldiers were holding down a West Indian man who was swearing in patois, words that the soldiers did not understand – but they knew these words were not polite.

Davis calmly walked over to the man, who was lying face down on the floor with four soldiers on top of him and said, 'My, my, my, you have been a hard nigger to catch. Cuff him.' Davis looked behind the boxes where the man had a bed and food. 'This is why you must bloody well follow my orders,' he shouted at the soldiers standing there. 'Take him to the Brig. One down, one to go.'

Knock, knock. 'Papers!' the soldiers shouted.

The door opened and the 6ft-tall, white-skinned, dapper-looking Dangle was standing there. The soldier took one look and said in a softer tone, 'May I see your papers, sir?'

'Yes, you can. Plus my guest.' He handed the soldier both sets of paperwork. The soldier looked at the paperwork, then looked over Dangle's shoulder to see the outline of a woman. He quickly gave the papers back and said, 'Sorry to disturb you, sir.'

... Roy ...
Knock, knock.

'Papers!' the soldiers shouted.

The card game stopped. Selwyn went to the door. As he opened it we could see three soldiers with guns standing outside.

'I need to see all the papers of the people in this cabin.'

The men took out their paperwork. The soldiers looked at them, then started with Selwyn.

'Who bought you the ticket?'

'I did.'

'Where did you buy it?'

'Kingston Harbour.'

The soldier handed back his papers, then moved on to Evans. He looked at the papers, looked at Evans, paused then handed the paperwork back to him, moving on to me. The soldier took my paperwork and looked at it.

'How long have you lived in Montego Bay?' Looking mi straight in the eye.

'All my life.'

'Who bought the ticket?'

'I did, at the Kingston Harbour.'

He looked at me, stared at the paperwork. There was a pause that felt like an hour, but it was seconds. Then he handed it back.

After the soldier had asked the same questions to everyone in the cabin he moved to the door.

'We need you all to stand outside while we search the cabin.'

I looked at Evans, who looked at Selwyn. The soldiers looked under the beds, in cupboards and drawers, then the order came to 'Move out', and as the last soldier left, all the men in the cabin exhaled then looked at the mess the soldiers had left behind. Selwyn gave mi a nod.

'How them never find the rum?' Selwyn said.

Evans moved the picture on the wall and behind it was shelving with rows of rum bottles.

I was shocked. 'You never tell mi you had rum in here.'

'If you did know you would have been nervous and that would have given us away.'

'Just cool, man,' Selwyn said to me. 'Just cool.'

I now understood why Selwyn had lots of paperwork and envelopes in a box, the box from which he had produced the ship's ticket he had given me. 'Problem solved, but you owe me,' Selwyn said.

I had helped him hide the box under a metal beam that needed two men to lift it up to put the box beneath it. This was on the way back to the cabin after our talk.

I sat down, looked at the men in the cabin then said, 'You are some very smart boys.'

All the team leaders and top brass were assembled in the ballroom in neat lines facing the stage.

'AA-TEN-SHUN !'

There was a sharp sounding of the boots. Out walked the captain on stage.

'At ease, gentlemen. We have captured the stowaways. There was obviously a counting error. We had two stowaways, not three. This is a job well done.'

'Yes, sir!' came the reply from all the soldiers.

'As a thank you for your hard work the bar will be open for one hour where you and your team may have free drinks. But anyone found drunk will spend a day in the Brig.'

'Yes, sir. Thank you, sir.'

'Dismissed.'

Captain Stanley walked off the stage towards his cabin. He knew there was one more stowaway, but he was not going to mess up his 100% record of a clean ship.

PART V
Games and Guns

CHAPTER 16

'YOU SENT FOR US'

'Do you think anyone will show up?'

'Well, we are here, so let's see.'

Norma, Betty, Lucretia and Doris were sitting in the same spot on the deck where they had met the others the previous morning.

'Here they come,' said Betty. 'Good morning, all. Did you have a good night's sleep?'

'Yes, we did.'

'I hear them caught the stowaways.'

'Yes, mi hear say that he put up a good fight.'

'You did know him?'

'No. I saw when they was dragging him down the hallway. He was cussing some bad words.'

'Well, he should have paid like the rest of us,' Norma said.

One of the men said, 'Sister, the man was trying to get a better life in the Mother Country.'

'So am I,' she said, 'but I still had to pay for my ticket. My family, like a lot of people here, had to sacrifice many things to get mi on this ship.'

'Don't be so hard ... The man was not doing anyone any harm. We all from the same place.'

'Well, I worked hard to be here.'

Then the conversation became a free-for-all. There was a big difference of opinions about whether the man should be arrested; at one point the arms were going, the voices got loud, the sucking of the teeth became a choir, and while this was happening in full view of everyone on the deck a reporter was watching, standing just out of sight. He could hear everything that was said. Sometimes he could not understand what they were saying because of their broad accents, but he got the gist of the discussion.

Just as the talk was dying down, the reporter walked over to the group of about fifteen people and said, 'Hello?'

Everyone stopped talking. By now most of the passengers knew he was a reporter from the *Daily Express* and that he was doing a story about the people on board. Word had got around the ship; people had heard that some Inglish had bad feeling about West Indians coming to Inglan and this was making them nervous.

The reporter said: 'Can I have an interview with anyone who wishes to express their thoughts and feelings about coming to England?' There was silence. 'I only want to show the English people the other side of the coin. I know you don't trust me. Other newspapers are writing stories about you and this ship and the government are debating you right now in London, so why not put your side of the story?'

A man's voice came out of the crowd. 'Why you Inglish people hate us so much?' Everyone looked around. The voice was coming from the Chef. 'I read in *The Gleaner* newspaper about how your people and how your government don't want us there. Is you and your king invite us. It you who sent the ship for us. It was our people who fight and died in the white-man wars alongside your Inglish people.'

'Yes,' said another woman. 'Many of our men and women gave their lives in the war. Where is the gratitude? Where is the "thank you"?'

The reporter was writing as fast as he could. 'You don't feel the British government has shown its gratitude to the West Indian soldiers who were lost in the war?' he asked.

'No respect, no respect,' a voice cried.

'Your country is bruk. You don't have enough people to man your hospitals, buses, building sites. We are a part of your Empire, but we had no choice when you took our many minerals and you have taken many slaves from our islands – and what have we got back?'

'Do you feel England has raped your islands?'

'You see,' said Norma in a loud voice, stepping forward towards the reporter, 'this is the headline you're looking for ... This is why no one trusts you. Why you a use the word "rape"? Why did you have to make us out to be the bad people, when we have been the victims of your brutal Empire for over four hundred years?' Norma turned to the group of people and said, 'Na bother with this ... he just putting words into your mouth for a good headline. You coming?' She looked at Doris, Betty and Lucretia who got up and walked away, followed by the rest of the group.

'I only want your side of the story,' the reporter said.

One man looked around at him and said, 'Devil man.'

Before you could say 'Bye, bye,' all the group had melted away.

But he had his story.

CHAPTER 17

'WHAT YOU SOW, SO YOU WILL REAP'

'We need to tell the captain that Pele is missing.'

'You mad? You want the soldiers looking into our business? Want them questioning us about the drugs man on the docks? No, no, we will look all over the ship for Pele – and look for that woman. She knows something.'

'You OK, Hyacinth?'

A mumble.

'Well, what happened last night? Or what didn't happen last night?'

Hyacinth lay on her bed looking at the wall. She said nothing.

'You sure you're OK?'

Hyacinth started to sob. Maria sat next to her. 'Did he hurt you?'

Hyacinth kept crying. Maria sat with her, rubbing her back.

'Never mind, sister, never mind.'

... Norma ...

What a nice morning, the sun is hot on my face and the sea is calm ... I am sitting on the deck of the ship in a wooden lounge chair reading a book with the blanket over my legs. Sometimes I just need some space and time away from Lucretia and the rest of the group.

As I was reading my book a voice said, 'You're looking well today.'

I looked up and there in front of me was a face I recognised.

'My Lord, I knew I saw you on the ship.'

Roy moved over to me and sat down next to me sideways on the lounge chair.

I put my book down on my lap. 'So how have you been?'

He looked me in the eye.

'It been hard, but some friends help me out.'

'So you was the stowaway the soldiers were looking for? How did you get past the MPs and the checks?'

'The brothers helped me.'

'That's it, that's it ... "The brothers helped me."' I took off mi glasses. 'You had no damn right being on this ship. You could have got mi in trouble.' Mi voice was getting vex and the Jamaican was coming out. 'Mi could have been sent to the almshouse as a co-conspirator. Wha sweet a mout' hat a belly.'

'Why you had to say that?' Roy said. 'You had nothing to do with mi staying on board this ship. A mi mek that decision not you, a mi took the risk not you, a me dem a put ina almshouse house and deport back a yard.'

'Good,' I said. 'You're lucky mi na tell soldier-man over there all about your backside.'

'Norma, it is Norma, isn't it? Mi never meant to put you in mi business. I just want to get to Inglan. I just want to get a job and find a new life. How that so bad?'

I suck mi teeth and started to get up from the lounge chair, picking up the blanket and book. 'It's wutless men like you that make life so hard for our people to get on in life. Them white people think we is all teefs and crooks.'

'What you care about what the white people think? It's what you think that matters,' he said, in a vex tone with a steely look.

'You is the tief,' I said.

He just looked at me. I sucked mi teeth and walked away.

He put his head in his hands and I heard him say: 'Lord a-what-wrong with that woman?'

'Look over there by the door, it's her.' The boys made their way over to the other side of the ship on the deck. 'Now be cool, don't make her suspicious. Let's see if she asks for Pele – if she don't, we will know she knows something.'

'Hi Anton,' she said. 'Is Pele with you? He said he would meet me yesterday but was a no-show.'

Anton and Verndo looked at her. 'So when was the last time you saw Pele?'

'At the bar,' she said. 'Why, what's happening?'

'Nothing,' Anton said, 'nothing. I just thought he was with you.'

'Come on, what's going on? If he got another woman then he should have the balls to tell me – not his little gang—'

Verndo interrupted, 'You don't know what the hell you're talking about and who the—'

Anton grabbed Verndo to stop him from saying any more. He looked him in the eye and said, 'Stop your noise!'

'You guys are messed up. I just met you and your boy is treating me like some piece of shit.' And she walked off, cussing in Mexican ... 'The little bastards,' she thought. 'I will teach them to talk to me like that! What you sow you will reap,' she thought as she walked away.

'Man, I told you to be cool. We don't know if she knows something.'

'She bloody well does,' Verndo said. 'I feel that she knows something, I just feel it.'

In Davis's cabin he was holding a meeting. 'We've got time before we get to London. We need to take all their money before we get there ... The game's on tonight, same place, same time. Let's not bloody well mess up this time,' he warned as he looked everyone in the eye. 'Don't mess it up!'

In the lower hall there were some men setting up equipment.
'Mi a play some tunes in the lower hall,' the DJ said to Selwyn.
'What you have?'
'Blue Beat, Mento, Calypso and some original White Label.'
'Sound good. I will drop in tonight to "drop some foot".'
'Bring some women with you.'
'Yes, man, mi know which women to bring.'

*

As Mavis walked down the corridor she turned around, and standing there was Edward in his brown uniform, looking very nice.

'Mavis, are you going to the dance tonight?'

'Who wants to know?' she said playfully.

He looked at her and said, 'This man does. Will you meet me on deck at seven thirty by the lifeboats?'

'Maybe, maybe not. Let's see,' she said with a smile as she walked away from him.

He stood still, just looking at her body and that Caribbean woman's walk that Mavis had perfected.

'Chef, we only have five days left of rice and four days left of meat ...'

'OK, then we have fe make do with what we have. Now you will learn what it is to be a chef. Now you will make something out of nothing ... (like you have been doing all this trip),' he added under his breath. 'Pull out the fish: we have hole-eep of fish ...'

'Yes, Chef, we can cook salt fish and season fish with vegetables for everyone tonight.'

'Then that's what we will do,' came the order from Chef.

'You been in bed most of the day. It time to get up.'

Hyacinth rolled over. 'What's the time?'

'Eleven a.m.,' Maria replied.

'Have I been sleeping all that time?'

'Yes. Sleeping and crying.'

Hyacinth wiped the sleep from her eyes. There was a long silence, then Hyacinth exhaled and spoke.

'He was rough, very rough.'

Maria stopped what she was doing and looked at Hyacinth sitting up in the bed, staring into space.

'I – I ... I just couldn't control him. He wanted me to do weird things to him ... I could not stop him. I felt as if I was drugged. I could see what was happening but I could not stop him ... !'

The words were tumbling from her mouth, she could not stop talking and crying at the same time.

'He hurt me, he hit me, he called me the worst things ... he wanted dirty sex.' The words came though the tears. He keep talking to me in a different language, I think it was German? I was just his plaything, his *experiment*.'

Tears were running down her face and she started to rock back and forwards as she talked. 'What did I do to deserve that? I could not stop him, Maria. I tried ... I really tried to stop him.' Her voice got louder.

'I need to wash, I need to wash, yes, wash ...' She got out of the bed and walked into the bathroom, slamming the door behind her.

Maria sat on the bed looking into the empty room, listening to the shower and the crying coming from the bathroom.

After ten minutes she got up and knocked on the door. 'You OK?' She knocked harder. 'You OK?'

The water kept running. Maria pushed the door, the room was full of steam. Through the steam she saw Hyacinth sitting in the corner of the shower crying, just crying ... Maria moved over to her and pulled her out of the shower, not stopping to turn off the water. She knew her friend was in a bad way, she knew that this animal had raped and hurt her. 'Come, my sister, come with me, we will get you cleaned up.'

Hyacinth pulled out of her daze. 'I got to clean, let me go, I got to clean myself.'

'Hyacinth, you been in the shower for over ten minutes, you're clean.'

'No, no, no, I'm, dirty, I'm dirty, I'm ... I must wash, I must wash.'

She was making no sense.

Maria let go of her and Hyacinth ran back into the bathroom. Maria stood still for a moment, then went outside the cabin and stopped the first soldier she saw. 'My roommate has been assaulted,' she said. 'Please get a doctor.'

'What cabin, madam?'

'438.'

'Stay with her till we come back.'

Maria ran back into the cabin. The water was still running, steam still filling the room. Looking into the shower, she could see Hyacinth rubbing her arm vigorously. There was red in the water.

'Shit.' She ran into the shower, pulled Hyacinth out with blood all over her naked body and her arm. 'Stop, Hyacinth, stop!'

But her friend did not hear, she did not see, she was in a dream state, she was reliving that terrible night over and over again. Maria wrapped her in towels.

Just then the doctor and a soldier burst into the cabin and saw the bloody towels all over the floor. Without a word the doctor moved over to Hyacinth.

'Soldier, wait outside. Let no one in,' he said.

... Norma ...

I was sitting on my bed in my cabin wondering what makes me say the things I say.

Why don't I feel any compassion for Roy and the stowaways? Why am I so hard and mixed-up? Why am I still thinking about

Roy, not knowing he was on board, then when I meet him I curse him out? In my heart I was glad to see him.

Jesus, Lord, awah wrong wid mi?

'She will sleep for several hours. Let me know when she wakes up.'

Maria looked at the doctor, who told her: 'I will have to inform the captain as she has many bruises and maybe a cracked rib. Where and how did she receive the injuries?'

Maria looked at the doctor, and replied, 'It not my place to say anything. When she wakes up she will tell you the story as I don't fully understand what happened.'

'Then tell me what you do know.'

Maria went silent.

'Listen,' said the doctor, 'this is very serious. If someone assaulted her we need to get him before he does it again.'

Maria looked down at her hands and said, 'She spent the night with a man called "Dat", no it was "Datgail" or was it "Dangle"? I only saw him once. he about six foot tall, blond hair—'

'OK, OK,' interrupted the doctor. 'I will inform the captain.'

'Why did you stop me describing the man?' Maria asked.

The doctor said nothing, just started to pick up his instruments.

'You know him, don't you? You damn-well know this man.'

The doctor said, 'I'm going to the captain right now. We will be back once she wakes up.' With that, he was out the door quicker than he came in. Maria just looked at the door and kept thinking, 'You damn-well know that man.'

'It's seven o'clock. You coming to the dance tonight, Doris?'

'Yes, I will be there once I put the kids to sleep.'

'Precious is already upstairs. She must have a hot date ... we must see who that is.'

'How do I look?'

'Your skin looks so nice next to the white dress ... I love the way the dress buffs out, and shows off your little waist.'

'Stop it, you're making me blush,' Betty said.

'Don't forget your gloves ... a lady always has her gloves.'

'Not tonight, I'm going bare-back.'

They both burst out laughing.

Precious was sitting at the table in the hall below the ballroom. Some people were in the hall hanging out, talking, drinking; she just needed some space. Some days the whole thing got on top of her. She wondered how Daddy was doing back home with the police. 'Will Mother be at the docks in London to meet us? Where will we stay?' she thought. 'How long?' She didn't like the stories everyone was hearing about Inglan and the white people who didn't want us there ... 'I'm just feeling so alone and missing my Daddy and Mother.'

'Can I get you a drink?' a deep voice said.

... *Doctor Tom* ...

As I entered the captain's HQ, he took one look at my face and said, 'In my study.' Captain Stanley then marched off towards his study with me in tow.

Stanley entered the private room, which was very basic with few personal things in sight – no family photos or anything that would link him to anyone; just a photo of Winston Churchill and one of his dog, Paddy. There were many books and paintings, and wooden panels somehow retained the cigar smoke, which hit you as you walked over the deep carpet. The honey-coloured wooden desk was old and well loved; it looked to me like the only personal thing that was in there, and it would not have looked out of place in a stately home. His desk was minimally covered, with pens, paper and folders neatly on the right-hand side, and on the left, the photo of the dog Paddy and an ashtray so clean you would have thought he just received it.

He moved over to a side table, which held four glasses and a jug of water; two decanters, one of whisky and one of brandy. He took two glasses and poured us a pair of stiff drinks, then added a little water. He did not need to ask me what my tipple was, as we had been in this space together many times before.

He then sat down behind his beloved desk and removed his hat. I closed the door, then I too sat down and took off my hat.

'Stanley,' I said, 'we've got a bad situation!'

The captain handed me a glass. We both raised our glasses and took a big drink.

'Right, Tom, what happened?'

'A West Indian woman has been assaulted and maybe raped.'

'Bloody hell,' said Stanley. 'Do we know who committed this crime?'

'Well, it has not been confirmed by the woman who was assaulted, but I believe it to be Mr Dangle.'

'Oh, my giddy aunt ... Not him!' he shouted. 'Not him!' We both took another drink.

'Stanley, it's time to let me know who this Mr Dangle is and why there was so much secrecy surrounding him.'

Although I'm one of his oldest friends, he shifted in his seat as if he was very uncomfortable. He said, 'Anything I tell you does not leave this room. You and the vice-captain are the only ones who will know who he is.'

'Agreed,' I said. 'Well, who the hell is he?' I asked.

'He's a double agent working for the British government. He's the reason we were over this side of the world. I have direct orders from HQ to make sure he gets to London in one piece. He has a lot of information that the government needs.'

I took another gulp of my drink. 'What am I supposed to do?' I said. 'As the ship's doctor I need to submit a report when things like this happen. The MPs need to be called in and ...'

'Hold on, hold on. We are in very murky waters here. We are dealing with the Official Secrets Act. That prohibits me from doing anything till I get orders from HQ. I need to radio London. This is bigger than me, you and the assaulted woman ... Where is the woman now?'

'Sleeping. I have given her a sleeping pill. She will be out most of the evening.'

'Who else knows?'

'The soldier who reported it to me, who is standing guard outside her cabin.'

'Right,' the captain said. 'Go and talk to him. Tell him he only reports to me and you. Is there anyone in the cabin with her?'

'Yes. One woman.'

'Please go back and talk to her as well. We *must* not let this get out. We need to contain this incident.'

I finished my drink quickly, then said, 'Very well, Stanley, I will take care of it.'

'Thanks. Come back to me when you have spoken to the poor woman.'

'Soldier,' the captain shouted from his study, 'get me the vice-captain this minute.'

'Yes, sir.'

Within two minutes the vice-captain walked into the captain's study.

'Please go to Cabin 334, and tell Mr Dangle that he must remain in his cabin till the morning. I will be visiting him then. Post two soldiers outside his cabin till I tell you to remove them. Dangle is not to leave his cabin under any circumstances. I will fill you in later tonight ...'

'Yes, sir.'

*

Precious looked up and standing there in his light blue shirt and grey trousers was a man she had seen at the dance two nights ago.

'Hello,' he said in a soft but deep voice, 'are you alone?'

'I'm just taking some time out from the group. The cabins can get crowded.'

'I completely understand. Would you like a drink?'

'Thank you. I will have a fruit juice if they have any, or I will try the English beer. Or a glass of wine. But before you buy me a drink, don't you think you should introduce yourself?'

'My name is Rodney Omari Bernard,' he said. As he walked off, Precious watched him strolling towards the bar in that manly Caribbean stride. She thought, 'Well, he looks good, but I can't get involved with anyone on this ship. I got the kids to look out for.'

Then she reconsidered what she was thinking and said to herself, 'Maybe Doris is right. I need to relax and a have some fun. What harm can it do?'

'Soldier, I need to send this top-secret message to London. When you get the reply you only give it to me. You find me, wherever I am. Do you understand?'

'Yes, sir.'

'Private Warren. You do not discuss this incident with anyone. If your commanding officer asks you why you're posted outside this cabin you say Captain's orders. Don't worry, he will go to the captain to check.'

'Yes, sir.'

Knock, knock. 'May I come in?' the doctor said. 'How is she?'

'Sleeping,' Maria replied.

'Till the captain investigates this incident please keep it to yourself. Now you need to tell me all you know. I will take notes.'

'I hope you like white wine. They didn't have red.'

'White is fine.'

'May I sit down?'

'Please do.' As he adjusted himself in a nervous way, Precious placed the drink in front of her. She looked at him, then went right in there with the question, 'Are you married?'

He nearly choked on his beer. 'You don't waste time, do you?'

'Well, are you?'

'No, I am not.'

'You have a "send-for-me-woman" back home?'

'No, I had a woman but that ended the day I got on this ship.' He looked her in the eye and asked, 'Are *you* married or do you have a "send-for-me-man" back home?'

Rodney was starting to get the flow of the conversation and a feel for Precious. Precious laughed. She liked his sense of humour, the way he held his ground.

As he was talking, she was looking at his face, noticed that he had a little scar on the left side of his face. You didn't spot it as fast because it sat in the groove of his laughter lines. His eyebrows were long for a man and jet-black, just like his skin. A very thin moustache, just on the top of his lips made his lips so kiss-a-ble ...

'What do you think, Precious?'

Precious was not listening. She was in her own world, looking this fine man up and down.

'Sorry,' she said. 'You'll have to repeat it.'

'I said, I feel sorry for the stowaway,' Rodney repeated.

'Yes, it must be hard to be lock up for that long.'

'That poor man was just trying to get a better him life, just like us. I hope we as a people can help them?'

'Yes, you're right.'

'I think I like this man even more,' she thought.

Knock, knock. 'Captain, sir, I have a message from London.'

The soldier entered the office, walked over to the captain at his desk and handed the paper to him in a sealed envelope.

'That will be all.'

'Yes, sir.'

The captain opened it hesitantly. 'Damn,' he thought, 'that's just what I thought the HQ would say. Damn.'

He went on the Tannoy. 'The vice-captain and the ship's doctor to report to my study at once.'

CHAPTER 18

A WEIRD SOUNDTRACK

Tannoy: 'This is the vice-captain. The entertainment and dance will start at 1900 hours in the main ballroom and the lower hall. Anyone found drunk will be placed in the Brig. Over and out.'

'Boy them na joke.'

'You see them white boys them must learn to hold them drinks,' Lucretia said as she was putting on her lipstick.

Norma was sitting on her bed, still mad with herself about the way she had talked to Roy, but she did not let anyone know that.

'Will you be in a better mood tonight, Norma?'

'Gal, I am always in a good mood.'

'Cha,' Lucretia said, 'me will find you a good man tonight. You need a good f—'

'Lucretia,' Norma shouted out, 'stop your noise.'

'Cha, you gwan like you don't want it?'

'I will meet you in the ballroom,' said Roy.

'You not coming to the game tonight?'

'Yes, man, but I need to talk to someone.'

'But wait. You find a woman on board this ship?'

Roy thought before he answered. 'I'm going to have a drink with a woman, that right, and she is better looking than you.'

'Ha haha ha. Gwan, you is bad man. Just make sure your backside is in the boiler room by eight thirty.'

'Easy na-man.'

'When I see Ada tonight I will have it out with her. I don't care what you say, she knows something – I can feel it.'

'Just be cool. You get more done with a cool head.'

... *Private Mickey* ...

I'm patrolling with Sergeant Davis's squad tonight, so I know there will be a lot of ducking and diving. I only got four hours' sleep. The pills the doctor gave me are not working. All the pills they give me is the same old shit.

I was sitting on my bed in my shirt with my jacket hanging on the door. I knew it was time to get ready for the patrol, but as I sat in the empty cabin I could see the German soldier running towards me ... I blinked, rubbed my face, got off the bed and put on my uniform. I looked in the mirror, at the lines under my eyes and the whiteness of my skin. Sometimes I wish I had died out there ... This is a living hell.

The longer I looked at my reflection in the mirror the more it seemed my reflection was moving away from me; I could see myself moving but standing still ... there I was, moving away far, far from myself. How can that be, I'm here, I'm here, come back ... I could see myself moving away, getting smaller and smaller and smaller. I slapped my face, hard, closed my eyes. As I opened them, there I was. Looking back at myself. 'I can't damn-well do this, I just can't,' I thought, still looking in the mirror.

Out came a shout, 'You ready? Private Ross said the squad's ready and we are late.'

I jumped up. 'I'm coming, I'm coming ...'

In the lower hall a group of men were putting together the PA for the dance. The lower hall was smaller than the ballroom. There was just a bar and some smaller tables, wooden floors and a platform stage. Fitzroy and Sir Noxson, a well-known DJ from Jamaica, took out their records, getting the microphone ready.

'Yes, man, we are playing some bad tunes tonight. You have all the records from mi box?'

'Yes, Noxson. Them is all here.'

'Give mi the new Buster Newman. Mek mi run the tune.'

He took the record out of the sleeve, cleaned it off with the record cleaner, placed it on the deck with its five-inch-thick cushion. He set the needle on the record and the big sound of Buster Newman tune 'Inna de Yard' ... fast, raw, with a thick backbeat played out.

'Bad tune, Noxson, bad tune.'

The sound was full-on in the hall. The white barmen looked up as the music hit their ears. They wondered how they got the sound so loud. Winston was sitting at the bar – once the music hit him he got up and started to shuffle to the record. The tables vibrated to the sound of the Caribbean.

In the ballroom the Pan Players were getting ready. Lord Pan had the team ready for the night's show. They could feel the loud vibration from Sir Noxson downstairs. Once again Elroy was missing.

'Where the rassclaat him da … every rass-time him late.'

No one said a thing, just got on with their pan adjustments, not looking up.

The bar people had all the drinks ready at the bar and the kitchen was emitting a wonderful tropical smell that had everyone licking their lips.

The stage manager sat down, looking at the Pan Players, not moving just looking at them with contempt. 'Hey, you know you're the only show on tonight?'

'Yes, man,' Lord Pan said. 'We ready.'

'It's seven fifteen,' a pan player said. 'We are playing people into the ballroom?'

'Yes man, let's warm them up.'

'But Elroy is not here.'

'Well, mi na wait, you all ready?'

'Yes, we ready.'

'After three: one, two, three …'

The sweet sound of the steel pans filled the ballroom. The sound went out of the ballroom into the corridors and up onto the decks and into the kitchen.

'Come on. They have started. You don't hear the music?'

'Yes, mi a come,' Norma said. 'Just ole on a minute, na?'

'Can you smell the food?'

'Yes, some good West Indian food a gwan tonight?'

'Yes, man. Come. Selwyn make us go and get some food. Mi want to see which woman Roy ha check.'

'Private Mickey, you take the lower levels and Edward, you stay near the ballroom, so if anything is happening you let me know. Keep an eye on the MPs, who will be inside the dance halls. Right, we have covered all the bases. We start the games at eight thirty. By then most of the passengers will be in the halls.'

7:15 p.m. People started to come into the ballroom, getting a table and grabbing drinks while the Pan Players were playing soft Caribbean songs.

Norma's group was sitting at a big round table. 'I love this song,' she said. '"Caribbean Sunset" ... it always reminds me of the beach at Runaway Bay, watching the sun go down.'

Then Lucretia burst into song. She was not a very good singer. Her voice had a high-pitched sound, the sound your mother made on a Sunday afternoon singing over Jim Reeves songs. Norma looked at Mavis, Mavis looked at Lucretia.

'She's one in a million,' Mavis said, looking at Norma with a smile. Lucretia kept singing badly, louder and louder. Mavis began to sing along with her.

'Sunset on the beach,' they all sang along to the song. The next table joined in; a good-looking man from that table got up, singing the song, and moved over to Norma and extended his hand for a dance. Norma looked at him, liked what she saw and moved Lucretia out the way.

'Gwan, gal,' Lucretia said.

He led Norma out onto the dance floor with one movement of his hand. He started to drop some foot, arms waving up and down, hips moving in time to the music, head nodding. Norma could move and felt light on her feet. Before you could say a word people were on the dance floor; women in their colourful dresses, men in their high-waisted trousers with shirts buttoned up to their necks, some in kipper ties with braces holding up their pleated trousers with a razor-sharp crease in the legs. Everyone was smiling and singing, the Pan Players were vibing off the crowd, playing one song into the next, not stopping, keeping everyone on the dance floor.

Lucretia's feet were now on the dance floor, dancing with two men at the same time. Mavis was moving to the music next to Norma singing her heart out; Norma spun around and, standing in front of her was Roy, big white teeth smiling with a 'please dance with me' look on his face. Roy was looking at her in her fitted all-in-one blue and yellow dress, with a neat belt around her waist and slingback white shoes, as she danced in front of him, not saying a word, just dancing. Lucretia looked over and danced across the floor to them; as she got closer, she took a good look at Roy then said in Norma's ear, 'Na-dat the man who took our bags onto the ship?'

Norma said, 'He does look like him but it not him.'

'Mmmmm,' Lucretia said as she danced away from them back to her two men she had left on the dance floor.

The sound of the music echoed down the corridor into the kitchen, where Chef was about to take out the food.

'Man, them a play some bad tunes tonight.' The members of Chef's team were dancing in their white aprons and white hats as they took out the food, singing and setting up the dishes. It looked like a scene from a Hollywood musical, with dancing chefs and servers placing food on the table with a dance move spinning and dipping to the music. For the first time the food-serving tables were empty as all the people were dancing on the packed dance floor.

In the lower hall one of the men came down from the ballroom.

'Noxson them a mush you-up upstairs dem a drop some tunes, man?'

Noxson looked around and there were only about eighty people in the hall with him.

'Cha, time to set this place on fire. Give mi the White Labels box.'

'What, so early you a go into the white box?'

'Yeh, man, mi have to show everyone Sir Noxson na ramp.' With one flick of his wrist he dropped the White Label record 'Spanish Town' and everyone was on their feet. People outside the hall who were on their way upstairs heard the bad tune and came into the hall right onto the dance floor.

'Yes, man, that's how you do it.'

The song got to the chorus when everyone joined in, 'Spanish Town, the place I love to be …' The music war was on and Sir Noxson was not going to lose to the Pan Players in the ballroom. The bar was flowing with drink, women were dancing with anyone who asked nicely, the men standing by the bar were nodding their heads, shouting out 'Tune, tune,' as the song came to an end. Sir Noxson took one record off and put the next on without dropping the beat. The Rhythm and Blues played. 'Feel the beat in your feet' … The room was buzzing, rocking, more people were coming into the room and the beat was on.

'After they start serving the food, it will be about seven forty-five. We will meet you all downstairs in the boiler room,' Selwyn said to Evans, Devon and Delroy.

The ballroom was full of a mixture of cigarette smoke and perfume, everyone was on their feet. Norma was still dancing.

'I'm thirsty,' she said to Roy.

'Let mi get you a drink,' Roy said as they walked over to the bar, moving between the people on the floor.

'What would you like?'

'I think I will try the rum, Jamaican rum that is.'

'Sure.' As she waited at the bar, watching the people dancing and singing she glanced to her left and saw the food being put out on the table. Roy handed her the drink; they clinked glasses.

'Have you eaten?' Norma asked.

'Not yet.'

They took a drink and looked at the people dancing, neither knowing what to say as they leant against the bar. Roy was about to say something when Norma said, 'I'm sorry about the way I talked to you yesterday. It was rude and uncalled for.' Roy was startled, not expecting that to come out of her mouth. That was the moment when they looked at each other eye to eye, then suddenly turned away ... as if this was not the time to be looking at each other like that.

'Thank you for saying that,' Roy said. 'I didn't mean to upset you or get you into trouble.'

The air around them felt fresh and clear ...

'So, who is this handsome man?' Mavis said, appearing from nowhere.

'Mavis, Roy; Roy, Mavis.'

Roy nodded his head. 'Would you like a drink?'

'My, thank you. A man with manners! You need to hang on to this one.' Norma blushed. 'A wine will do.' When Roy turned to the bar, Norma and Mavis started to talk. Then Lucretia appeared with a man.

'So the party over here? No one invited me ...' Roy had his back to Lucretia; Norma thought Lucretia could blow Roy's cover. She never could keep her big mouth shut. Roy turned around and gave Mavis the drink.

'And who is you?' Lucretia said before Norma or Roy could say a word. 'You sure look like someone I meet on the docks in Jamaica?'

Norma moved quickly over to Roy. 'Roy, this is Lucretia, my mad sister-friend.' Roy nodded. Before Lucretia could say another word Norma said, 'You not going to introduce us to your companion with you?'

'Of course. This is Michael from Trinidad.'

'Wha-gawn everyone?' he said.

'Come, ladies,' Norma said. 'Let's go to the ladies' room. We soon come.'

'I'm hungry. Let's get something to eat,' Anton said as he and Verndo walked over to the food table, moving out of the way of the dancers, looking at the colourful display of dishes. 'What's that?' he asked.

'That vegetable-stew.'

'And that?'

'Yam and dumpling. You don't know what yam is?' Verndo asked.

'Of course I do. But it looks different.'

Chef looked at the two men and thought, 'I understand the Inglish boys asking mi about Caribbean food – but them two is Caribbean men?'

'Where you find that man?'

Norma kept looking into the mirror inside the women's toilet, replacing her lipstick, thinking she can't trust Lucretia with this important information. Her lips are too loose.

'You don't remember? We met him on the first night of the dance. You were too interested in another man you were talking to.'

'He looks nice,' Mavis said. 'Anyway, who's the man with you?'

'He just some man who will not leave mi alone,' Lucretia said, throwing back her hair and rubbing the lipstick off her teeth. 'Well, if you don't see mi later tonight you know things a-gawn.'

All the women laughed as they made their way out of the toilets. That should hold her for now, Norma thought.

'I thought only my mother could cook like this ... If you're not eating that, I will.'

'Don't touch my food,' Anton said as he looked around the ballroom. There were lots of people eating and dancing. 'Look,' he said loudly, 'look over there!'

Verndo looked up. 'Hell! That's her!' He went to get up. Anton held his arm.

'Sit down. I told you we need to play this cool. Let's just keep an eye on her, then when the time is right we will talk to her.'

'We are going to get some food, you a come?' Lucretia said to everyone by the bar. They started to follow her. Roy looked at Norma for approval.

'You got to eat,' she said as she moved towards the food tables. Suddenly Roy took hold of her arm. That stopped Norma from moving forward. She looked down at his hand, then up at him in a way that said, 'Is who you a hold like that?'

Roy released her arm. 'Sorry, Norma, but will your friend tell on me?'

'Don't worry, I told her she had met you on the first night at the dance so keep to that story.'

The boiler room was laid out with two tables and four chairs around each. The card table had a green cloth over the top, two ashtrays and two boxes of cards; the dominoes table had a hard board on top of the table to take the impact of the dominoes hitting the surface, two ashtrays and two long wooden boxes of dominoes. Cases of rum and beer were in the corner, with a table of glasses. There were no windows in the room, just pipes and valves, with the low frapping sound of the ship's engine, which sounded like a heartbeat and was always in your ear.

'Right, it's ten past eight. The coons will be coming downstairs soon. Don't forget – no fighting.'

Colin the prize dominoes player was pacing up and down. 'I'm ready to take their money tonight.'

'You just remember to lose the first game then we up the pot money after the drinks have set in.'

'We're all good now. I'm taking one more look around the corridor then let the games begin.'

Selwyn was making his way downstairs with the group. Devon remained at the top of the stairs as a lookout.

'Where is Roy?'

'Don't worry, he will be here.'

'Please can you pass the hot pepper?'

Norma passed it over to Michael. They sat at the table, eating, talking and looking at people dancing. Roy felt very comfortable in the company of the ladies, they were making small talk and just being friendly ... as he took a mouthful of rice and peas, he looked at the big clock on the wall.

'Shit,' he thought. 'Is that the time? I need to get to the game.' He said, 'Norma, please don't think I'm being rude, but I need to go somewhere.'

This was overheard by Lucretia. 'Is where you need to be? And you don't finish your food?'

Roy kept looking at Norma, whose face was not friendly. She put down her knife and fork and said, 'It must be important for you to leave in the middle of your dinner.'

'Sorry, Norma.' The whole table looked at Roy, who was feeling really bad. But he could not let down the boys. He whispered in Norma's ear, 'I'm part of a big dominoes and cards game tonight in the bottom of the ship. I don't want to lie to you, but I need to go.'

Norma moved out the way and Roy stood up and said, 'Please excuse mi, ladies and gent.'

As he moved away Norma quietly said, 'Good luck!' and smiled.

Selwyn, Evans and Delroy walked into the boiler room.

'Inglish boys you ready to lose some money tonight?'

All four Englishmen smiled.

Roy was making his way downstairs, thinking about Norma and the way she looked so good. He'd wanted to stay with her, but he needed the money ... and he knew he was going to win tonight. He pushed the boiler room door open, and Davis, Bill, Tommy and Colin were standing drinking and smoking. They all looked at Roy.

'Cha, man, now we a start the games,' Selwyn said.

'She going out of the ballroom.'

'OK, let's follow her.' Anton and Verndo calmly walked out of the hall, watching her going down the corridor then into the women's toilets.

'Wait here: when she comes out, I will tell her that Pele wants to talk to her on the deck ... just play along.'

'You boys are on form tonight,' Davis said to the smoky room, with a grin on his face. Selwyn looked at Evans, who was on the same dominoes table as Bill and Colin.

'You win the first game,' Colin said.

'How you doing on the cards table?'

'Not bloody well,' Tommy said.

Roy was smiling and rubbing his hands, having won the first game. Delroy and Davis looked on.

'Let's all top up our drinks and then start the next round.'

'Hi, Ada. Pele gave me a message for you.'

'Did he?' she said. 'And what was that? If he saying he sorry, I don't want to hear it.'

'No, it not that. Come upstairs on the deck, let's all talk.'

'Why can't we talk here? Is Pele upstairs?'

'Yes, he is,' Verndo said.

Alarm bells went off in Ada's head. She knew Pele was dead, so ... A) these clowns are going to kill me? ... or B) they trying to spook me ... or C) they know nothing about nothing? 'So, play along,' she thought.

'OK, OK, just going to get my jacket. It cold up there. Meet you at the top of the stairs.'

Ada went into the ballroom, picked up her jacket, tapped the side to make sure she had it in her pocket. Then she calmly walked out of the hall, down the corridor and up the stairs to the deck. The air was fresh and cold, the sea was black.

'Hi, guys,' she said, smiling. 'Where Pele?' she said, looking around.

Verndo could not hold it in any longer. He grabbed her by the throat: 'Listen, I know you had something to do with Pele going missing.'

'What? What you talking about? And Get the hell off me!'

'You don't fool me,' Verndo said. 'You bloody well better talk …'

Anton pulled Verndo off the woman. 'Calm down, everyone bloody well calm down,' he said. He looked at Ada dead calmly in the eye. 'Please tell us what you know.'

She adjusted her jacket, looked at both of them and said, 'Go to hell!' and walked off. As she did this Verndo was about to stop her, but Anton put his hand on Verndo's shoulder, stopping him. He turned him around and said, 'She knows.'

'If you think she damn well knows, why you stopping me?'

'Because she had a knife in her jacket.'

Private Mickey was walking downstairs, near the boiler room. He was looking out for the MPs and talking to himself. 'I got to get more pills. My head's well messed up.'

He turned around, saw a shadow moving just out of his eyesight …

'Stop! Who goes there?' No answer. 'Who the hell is there?' He kept on looking, but no one was there … He rubbed his head, it was covered with sweat, so much sweat.

'Is where him a go?'

'He be back soon,' Norma said, eating her food and not looking at Lucretia.

'I like him,' Mavis said. 'There something cool about him, something you can trust.'

Norma just looked at her.

'Let's up the pot?'

'How much?' Selwyn said.

'Two dollars more? You guys good for that?'

'Yes, man.'

'OK, the winner must be the best out of three games on both tables.'

Selwyn looked at Roy with a knowing look that said they up to something. But he had told the boys to be ready for a move by the Inglish boys.

'You deal,' Davis said.

Roy picked up the cards and shuffled. He gave out the cards to the four players; everyone looked at their hand. Roy raised his left eyebrow; that meant he had a good hand, so Delroy knew he had to play out his hand so the English boys use up their best cards ...

'Two cards left,' Roy said. He put the cards on the table face down. Davis and Tommy looked at each other. Tommy put down a Queen of Hearts. Delroy knocked the table, meaning he could not play. Davis played the five of Clubs.

Roy coolly turned over his two cards. 'Game done,' he said.

Davis looked at Tommy and said, 'What! How the hell did you have that hand?'

'You must know you're playing with the master. Two more games and I win this table.'

Selwyn and Evans were still playing dominoes. Selwyn had one domino in his hand; he looked at Evans who looked at him with a 'I don't know if they have it' look.

'You bloody well playing that domino?' Colin said impatiently.

'Yes, man, I'm just thinking.'

Bang. Evans put down a six and four. Hopefully, Selwyn had the winning hand. There was a silence ... everyone was waiting for Colin to play. He dropped a six and three, and Selwyn looked at his hand, looked at Evans and Colin and '*bang*' slammed down the winning domino.

'D-E-U-C-E,' he said. 'We win, man, WE WIN ...'

'NO damn way, no damn way – you had that?'

'Is what you saying I is cheating, man? You say mi is a cheat?' Selwyn said in an angry voice. Davis and Roy looked over from their table.

Colin got up, banged on the table and walked over to the drinks.

'Come, man, you must learn how to lose ... it no shame, it just that I'm better than you,' Selwyn said.

Colin turned around with red eyes and a look that was mean on a six-foot man who was very well built and did not like to lose.

Davis leapt up. Roy was standing too.

'You guys, cool down, just cool down.'

'No damn way am I playing with them two bastards! I don't know how but they're cheating.'

'I did tell you not to call mi that, you rassclaat.'

'What you call me, you coon?!'

By this time Davis was moving over to Colin, and Roy was going over to Selwyn.

'Time out,' Tommy said, 'just cool down.'

'No bloody time out! I want my money back. Them jokers are up to something.'

'How? You is a bad loser.'

'You na take the money, we have one more game, if you na restart the game then we win the money.'

Now Davis had a bad look on his face. 'No bloody way.'

Delroy said, 'If you feel we is a tief you open that new pack of cards and dominoes and the winner of the next card game win it all.'

Selwyn said, 'What about me? I'm up on my table. Then the winner of each table takes that table's pot. We cool with that? ... You cool, Davis?' He looked at Colin. 'OK, let's play.'

*

'Who the hell does he think he is, putting his hand on me? I will give him what that other idiot got. He will get it and I will get the $1,000 bounty on their heads.'

Ada remembered being on the docks in Mexico with her bags, watching the soldiers telling the drugs gang to get on the floor, seeing the boss-man standing there regal and proud, surrounded by soldiers. Just then De Anglo had tapped her on the shoulder looking very serious. He said, 'Ada, you're going on the ship?'

'Yes, I am.'

'You know I have to get out of town because of that shooting in the club? ... Well, we have one more job for you and the boss-man will pay you very well.'

Mavis was talking to the group. Then over came Junior, whom she had met at the dance, looking dapper in his white shirt with cravat, neat trousers held up by yellow and red braces. 'Hello, Mavis. May I get you a drink?' he said, while on either side of her Norma and Lucretia were standing.

Junior only had eyes for Mavis.

'So you na asks us two lady if we a drink?'

'What we is – just bookends?' Lucretia said.

Mavis gave her a bad look. Norma was just looking on, wondering if Roy was OK ...

'Forgive my bad manners. I was dazzled by the beauty of this woman.'

'LORD, the man has words, just for that I will forgive you.'

Everyone burst out laughing.

Junior said, 'Is that rum and wine all around?' Everyone just nodded. The women moved back together and watched Junior walk over to the bar.

'Him nice?'

'We will see ... we will see ...'

Davis had a good hand. This time the game was blackjack. Roy looked at his cards, and looked at Delroy, who was not happy with his hand ... the cards went on the table one by one.

Roy tapped the table, meaning he could not play. Delroy looked at him, then at his cards. He thought, 'If I don't play the next card we will lose the game.'

Selwyn was looking at his partner who had his poker face on. Then he thought, 'He must have the key domino in his hand.'

Roy had two cards left. He placed them on the table face down to show the other players he was ready to win the game and spook them at the same time. Davis had a bead of sweat on his face, his palms were getting wet and his mouth was dry. Everyone was looking at everyone for answers. You could cut the air with a knife.

Delroy looked at Roy. Roy looked back at Delroy. It was his play; he slowly dropped the ace. Roy tried not to show his disappointment.

Tommy went, 'Bang! I got this game!' He had one card in his hand and was so confident he had won.

Selwyn looked at Evans who looked at the dominoes.

Evans went 'BANG! You messed up!' Then he banged it again. It was a double six.

Colin's eyes were popping out of his head. 'What the hell, no bloody way!'

Colin got up, pushing the table over. 'No way is a coon going to beat me – I'm the champion of the army!' As he said this the table went flying, the dominoes were on the floor, the chair went backwards.

Selwyn let out a shout. 'Give mi my rassclaat money! You na play mi as some fool!'

By now Davis, Roy, Evans and Tommy were all on their feet. Selwyn was standing by Roy, Davis went over to Colin, trying to calm him down. Roy was furious, Colin was raging – and the rest were trying to keep the two men apart. Voices got high. Colin went over to the drinks table and picked up a bottle ready to hit Selwyn.

'Put that down,' Davis said.

'He cheated!' he shouted, looking at Selwyn.

Selwyn had now lost it. 'What the bloodclaat ... mi a chop up him rass!' Now the boys were holding back Selwyn.

Private Mickey was in the corridor and heard the big noise coming from the boiler room. Walking towards the door all he saw in his head was the German soldier taking up a gun and preparing to shoot him ... He looked behind him – there was the squad of Englishmen on the battlefield following him. 'The German soldiers are inside that building!' someone shouted. Mickey lifted up his foot with his big boots on and gave one big kick at the boiler room door, bursting it open ... Time was not real time at this point, everything became slow motion. The door slowly opened – Private Mickey saw the German soldiers pointing their guns at him and his fellow English soldiers behind him; he heard the Germans talking German: 'Komm zuruck.' Private Mickey looked at them, took aim and slowly pulled the trigger of the gun.

In the time it took for the trigger to go to the back of the gun all the men in the room stopped what they were doing: Roy was being held back by Selwyn, Delroy and Evans, while Davis, Bill and Tommy were holding Colin down, with bottles, cards and tables on the floor. They all heard the bang and they all looked at the door flying open then froze like a deer in headlights as they all saw the gun pointing at them.

'What the hell' – before Davis could say it or the men could move, the sound of gunshots filled the room, and suddenly there was no sound, just men diving for cover. There was no human sound coming into Private Mickey's ears, just the Nazi soldiers diving for cover ...

'Die – you – bloody – Nazi – pigs – die!' he shouted as he kept on shooting.

There was an eerie silence.

Then the sound of the throbbing ship's engine filled the room ... You could hear the distant sound of the steel pans from the dance floor playing a soft melody that somehow matched the throbbing of the ship's engine ... Reality had now returned to Private Mickey's mind as he looked at the blood and bodies lying on the floor and smelled the reek of gun smoke in the room. The boiler room was still.

Devon was at the top of the stairs and jumped up. 'A what de rass was that gunshot?' he thought, and he ran down the stairs, falling down the last steps onto his face. When he raised his head up from the floor he saw the back of a soldier standing in the doorway with a gun by his side and in the room were bodies on the floor.

'Shots reported in the lower levels of the ship,' came on the radio of the MPs.

*

... MP Alex Simpson ...
'All doctors report to the boiler room.' I was in the ballroom when the order came in code ... *45 boiler room*. 45 meant a top emergency, stop what you're doing and get to the call.

No one expected to see what they saw.

I came clattering down the stairs. All I saw was MPs holding down a soldier to my right who was ranting about Nazis coming and all manner of things that no one understood ... they were calling him 'Private Mickey'. As I walked into the boiler room the doctors were helping people lying on the floor. There was blood everywhere.

'Soldier, come here, hold this down on this man, keep the pressure on,' the doctor said. I was pressing down on a bandage on a West Indian man who was bleeding out. One, two, three ... I counted six or seven bodies in the boiler room. No one was moving.

The two doctors and three nurses were moving from body to body. Some were West Indian men, some were white men, some had so much blood on them I did not know if they were black or white.

As I looked up there were MPs lining the corridor. In all this madness in stepped the captain in his white uniform. 'What the hell happened here?' he said to anyone.

'Captain, Private Mickey Morton shot the men in the boiler room. We have him under arrest. That's all we know at this time, sir.'

'Is anyone dead?'

'We don't know,' the head doctor replied.

'Where are the stretchers?'

'They're just coming, sir.'

'Right, get all the men to the infirmary.' The captain took a good look around at the carnage and ordered the boiler room and the floor to be sealed off.

'No one is to come down here. All the MPs seal the damn floor. I want a full report with the heads of departments in my office in one hour.'

'Yes sir.'

The captain walked over to Private Mickey, who was being held against the wall by four MPs. He looked Mickey in the eye. 'Did you shoot these men?'

Private Mickey kept saying over and over again, 'It's the Nazis ... it's them Nazis ... we must stop them ... bastards ...'

The MP told the captain, 'This is all he keeps on saying, sir. I think he's gone mad.'

'That's not for you to say, soldier. Take him to the Brig and put four soldiers on suicide watch.'

The captain stood back as the wounded men were lifted up and put on stretchers and moved to the infirmary.

'MPs! I want you to clear the corridors. I don't want any passengers to see bodies being moved to the infirmary.'

'Yes, sir.'

Orders were being passed everywhere. MPs were moving out of the boiler room into the corridors leading to the infirmary. Devon was being held and questioned by the MPs.

'What did you see? Who started shooting? Where were you?'

Devon was in a daze ... he had his head in his hands. He could not believe what he had seen.

'Who's that you're talking to?' the captain asked.

'He is the only witness to the shooting.'

'Then get that man into the interview room under guard. Take his statement. I will join you there shortly.'

He then walked over to Tom, the ship's head doctor, and asked, 'Will anyone live?'

'I don't know. I will be in the infirmary. Then I will join you later with my report,' he said as he hurriedly walked off beside a man on a stretcher covered in blood.

'I don't goddamn-well believe this!' the captain said under his breath.

As all this was happening the music from the dance hall drifted down into the boiler room, providing a weird soundtrack to the scenes of blood and gore. At one point there was a silence in the boiler room, just the sound of Caribbean steel pan playing a soft tune as the bodies were being moved. It felt angelic and disgusting all at once ...

*

The dance was in full swing. In the two halls people were drinking, dancing and eating, oblivious to what was going on in the lower part of the ship. Norma kept looking at the door, expecting Roy to appear any time. She was anxious and annoyed at the same time.

'Looks like he na come back,' Lucretia barked.

Norma just cut her eye at her. Mavis had given Junior the slip; he was getting amorous with her. She was looking around the hall for Edward, who had said he would have a drink with her tonight. She noticed that there were no MPs standing by the doors – in fact, there were no white soldiers anywhere in the ballroom.

'Hey girls, something's going on!'

'What you mean?' Norma said.

'Well, the MPs by the door have disappeared and there are no white soldiers anywhere. This has not happened before, from day one.'

'Maybe them believe we can behave our self.'

'Maybe,' Mavis replied. 'Maybe.'

'Captain, should we stop the dance, sir?'

'No, let them carry on. I don't want a mob of West Indian people going mad about a shooting – especially as it is one of our soldiers doing the shooting. Post some men back in the halls and put all the soldiers on full alert. I will report to all the men in the morning once I have the facts.'

'Yes, sir.'

The infirmary was full of doctors and nurses injecting, sewing up wounded men, giving blood transfusions, extracting bullets. It was a fully equipped hospital for the rich people who used to sail on this luxury liner.

They were pumping a patient's chest to try to get his heart going.

'Is there a pulse?'

'No, sir.'

'Try again!'

Nurse Maureen put a stethoscope to the man's heart. 'Sir, we've lost this one ...'

'What time is it, Nurse Dionne?'

'Twenty-two forty-five hours, doctor.'

'Please note the time of death and then move him to the morgue. May God have mercy on his soul. Is there any ID on this West Indian man?'

Nurse Sharon unwrapped the face of a soldier on the next examination table and instantly recognised him. She gave out a shout, 'Oh my God! Not you!'

The doctor looked around. 'What's happening?'

'Doctor, I know this man.'

The doctor said, without any compassion, 'Nurses, I need you all to do your job without emotion.'

'Yes, doctor,' Nurse Sharon said through her tears.

'Doctor, I need you over here – I'm losing this man!'

'This is the last record of the night,' came over the microphone.

'Will all the passengers return to their cabins. There will be a lockdown tonight. Anyone found out of their cabin will be placed in the Brig. All soldiers report to their stations.'

'I mash -up ... mi never dance so much,' Lucretia said as she came off the dance floor with two men in tow. 'See you two bad men tomorrow.' She looked at Mavis and Norma, who were sitting at the table with a pensive look on their faces. Edward was a no-show, Mavis thought; Roy did not have the manners to return to say, 'Good night'. Anyway, his loss, Norma thought. 'You all ready?' Lucretia said as she walked towards the door.

'Precious, thank you for a lovely evening. It was nice to get to know you and your group. May I walk you to your cabin?'

'That would be nice,' she said.

'I don't see any of them men tonight,' Sir Noxson thought. 'No Roy, Selwyn, Delroy, none of them come to support mi tonight. Cha, wurt-less man, dat.'

As Norma was walking back to her cabin she was having an argument in her head. 'What was I thinking? That man Roy is a crook, he conned his way onto the ship through me and now he's conning me to keep me quiet by being nice to me. I just know he was with some woman tonight. Damn womaniser, I done with him, DONE.'

'Doctor, we lost this man!'

'Please note the time of death and tag him. Thank God the rest of the men are stable.'

'Doctor, we have removed all the bullets from their bodies. The rest of the men are under observation,' Nurse Dionne said.

Doctor Tom pulled off his gloves and threw them angrily in the bin. 'We lost two men tonight and two more may not make it,' he thought. 'Infirmary team, you did the best you could do. Please set up an observation rota throughout the night. Send me your reports for 0900 hours tomorrow. If you need me I am going to report to the captain.'

Knock, knock. 'May I enter?'

'Come in. Come in, sit down, man. You must be exhausted.' Captain Stanley placed one more glass on the table next to his full glass of whisky, then poured the spirit into it.

Tom held up his glass of whisky and suggested the toast, 'To two good men.'

The captain looked at him and clinked his glass. He leaned back in his chair and lit a fat cigar.

'OK, Tom, let's hear your medical side of this sad story – from the top ...'

PART VI
Aftermath

CHAPTER 19

THE FALLOUT

Doctor Tom had about three hours sleep. He got up at 4 a.m. to check on the men in the infirmary. He sat down in his office, looking out to sea, watching the sunrise – his mind thinking about what just happened. In forty-eight hours, just two days ... the ship had fallen into a state of madness. Rape, assault, shootings, corpses ... he slumped back into his chair. These poor men, who had escaped being killed in the war by Nazis only to be killed by their own people. Tom finished off his report for the ship records and the team meeting at 0900 hours. He knew the rape case would be put under 'Classified/Top Secret'. He placed the shooting folder to the right of his desk, then slowly picking up the folder for the rape victim, opened it to add more information.

'What time is it'?

'Eight thirty,' Maria said.

'Have I been sleeping all night?'

'Yes, you have.'

'I feel very dizzy.'

'The doctor said you must stay in bed till he comes back to see you this morning. Here is some water ... you must be dehydrated.'

'Thank you, thank you.'

*

The Tannoy woke up most of the passengers: 'Good morning. This is your captain. There will be a ship team and soldiers meeting at 0900 to 1000 hours. I am asking all passengers to remain in their cabins until you get the "all clear" between 1000 to 1100 hours this morning. Over and out.'

'What the man a say?'

'Dem are lock us up like we is in prisons. Lockdown last night, lockdown this morning.'

'Cha, wake me up at nine,' Chef said.

'That man, that man ... he really upset me, but still he's in my head,' Norma thought as she lay on her back on her bed. 'He mek mi look a fool in front of the girls, them must think I is a damn fool. You have three men to one woman on this ship and mi have fe go and take up with the damn stowaway. Thank the Lord Mother was not here to see this and she would a lick mi in the head' ... Norma let out a giggle.

'A what sweet you so?' Lucretia asked.

'None of your business.'

'Mavis? You awake? You hear the mad woman laughing with herself?' Lucretia shouted across the cabin.

There was silence.

'Mavis? Mavis! You not hear me? What the hell happen to you two pickney?'

... *Captain Stanley* ...

At 9 a.m. I assembled the soldiers in the ballroom. Rumours about a shooting must have been on all their minds.

'Attention,' came the order from the vice-captain.

Then I walked out on stage.

'At ease. I have some bad news. At 2145 hours yesterday Private Mickey Morton shot and killed two men: Private Colin Matthews and a passenger named Mr Selwyn Carter. Wounded were Private Thomas Francis, Sergeant Andrew Davis and Private Bill Nixon, as well as passengers Mr Evans Michele, Mr Gladstone Vincent Carman, Mr Delroy Spencer. All the wounded are in intensive care. Private Morton is under arrest in the Brig. So far, the passengers do not know of this shooting as it happened late last night when the entertainment was on.

'I will be making a shipwide announcement after this meeting to the passengers. Your orders are: if any passengers ask you for any information about this shooting you say that it's in the hands of the captain and the MPs.

'If anyone claims to be a relative or friend of the dead and says they wish to see them, you take them to my office. This is a sad day on this ship and we will now have a minute's silence for the dead and wounded.

'Thank you.

'We will maintain normality as much as possible and will continue the entertainment. But everyone will be on full alert until we get to London. There is a newspaper reporter from the *Daily Express* on board this ship. No one is to talk to him. If you see him trying in any way to get into the infirmary or trying to get a story out of a passenger, report him to your sergeants. I will take the newspaperman in hand and that may mean confining him to his cabin.

'I don't need to tell you how deeply we all feel the loss of our fallen soldiers and passengers. I will be contacting the relatives when we get to London. Under these unusual circumstances I will allow some questions.'

A hand went up at the back. 'Sir, can we visit the soldiers?'

'Not at this time. Perhaps when they are in recovery – we will keep you all posted. Yes, soldier?'

'Sir, do we know definitely that Private Morton was a lone shooter?'

'Yes. Yes, he was. Next?'

'Sir, what happened to make Private Morton shoot them? Was there a fight?'

'No, soldier, there was no fight. I cannot say any more than that as this will be a legal matter in London. Last question. Yes, soldier?'

'Sir? There is a rumour that a woman was assaulted on the ship and you have the man in custody?'

The captain looked at the vice-captain, then at the soldiers. 'Yes, this is true. There was an assault and a man is under cabin arrest. This matter is not to be talked about with the passengers, or anybody. This now comes under the National Security Act, and anyone revealing the identity of the woman or the man involved will be in breach of this Act and will be imprisoned. That is all. Soldiers, may God have mercy on our dead soldiers' souls. Dismissed.'

'When can we go out, Aunty Precious?'

'The captain said later this morning. Be patient...'

'I get the feeling that something happened last night. Did you see all the soldiers telling everyone to use the other stairway?'

'Yes,' Betty said, 'I did notice that there were more soldiers around than normal last night. I hope our people are not involved.'

'Mmmm.'

Knock, knock. 'It's the doctor. May I come in?'

'Yes,' Maria said.

Hyacinth was sitting in a chair and Maria went over and stood by her.

'I have come to see how you are doing today. Do your ribs still hurt?'

Hyacinth looked the doctor in the eye. 'I want that man in prison. He is a rapist and a sodomite. I want to see the captain. I was told he was coming to see me.' She stopped talking and looked at the doctor.

'The captain will be seeing you today. And the accused man is under arrest. May I do my medical checks?'

'OK.'

The doctor could see that she had received a good beating. She had damaged ribs and a swollen mouth, and she was bleeding from the anus and vagina.

'I need you to come with me to the infirmary as you need more medical attention.'

'I don't want anyone to know about this so I will walk to the infirmary with no guards.'

'As you wish. But your roommate must walk with you as you're far too weak to walk alone. Once you've been to the infirmary the captain will come to see you.'

'I want to see him and the MPs today. I want to make a statement. That bastard will not get away with this.' Hyacinth had fire in her eyes and hurt in her heart.

*

... *Captain Stanley* ...

After only three hours' sleep I was sitting at my desk. The shooting and the rape went round and round in my head. I couldn't believe that in forty-eight hours all this could have happened. I have seen good men killed on the battlefield, I have lost good friends to the war, but somehow this felt worse. I felt so helpless ...

I sat at the desk in my study reading the telegram from London about Dangle and the rape. I laid it out before me on the desk.

London HQ. Captain Stanley under no circumstances are you to imprison, interrogate or have any interaction with Dangle. Put him under cabin arrest until you get to London, when he will be escorted off the ship by MI5 END

Not a word about the poor woman who was raped. Would they have sent me a telegram like this if it was an Englishwoman? I placed the telegram in the rape folder then looked at the wording for the Tannoy announcement about the shooting. I picked up the microphone and flicked the switch.

'Good morning, passengers, this is your captain. I have some sad news. At 2145 hours last night there was a shooting on the lower deck. One soldier and one passenger were killed and four men were injured. They are in the infirmary.

'The MPs are investigating the incident. The lower level of the ship is out of bounds until further notice. Our thoughts are with the families of the deceased.

'At 1200 hours today there will be a minute's silence throughout the ship. Captain Stanley: Over and Out.'

There was a shocked silence before the talking began.

'They never give the names of the dead people. Why didn't he say their names?'

'I don't know,' Norma replied. 'I don't know,' she said again, but this time more slowly and thoughtfully. Roy, she thought, he did not come back to the table last night; he said he was in a cards game in the lower part of the ship. Roy, she thought again ... He wouldn't be known as Roy, would he, if they found papers in his pocket ... what was that name he mentioned? She trawled through her memory, then she had it! Gladstone ... Gladstone Vincent Carman. 'My God!' Norma shouted out. It just came out of her mouth.

'What the hell wrong with you! Why you shouting out "My God"?' Lucretia said.

Norma got up. 'Soon come,' she said as she picked up a jumper and walked out of the cabin. Mavis and Lucretia just looked on.

As she went down the corridor she saw a soldier. 'Please, sir, can you tell me where the infirmary is?'

The soldier stopped, thought about it then said, 'Do you have a relative there?'

'My friend did not come back last night and he said he was going to the lower part of the ship.'

'OK. Follow me.'

Devon woke up in a different cabin all alone, with a guard outside. The MP had told him last night, 'You're not under arrest, but they need to keep you away from the passengers till the captain has told the ship about the shooting.'

As he sat up in bed he thought, 'It was all a dream ... did I see the dead bodies of my friends? Was that white soldier holding a gun? No, man, I can't believe it, I can't take it in. There was blood everywhere, everywhere. Just as he was thinking this there was a knock on his cabin door and in walked two MPs.

'Good morning. Here is your breakfast ... At 1300 hours you will be taken to the captain, who will interview you about the shooting.'

'Soldier-man, I told you all I know. What more can I say?'

'This is the order from the captain. I will pick you up at 1255 hours.'

With that, the men turned and walked back to the door. It then dawned on Devon: they must feel it mi do the shooting?

Sir Noxson knocked on Selwyn's cabin door. He was ready to cuss him about not coming to support him the previous night. He kept on knocking but no one came out. As he walked away, he thought, 'Bombo, I wonder if him get caught up in the shooting. Mek mi go down to the doctor ...' His walking pace picked up as he went down the corridors.

Where am I ? Wa dis? Who is you? Roy was coming around to see tubes in his arm and bandages around his body. His head felt heavy as he laid back on the pillow. 'My body aches,' he thought. 'I can't talk. What's down my throat? What's wrong with my voice? Why can't I talk?' He fell into a panic.

A white face appeared over his bed.

'You're awake?' asked Nurse Sharon. 'You are in the infirmary with a tube down your throat. Don't try to talk.'

Roy's eyes just got bigger. 'You have been in a shooting,' she explained, 'and you are in recovery. I will call the doctor. Please stay still.'

Roy looked to his right and saw Delroy bandaged up with tubes in his arm. He then looked to his left and Evans was lying on the bed with a bandaged head.

'Where was Selwyn? What the hell happened?' he thought, then he remembered the gun ... and the soldier – and he blacked out.

'That's the infirmary,' the female soldier said. She knocked on the door. A passing nurse saw her through the glass.

'Yes? How can I help you?'

'I am looking for Gladstone Vincent Carman. Is he inside?'

'Are you a relative?'

Norma quickly said, 'I am his cousin.'

'Please wait here.' The nurse walked away. There was a wait, then the doctor and MP came outside.

'Miss Norma, you say you're the cousin of Mr Carman?'

'That's right. Well, I'm sorry to say ...' Before the MP could say another word Norma was crying. The MP went on: 'He was involved in the shooting last night and sustained gunshot wounds, but,' more tears were running down her face, 'he is alive ...' That's all Norma could hear – he was alive '... but not out of the woods yet. We will be keeping him here for the rest of the voyage.'

'May I see him?'

'Not now. Maybe later today.'

'She can't get away with it. I just know Pele dead – if he wasn't we would have seen him on the ship. It not like Pele not to let us know what's going on ... We need to get bad on her ass, get her somewhere quiet so we can work her over. I bet she working for the gang back home – I bet you they put out a bounty on our heads. If you don't help me I'm doing her myself.'

Anton adjusted his shirt and trousers, opened the cabin door, then coolly said, 'After you, Verndo, and don't forget your knife.'

Verndo had forgotten that Anton could be very dangerous while also keeping his cool.

'How we a cook food when we just get in the kitchen?' The English chief said, 'Put up a sign at the door saying, "No breakfast today – just tea and bread". There's no time to do breakfast. So start on dinner,' he added as he walked away.

'Chef, then we a start pan the evening dinner?' Junior said.

'Yes, man.'

'We have some goat left and rice.'

'OK, who is doing the dumplings tonight? I beg you no badda put in too much salt in the damn dumplings and everybody must go easy on the scotch-bonnet pepper as we only have two days' left of supplies'

'Yes, Chef,' came back the team.

Knock, knock. Maria opened the door. Standing outside was an MP.

'Please let Miss Hyacinth know that the captain will see her at 1500 hours today. The guard will escort her.'

'No,' came a voice from the back of the room. 'I will walk there myself.'

Hyacinth was sitting at the dressing table looking at her face in the mirror, taking in the injuries that man had inflicted on her. The MP turned and walked away.

'You know I'm coming with you,' Maria said with a 'try and stop me' tone.

'You have been my rock. I just met you. You don't have to live this nightmare that I'm going through.'

'Sister, be still.'

'I demand to see the captain. How dare you stop me from leaving my cabin? I will report you.' When Dangle raised his voice he expected to get his way.

Two very big MPs just looked him in the eye as they stood outside his cabin. He was standing at the doorway in his fine suit and cravat, wanting to go out to search for another victim.

'We are under captain's orders that you must not leave your cabin under any circumstances.'

'How dare the captain put me under arrest? What have I done to deserve this treatment? I am working for the British government. I will let the captain know that they will not get any information if I'm not allowed to move around this ship,' Dangle thought. 'Get me your captain now!' he shouted to the soldiers, then slammed the door.

'That's all I know,' Devon said to the captain, who gave him a 'I don't believe you' look.

'What more you want from me? You have a mad soldier who shoot up everyone in the room …'

'Are you sure there was not a fight before the shooting?'

'I don't know. I was at the top of the stairs looking out for MPs … it the gunshot that got me downstairs.'

'OK, Mr Devon. I have your statement. Please read it then sign it.'

'What you a do with the mad soldier-man?' Devon asked. The captain and the soldier in the captain's office looked up.

'He will be dealt with in the English courts. We will need your address in England as you may be called as a witness,' the captain replied.

'May, may. I am the only witness?' he said in a vex voice. 'So you think your mad soldier is going to tell the truth about the shooting? Cha, you soldier-men always stick together ... I can see there will be no justice for my brothers.' Devon signed his statement then said, 'You done with me?'

'Yes, we are.' Devon left the captain's office knowing there was going to be a cover-up.

'It two fifty p.m. You ready, Hyacinth?'

Hyacinth stepped out of the toilet, looking every inch a battered woman. But she somehow also had a steely aspect about her: she looked like she was ready to take on anyone who would get in her way today. Maria opened the cabin door. Hyacinth took a deep breath, then stepped out into the corridor. Maria led the way to the captain's study.

As they approached the corridor leading to the captain's office they encountered two soldiers. Hyacinth paused, looked at Maria. 'How do I look?'

'Wonderful.' Hyacinth straightened her back, fixed her dress, and her shoulders went back with her head held high.

'Please come in,' the captain said. Hyacinth and Maria walked into his office. Looking around at his furniture it felt like someone's study in a private house. 'Please take a seat.'

This was the first time the captain had had an opportunity to take a look at the raped woman and what injuries she had suffered. 'My God, what animal did this?' he thought. He tried not to let his feelings show on his face.

The door opened and the doctor walked in, greeting them as he stepped into the study with a female MP. 'Sergeant Christina will be recording your statement.'

'Good afternoon, ladies,' she said.

The ladies just nodded their heads.

'We are here for you to give your signed statement about the incident,' the captain said.

'INCIDENT?INCIDENT!!! That man raped and assaulted me and I want him in prison.' Hyacinth let her frustration out.

'Miss Hyacinth, we have to have a statement from you so the charges can be put to this gentlem …' the captain stopped in mid-sentence, '… the person we have under arrest. When you're ready, in your own time, please tell me what happened.'

Hyacinth looked at the captain sitting behind his desk, the woman soldier sitting behind dictation equipment, The doctor sitting in the corner of the room and Maria sitting next to her, holding her hand. She took a deep breath then started to tell her story … The doctor sat quietly in his chair and listened to Hyacinth's statement, which she gave in full detail – not sparing any words or depravity she underwent. Sergeant Christina took down every word that came out of Hyacinth's mouth; when Hyacinth got to the part about anal sex and being beaten, Sergeant Christina made a noise that slipped out of her mouth; she just wasn't able to hold it in – a sharp intake of air mixed with pain. Everyone in the office looked at her. She just kept her head down and carried on typing.

'That's my full statement.'

'Thank you,' the captain said. 'I now have some questions I need to put to you.'

Hyacinth looked him in the eye.

Captain: 'Was there anyone else in the cabin with you?'

Hyacinth: 'No.'

Captain: 'Were you drunk?'

Hyacinth: 'No.'

Captain: 'Do you feel you were drugged?'

Hyacinth: 'Yes.'

Captain: 'At any time did you consent to have sex?'

Hyacinth: 'No.'

Captain: 'Did he force you to go to his cabin?'

Hyacinth: 'No, I went there freely but that does not give him the right to rape me.'

Captain: 'Did you lead him on?'

Hyacinth: 'No, having a drink with a man is not leading him on.'

Captain: 'Are you willing to testify in an English court?'

Hyacinth: 'Yes! Just try and stop me!'

Captain: 'Did you have sex or any sexual contact with this man before the assault?'

Hyacinth hesitated. 'I did go to his cabin once before, we did kiss ...' She paused as she knew how it would sound to a person who was not there. 'I stop him before it got out of hand. We had a drink then I left the cabin.'

Captain: 'Thank you, Miss Hyacinth, for the detailed statement. May I have the doctor's report added to the statement you just made?'

As the doctor read out her injuries Hyacinth kept looking at the pattern in the carpet, the way the colours intertwined. She was trying to work out how they did that. Maria looked at her, knowing she had zoned out to escape all these gruesome details of the injuries to her body. She knew this was her way of protecting herself. The doctor's report was factual and curt, she thought. Just where should Hyacinth put her head when a white man you don't know is telling a room full of people about your vagina and blood from your anus? Somehow it felt as if she was being raped all over again.

'That's my report, Captain,' the doctor said.

There was a silence in the room. Then the captain got to his feet to deliver his official speech.

'On behalf of the King of England and the King's Navy I would ...'

'PLEASE PLEASE!' Hyacinth stopped him in his tracks. 'Don't say what you're about to say! Have we done here?'

'Yes,' the doctor said to Hyacinth. The captain was standing there with his mouth open, feeling ashamed about what had happened to this young woman – on his watch, on his ship, by a Nazi.

'Yes, yes, quite, quite,' he said. 'The Navy's medical team and the MP will meet you at the docks in London. When we dock, please stay in your cabin. We will collect you.'

Hyacinth got to her feet, followed by Maria. The doctor held open the door and said, 'I will visit you tomorrow.'

Hyacinth and Maria walked out of the captain's study without another word being said.

Doctor Tom closed the door. Captain Stanley slumped into his chair. The soldier taking the dictation wiped a tear from her eye, put her equipment together, then said, 'I will have the transcription ready tomorrow morning, sir,' as she walked out of the office. When Tom sat down, Captain Stanley reached into his bottom drawer and took out the old single malt whisky he kept for very important or trying times.

'I'm not sure if she led him on,' he said. 'She did admit to kissing him and went back to his cabin.'

Tom looked at Captain Stanley. 'I don't believe you just said that, Rick. Look at the list of the woman's injuries, then tell me again she asked for that treatment. I am ashamed as a man, and I feel so sorry for that poor woman.'

Captain Stanley poured out two drinks, and both men sat there drinking and saying nothing. Their faces said it all.

There was a knock at the captain's door.

'Come in,' the captain said.

'Sir, Mr Dangle is insisting that he be let out of his cabin. He's making merry hell, sir!'

The captain put down his drink. The doctor, who was sitting opposite, saw the rage in his eyes and said, 'Calm down, Rick, calm down.'

'Can you believe this?!' He looked at the soldier. 'Go back to your post. I will be there shortly.'

'Rick, Captain Stanley, calm down.'

'What the hell is wrong with that man? So he wants to see me, does he? Then let's go!'

He picked up his hat and his black stick that never left his side and stormed out the door, followed by a very concerned doctor who knew that Captain Rick Stanley was not a man you got angry.

CHAPTER 20

A BAD SMELL

Mavis was sitting on the deck of the ship in the sunshine, looking out to sea.

'How are you today?' a man's voice said. She looked up, but the sun was behind him; all she could see was an outline. Then he moved forward so she could see his face. It was Edward.

Mavis smiled. 'It nice to see you – where you been?'

'I'm so sorry I did not get the opportunity to buy you a drink. As you know there was a shooting that night I was meant to meet you.'

'Yes,' Mavis said, 'so sad to hear that. Are you OK?'

'Yes, I'm fine, thank you. It's good to know you care.'

Mavis blushed like a little girl. She stood up and gave him a hug. She whispered in his ear, 'So good to see you,' then gave him a little kiss on the cheek.

'This is the vice-captain,' the Tannoy bellowed out across the ship. 'Tonight we will not have entertainment in respect of our fallen soldiers and passengers. The bar will be open and there will be background music from 1900 to 2200 hours.'

'Aunty Precious, please can we go to the captain's headquarters?'

'No, not today. We will be playing games this evening.'

'Yes! That will be fun.'

'I will meet you in the ballroom,' Doris said as she left the cabin.

Precious looked at the door and said, 'Am I the only one looking after the pickney dem? Why is it always me?' she said.

'That's not fair, Precious,' Betty said. 'We have all been helping out with the kids – it's not just you.'

Precious was surprised at the way Betty talked back to her. Betty turned to the kids and said, 'Are you all ready?'

'Yes, Aunty.'

'Then let's go.' Betty moved to the door without a backwards glance at Precious as she stepped out of the cabin.

'No pan playing tonight, so let's meet in the bar,' Lord Pan said.

'OK,' one or two members of the team replied.

'It's about time I meet me a nice woman,' Elroy said.

The men agreed. 'It been too long time mi na have a woman in mi bed.'

'Yes, man.'

'Mi ball a drop because them na get no use ...' All the men burst out laughing.

'Mi a put on my new shirt tonight. Mi have mi eye on one good-looking woman,' Lord Pan announced.

'Soldier, do not let anyone inside,' the captain said as he opened the door to Dangle's cabin.

'At last you found the time to see me,' Dangle said. 'This is outrageous – to think you have put *me* under arrest?'

'Sit down,' Captain Stanley said, looking him in the eye.

Dangle did not move. He took another sip of his drink, totally ignoring what the captain was saying.

'You know I am under government protection,' Dangle said.

The captain saw red. He pointed his black stick at Dangle's chest. 'Sit down! Or I will make you sit down!'

Doctor Tom was standing behind the captain. He calmly said, 'Mr Dangle, you had better sit down.'

Dangle slowly sat down on his sofa in a very relaxed, almost contemptuous way.

'There have been allegations of rape made against you by a woman.'

Dangle looked up at the captain with an unruffled expression.

'You must be mistaken. I don't need to rape any woman. This is an outright lie.'

'We have her statement, and the doctor has examined her and reported her injuries. Do you deny being with a woman in your cabin last night?'

'No, I don't. A woman named Miss Hyacinth was in my cabin. I did not force her to be in my cabin. Come on, we are all men here, and educated. These inferior people are like animals, they just love sex. Your country used to keep them as slaves. They are beneath the white race! That woman wanted to have sex with me. I did not have to force her.'

'My God, man, have you seen her injuries?!' the doctor said from behind the captain. 'This woman has sustained more than fifteen injuries to her body, including a cracked rib and anal injuries.'

Dangle picked up the bottle of wine from the table and poured himself a drink. 'I have diplomatic immunity. You can't arrest me or imprison me.'

'Well, Mr Dangle,' Captain Stanley said, 'while you're on my ship you're in international waters so you're in my kingdom – and you will stay in your cabin under guard until we get to London. If you make any attempt to leave this cabin I have given the MPs orders to use any force they deem necessary to restrain you,' he said in a very firm voice.

'This is outrageous! You don't know who you're dealing with! I want to talk to your superior in London.'

'This order has come from HQ London. You will be escorted off the ship by my MPs. Then you will be handed over to MI5. Until then you're under my authority and, let me be very clear, you give me a good reason and I will shoot you myself like an animal.'

Dangle did not like being called an animal. He leapt to his feet but as he did this Captain Stanley raised his black stick in readiness to bring it down on the man's head. Suddenly Doctor Tom's hand appeared, holding back the captain's arm, stopping him from hitting Dangle.

'He's not worth it!' Tom said.

Dangle fell backwards into the chair with a frightened look on his face.

'Just give me the reason,' the captain said.

Looking into the captain's eyes Dangle saw a man who would not hesitate to kill him. He had seen that look before.

The captain took a step backwards, then adjusted his uniform, putting the black stick back under his arm. 'We are done here, doctor.'

'Yes we are, Captain. Let's get out of here. There is a bad smell in this cabin.'

PART VII
Not Welcome?

CHAPTER 21

THE VICTIM ... AND KISSES

'Captain? New orders from London.' The vice-captain handed a telegram to Captain Stanley, who was sitting behind his wooden desk in his study and smoking a cigar. He opened the envelope and read it two times.

'What the hell is going on in London?!' he said out loud. 'Why the hell must we wait in the Thames till we get an all-clear from HQ? What the hell am I supposed to tell the passengers?'

'Captain, there seems to be one hell of a disagreement about this ship. I have been moderating the radio from London and the word is that some MPs who are connected to Lord Mosley and his Union movement do not want this ship of West Indians to dock. The Mosley supporters and remnants of his old Fascist Blackshirts are stirring up bad feeling towards the West Indians.'

'Bloody MPs,' the captain said. 'They forget that a lot of the West Indians fought and died for our country. Mosley's types did not turn them away when they were on the battlefield in Europe and Africa ...'

Captain Stanley did not like injustice anywhere. He was not particularly a supporter of the West Indian people or them living in England, but he respected the brave men and women who had stood side by side with his people on the battlefield. 'I feel it's maybe best if we keep this to ourselves. We can always say the docks are full and that we are waiting for a docking port. Bloody Blackshirts.'

*

'In four days we will be in London and Pele not coming back. We know someone got to him, and they coming for us, on this ship or in London.'

'She knows something all right. I told you – before we get off this ship we need to get her!'

'You mean talk to her?' Anton said.

'You talk – I will beat the shit out of her then throw her overboard!'

'I still think we should let the captain know.'

'And what's the point of that?'

'We need to find out if Pele is still on board this ship.'

'By now he would have got word to us. There's no way he would have left us like this ... Let's face it, he dead – and we got to be alert all the time until we get off this bloody ship.'

... Norma ...
'Norma, that yellow dress with the red scarf looks great on you. I do like the touch of red around your neck... Where you going?' Lucretia said.

I thought long and hard then said, 'Sit down. I need to talk to you. Please don't say a word till I have finished.'

We sat in the cabin and I talked Lucretia through the whole story about Roy, from the time he carried my grips and bags on board the ship to the shooting. I ended with: 'He getting better now. So I'm going to see him in the infirmary today.'

I sat back. Lucretia did the same. We looked at one other ... I was waiting for an outburst from her, but it never came. She just said, 'What a romantic story! It like Romeo and Janet ... No, no, I mean Juliet!' She started sobbing. I was lost for words. Lucretia never ceases to amaze me.

'This man is meant to be in your life,' she said. 'I know these things ... I have the power to see these things!' I gave her one of my 'here we go' looks. 'This is more than a coincidence, it fate, it in the stars, it ...'

'OK, Lucretia, I get it.'

'Sister, I hope Roy or what-ever his name is now get better. You know I will keep his and your secrets!'

I gave Lucretia a big hug then we both let out a long, slow breath.

'Doctor! The bodies of Private Colin Matthews and passenger Mr Selwyn Carter have been moved to the morgue. We have taken Sergeant Andy Davis, Private Thomas Francis, the passengers Delroy Spencer and Gladstone Carman off the danger list but Private Bill Nixon is still not responding.'

The doctor looked at the notes then went over to Private Nixon and took his pulse. 'We need to have an ambulance and a medical team on standby when we get to London. He's not looking good.'

He then went over to Roy. The patient they thought was called Gladstone Carman was awake. 'Hello, do you know what day it is?' Tom asked.

Roy sat up and looked around. 'What happened to me? How did I end up here?' Nurse Sharon sat down next to him and told him what had happened. Roy lay there looking into space. Then he said, 'How are my friends?' He gestured across at Evans.

'He is making a good improvement, just like you, Mr Carman,' Nurse Sharon said. 'I need you to lie still. You're not out of the woods yet and you need to build up your strength.'

'Doctor,' a different nurse said, 'Mr Carman has a visitor. It's his cousin.'

Roy overheard this, but was in no state to question it.

'Can she come inside?'

'Yes, but not for too long. He needs to rest.'

As the nurse walked off to get the cousin, the doctor said, 'I will be back later.'

Roy sat up, looking at the door, wondering if he was dreaming. Who was this cousin? It must be a person related to the dead man's identity he had stolen. 'When dem see mi the game will be up, mi a go to prison.' His eyes were fixed on the door. It slowly opened and in walked Norma, almost in slow motion. Roy adjusted his eyes, to see a woman in a yellow dress with a red scarf and a red head wrap. It was a face he recognised. As she got closer he saw the almost tearful face of Norma. She walked over to his bed and took his hand.

'You're one man who knows how to get himself into problems, *Mr Carman*,' she said.

Roy smiled and a tear came down his face. He did not feel the tear making its way down to his chin. Norma wiped away the line of his tear, then touched her handkerchief to her own eyes. 'What a pair we are!'

Roy just looked at her, with a mixed look of happiness and sadness.

'When you get out of here I'm going to beat you because your ears too hard. The last thing I said to you was "take care", now look at you!'

For the first time, Roy smiled. He forgot about his pain, just kept holding Norma's hand and looking into her face as she was talking. He was focusing not on her words but on the colour of her skin, the very faint freckles, the colour of her eyes, the soft lines by her eyes, the way her glasses sat on her nose, the way her full lips moved when she talked, her warm soft hand ...

'I said, how is your friend doing?'

'The nurse said he doing well.'

'Glad to hear that. Everyone been talking about the shooting. Is it true that it was a soldier-man who shoot all of you?' Roy nodded his head. 'People don't know who got shot. For some reason they're not telling anyone.'

'Well, I'm glad about that,' Roy said quietly. 'I don't need anyone in mi business.'

Norma sat down and asked, 'Do you want anything?'

'No, I'm good right now. I just need to get better.'

'When you feel better you can tell me all about what happened with the gunman in the boiler room. I knew there were mad people in this world, but I never thought I would live to see a day like this!'

'Me either,' Roy said, 'me either.'

'Remember me?'

The voice of a short man in a light blue shirt and white trousers, with white braces holding up his trousers. Lucretia stopped, as she was walking down the corridor holding on to the railing because the ship was tossing around all over the place. She took a good look at him.

'Chef, how could I forget you?'

'Well, you seem to have many admirers!'

'What do you mean?'

'I saw you on the dance floor. You were putting down some bad moves with two men.'

'I never knew I was promise to you? I is a free woman and I don't need you telling mi about who I is dancing with.'

'No no no, mi never mean it that way. I admire you. You did look so good dancing ...'

'Oh, you really think so?'

'Yes, sister. I love the way you move and you groove. Mi like you, honey,' he said in a sweet-boy tone.

'Man, you is very forward.'

'Well, you have to be. I can't let a nice piece of woman like you get away from me.'

'But stop,' Lucretia said. 'You really is a bosey-man. How you know I like you?'

'Tell mi you don't and I gwan ...'

Lucretia looked at him, then Mavis's voice came in her head: 'Look at the man, not the height.'

'You're not bad, but I is not looking for a man right now. I want to work in Inglan then come home to Grandma ... But if and when I am looking for a man in Inglan I will look you up.'

'Let's just get to know each other.'

'Cool with me. Let's go to the bar.'

'Where you been?' Doris asked Devon, who was sitting at the bar.

'I been to hell and back.'

'You telling me you was mixed up in the shooting?'

'Yes. I was the lookout man. Doris, it was bad – very, very bad. Dem lock mi up like mi is the gunman. It just now dem let mi go.'

'Cha, did any of your friends get shoot?'

'Yes, them is in the infirmary. I don't know who is dead and how them a do; them won't let mi see them.'

Doris moved over to Devon and hugged him.

'Come and sit over here, mek we talk.'

Devon moved like an old man, even though he was only twenty years old. He was in shock. He had never seen anyone shot before, never seen any dead bodies.

'Were you in the room when the gunman started to shoot?'

'No, mi was on the stairs looking out. It's when mi hear the gunshots mi get down the stairs to see the bodies and soldier-man standing over them.'

'He never tried to shoot you?' Doris asked softly.

'No, he just stood there with the gun in his hand ranting about Germans and shooting them.'

'What a thing this!' Doris looked at his hands shaking. She could see he was still in shock. 'Come, Devon, you need to lie down. Let's go to your cabin, so you can sleep. I will sit with you.'

Devon looked at Doris like a lost child. She looked back at him with a caring expression.

When they got to his empty cabin, no one else was there. He sat on his bed, and Doris told him to lie down to sleep.

'I will be here when you wake up,' she said. As Devon dozed off, Doris remembered meeting him on the first day on the ship; she'd been taking a walk around the vessel, looking at the decks, the lifeboats and the view of the ocean when she saw a nice young man silently praying as he sat in a chair on the deck. He made a sign of the cross then was about to get up when Doris said, 'Are you Catholic?'

He looked up at her pleasant, smiling face and said, 'No, I'm a Seventh Day Adventist. But I like to make the sign of the cross as it makes me feel like I have had a good prayer.'

'I never looked at it that way ... I am also a Seventh Day Adventist! I am Doris, from Bermuda, and you are?' She extended her hand.

'I'm Devon, from Trinidad.'

Every day after that they met at that part of the ship just under the stairs to have a morning prayer together. Doris decided then and there that this would be her private time that was not for Precious or Betty ... Every morning she would say, 'I'm going for my walk.' She looked forward to the prayer time and talk time with Devon. They chatted about family, the islands, religion, God ... and their dreams for Inglan.

'I want to open a car repair business in Inglan. There going to be a boom in cars – they're making new roads for them. Back home I could fix any motor car, and sometime if I couldn't get the parts I would make them.'

Doris was transfixed by his stories, his view of life, his life mission. It was very close to her own story. She also wanted to go back home, but was looking forward to being in Inglan until the mess the fathers had made had been cleared up.

She knew she was developing feelings for this man. She could not stop thinking about him ... the way he walked; the way he had a parting on the left-hand side of his head; his Trinidad mixed-race skin, part-native Indian, part-African, part-white; the very pointed nose and wavy hair; he always had a tank top on and always looked clean and tidy and smart – so nice. She had not felt this way before about any man or boy, and knew this was not going to stop once they were off the ship.

As Devon slept Doris had a long talk with God about Devon and the men who were dead and were shot. She was very clear with God that she did not want any more people dying – and asked Him to bless Devon with love. She just sat there looking at Devon sleeping.

... *Precious* ...

I saw Betty take out the children to the deck of the ship where they could run around. I finally had a few minutes to walk around the ship; on the deck I leant on the railing, looking out to the sea, thinking about Mum and Dad, where the ship was going and what I would do with the kids once in London. I saw an empty deckchair positioned to look out to sea and sat down, pulling the blanket that was on the chair over my legs. This felt so good – the sea air on my face and time to think ... Maybe I had been hard on Betty and Doris; maybe I had been hard on the kids, but I did it for their own good ...

Suddenly I was having a conversation with myself: 'Why does no one like me?'

'Because you're so bossy?'

'You think you're all that?'

'You too much?'

'You think you know it all?'

'You think you're better than everyone else?'

'You're spoiled.'

'I really love my friends Betty and Doris – they are a big part of my life. I need to be less bossy and talk and listen to my sisters ...'

'I just want to get to Inglan and see Mother. She will know what to do. I'm twenty-two years old with my whole life in front of me.'

I sat there alone, watching the waves, debating inside my head.

'What the bloody hell happened?' Sergeant Davis said to the doctor. He sat up on the bed. 'How long have I been out? My leg, my leg hurts!'

'Sergeant Davis, you were shot in the leg and banged your head badly as you fell ... You have been sleeping on and off for several days.'

Davis looked around the room. He saw Tommy Francis and Bill Nixon. 'How are they doing? Not well? Who else got shot?'

'We lost Private Colin Matthews.'

'Colin? No, no, no! Colin! No!'

The doctor talked Davis through the shooting.

'I *told* them that Mickey was not all there! You could see he was not all there! Where is he now?'

'He's under MP guard in the Brig.'

'He'd better stay there – if I get my hands on him, he's dead.'

The doctor looked on calmly. 'As soon as you feel up to it we need you to make a statement about the shooting. Who were the other men that were in the boiler room?'

'You mean the West Indian men?'

'Yes. There were four of them. One is dead and the other three are in the other part of the infirmary.'

'Shit, this is bad – bloody bad.'

'Please lie down. We need to change the dressing on your leg.'

Davis lay down looking at the ceiling wondering how the hell this shit had happened. He thought, 'It was just a game of cards, just a game of cards.'

Knock. knock. 'Enter,' the captain said. 'Hello, Tom, please sit down. So what's the news on Private Morton?'

'I have tried to talk to him but he is not mentally stable. He still sees German soldiers everywhere. He feels he's in the war zone. We need to keep a suicide watch on him until we get to London. He a sick young man.'

'Any more news about the passengers in the infirmary? And how is the young lady who was assaulted?'

'She is getting better. I have had a nurse visit her every day. She does not want to leave her cabin,' the doctor said.

'I will have an ambulance at the docks for this lady,' the captain said in a soft voice. 'Tom, London wants us to hold the ship at the mouth of the Thames – some MPs and old Blackshirt followers of Oswald Mosley are trying to stop this ship from landing.'

'What?!' said Tom. 'What the hell are they playing at? We've got sick people on board. We can't lose time because of some political game.'

'You're right, Tom. You're damn right. As soon as we get to the Thames I will let them know we have injured men aboard who need urgent surgery. Damn Mosley and his Blackshirts. Just a few days to go… we have been on many voyages together, but none like this, Tom, none like this.'

Mavis made her way to cabin 366. She knocked on the door; it slowly opened. Standing there was Edward with that 'look' in his black trousers and white open-necked shirt, rolled-up sleeves with brown braces attached to his trousers.

'Please come in, Mavis.'

As she stepped into the cabin she saw boxes at the back of the two-room cabin. There was a sofa with a table and a vase of flowers, some bottles of wine and rum with two glasses. 'I have tried to make it homely for you, I hope you like it.'

'Edward, where did you get the flowers from?'

'I picked them in Bermuda. I kept them in water. I thought you might like them.'

Mavis smelt the flowers, and sat down. Edward poured them both a glass of wine and sat next to her on the sofa.

'To your health.'

They clinked glasses.

'This is where they store the officers' uniform and papers,' he said.

Mavis thought she would be nervous, but felt fine in Edward's company. He was looking as handsome as the first day she saw him. Edward himself was thinking, 'Be cool, don't mess this up.'

'Tell me about your family?' Mavis said.

The conversation went on to Mavis's life, her ambitions, Edward's home-town life as a soldier, the shooting. An hour went by, but it felt like ten minutes, the bottle of wine was done and the rum was kicking in.

'I like you, Mavis,' he said, as he looked into her eyes.

'I like you, Edward, you're a fine-looking man.'

'And you're a gorgeous woman.'

Mavis put down her glass, moved over to his side of the sofa and kissed him. Edward sat there tasting this sexy woman; he had never kissed a West Indian woman – but he could get used to it ... Mavis pulled back, thinking she had been too forward. She sat still, looking at him in his white shirt; he put down his glass then slowly moved over to her and kissed her again. It was a long kiss, a loving kiss ... her hands were begging to move up and down his back. Mavis fell back on the sofa with Edward on top of her. The kissing was deep and very sexual. Edward was trying to contain his passion, his manhood standing to attention and ready for action. His hands were moving towards her breasts ... Mavis came up for air.

'Wow, you're a good kisser. But let's take our time. I want you, but I don't just sleep with anyone I like.'

'I'm glad to hear that,' said Edward. 'I have a lot of respect for you. I am willing to wait until we get to know each other. We could have a drink at my pub back home?'

'What's a pub – and how will your people feel about you having a West Indian woman friend?'

'It's my mother who will have something to say!! But I don't care – I want to get to know you. We could meet in London, and I will show you what a pub is.'

'Yes, I would like that,' she said, adjusting her blouse. She then just lay in his arms, nothing more was said. They just lay there, listening to the sea.

CHAPTER 22

JOHN-CROW-BATTY, STOWAWAYS AND A POWERFUL LADY

'You have the pans ready for tonight's event?'

'Yes, man,' Lord Pan said to the stage manager. 'We're going to play the night out – this will be a real Caribbean Blues ... I feel we all need to have some fun. This shooting has got a lot of people down.'

'Yes, I agree with that,' the stage manager said. This was the first time the English stage manager had had a conversion with Lord Pan; before he'd always had a bad attitude and tone. If he lived in Jamaica he would have been box down, Lord Pan thought. The shooting had made people rethink how they dealt with other human beings.

'They're playing bad tunes in the lower hall. We only got one more night on this ship, so let's jam-down.'

Sir Noxson was getting his records ready. He was going for it tonight. Chef and the team were in the kitchen cooking up the last of the food supplies he had taken from Jamaica: he had sweet potatoes, callaloo, fresh seasoned fish, green banana, with some goat meat that was left in the freezer. The smell of curry goat went around the ship. Even the English boys, who did not eat 'that foreign muck' wanted to know where that wonderful smell was coming from. 'I soon come,' Chef said as he went out the backdoor exit of the kitchen.

*

Everyone wanted to lift the dark cloud that was on the ship. Tonight was going to be a night for celebrating the lives of the dead; it would be like a nine night so the West Indians were going to give the dead a West Indian send-off.

Hyacinth sat in her cabin looking at the walls. Then she looked in the mirror. Her face had healed, most of the bruising had gone down — but she had pains in her body.

'I need to get out,' she said to Maria. 'I need some fresh air. I will not be the victim of this. Let's take a walk on deck, then find two chairs in the ballroom so I can take my mind off it all.'

Maria looked shocked. 'Are you sure?'

'Yes. None of the passengers know about the attack. So why should I hide? I need to get out of this cabin.'

'OK, OK, let's get you a nice dress and some lipstick. If we going out let's "fix up".'

Lucretia was coming back from the cabin. She needed to get her jumper as the weather was turning cold. She was walking down the long corridor to towards the ballroom; there was no one in sight.

'Lord, mi stomach a hot mi,' she thought. 'The English-man food just give mi wind. Lord, I can't stop it coming out of my body ... There was a farting sound. Mmm Mmm, that sound bad. She looked around to make sure no one could hear or smell her passing wind. As she got to the end of the corridor her stomach gave her a sharp pain then she let out an almighty gust of wind from her bottom and just as the wind was leaving her body Chef came out of a side door that the staff used to get around the ship very quickly. He saw that big-mother African backside walking down the corridor and knew it was Lucretia ... he slink up behind her, then throws his arms around her just as the wind was leaving her body. She jump, he let go, she look around to see Chef taking in a mouthful of her wind that smelled real bad.

'Ahhhh – Ahhhh ....'

'A you dat?' she said, as she turned around.

'Woman, you is a powerful lady!'

Lucretia fell against the wall then slowly slid down to the floor, belly-laughing her head off. Chef was bending over, laughing, then collapsed on the floor alongside Lucretia. As they sat there, she said, 'It not me, it the damn Inglish food – it just keep give mi wind!'

Chef had tears rolling down his cheeks. Lucretia could not stop laughing. Every time she looked at Chef on the floor laughing his head off, she burst out again. They looked like a couple of schoolkids who had been naughty. As they caught their breath, sitting on the floor in the corridor, Chef said, 'You best marry me, so I can cook you some good yard food, so you don't have to pass wind like that.'

Lucretia replied, 'You're right – a man who can cook yard food and save mi from wind must be good for mi!'

Chef got to his feet, then extended a hand to Lucretia to help her off the floor. They looked deep into each other's eyes as she got up and something happened at that moment.

You can't describe it. You just feel it.

'A drink?'

'Yes. And I'm paying,' she said with a big smile.

'Attention...' The ballroom was full of soldiers standing to attention. 'One more day, then we dock in London. Soldiers, it's been a challenging voyage for all of us. I want you to be on full alert tonight as there is still a lot of bad feeling about the shooting. I need you to keep an eye on anyone playing up. The ballroom and bar are open tonight and anyone getting drunk or out of order will be put in the Brig.'

The vice-captain looked at the faces of his tired soldiers, weary and homesick; they had been on the front line and just wanted to go home. 'The good news is your fellow soldiers in the infirmary are slowly making a recovery and after your patrol tonight the lower bar will remain open just for soldiers only, no passengers, till 0130 hours.'

'Dismissed.'

The ballroom was filling up with people. The lower hall was blasting out tune after tune and two of the demobbed West Indian soldiers, Desmond and Bailey, were sitting at the bar talking about life in the Inglish army, home, Inglan and what they will face in London. They all wanted to go home, but there was no money back home; the offer from Inglan to come and work was too good to turn down.

'Mi a make some money and send back some to mi family,' Bailey said.

'Mi feel them is a wicked people to mek we dock in Jamaica and not let us off the ship. What kind of bloodclaat ting-a-gwan?'

'You did feel the heat, smell the fruits, see the palms trees; after all we did go and fight in the white-man's war and them just a shit pon we?'

Desmond put down his glass and lit a cigarette. 'Man, this is messed-up.'

One of the barmen, Cliff, was dancing behind the bar.

'I'm getting to like this West Indian Man-too music,' he said to the West Indian soldiers sitting on a stool at the bar. The soldiers looked at each other. 'Man, it called Mento, it a mix of Jamaican folk and African sound. It big back home but mi is hearing this new slower beat coming out of Kingston ...'

'Well, I'm tired of it. Where is the good old singalong English music?' said Simon, the other barman. Cliff walked to the back of the bar leaving the soldiers in a deep talk about music.

'Come on, look around you – the only white people in here are you, me and the MPs in the hallway so why would they playing "Knees Up, Mother Brown"?'

'Bloody coons,' Simon said under his breath as they got drinks from the back of the bar.

'You really can be a bloody dickhead sometimes!' Cliff said. 'Just get to know them, mate – they're humans just like you.' As he walked back to the front of the bar, he said, 'Look what I found. He placed a bottle of John-Crow-Batty rum on the bar. 'What is it? I have never seen this type of rum before.'

This stopped the discussion about music instantly.

'Huuoooo...!' Desmond and Bailey burst out laughing as they looked at the barman. 'This is the famous JA rum that's made in the hills of Jamaica – you Inglish call it moonshine, we call it John-Crow-Batty...'

'What the hell is a John-Crow-Batty?' Cliff said.

'Let me show you.'

The soldier took the bottle and opened it. 'Line up four shot glasses,' Desmond said to the barman. 'They call it John-Crow-Batty because you had to have the stomach as strong as a vulture to drink it and it smelled like what comes out of the vulture's batty.'

Cliff looked dazed. 'You taking the mickey? You're saying this rum is made from the bottom of a vulture?'

Now the two men were laughing so hard that a few other men came over and shared the joke.

'No, man, no ... not *from* the bottom!' Tears were coming from all the men's eyes. Cliff and Simon looked at the men laughing at them, then joined in the laughter. Four drinks were poured and the four men held up the white rum that looked like water, still laughing. Desmond said, 'Cheers to your king and our islands ...!' Then all four downed the shot in one. There was a moment's silence, then Simon let out, 'Gordon Bennett!' 'Bloody Norah!' said Cliff, and started coughing. 'My mouth is on fire ...' 'It's so bloody hot ...' The barmen were gasping as they ran to the water-tap, both putting their mouth under the tap at the same time. This was witnessed by the West Indian men standing at the bar who were all laughing at the white boys. 'You drinking "Big Man" drink!' Desmond said. 'Now you have tasted the West Indies!'

Simon and Cliff were getting as much water down their necks as they could and fanning their mouths. 'Bloody hell!' 'Cor blimey!' they said again. 'Jesus wept.' That's all you could get out of them.

All the people in the bar were laughing together, feeling like one human race. 'John-Crow-Batty rum is a drink them English boys will never forget,' chuckled Desmond.

'Hyacinth, you ready for this?'

'Please don't ask me again. I said I want to go out, so let's go ...' Hyacinth got to her feet, walked over to the door, looked back and said, 'You coming?'

As she walked down the corridor with Maria, every time someone passed her Hyacinth would flinch. She was still on edge. They made their way to the ballroom door. Hyacinth stopped, looked inside the room, shook her head, pushed back her shoulders then walked into the room. Maria was looking at her in amazement ... This woman had been badly injured and had been violently raped, but she will not be the victim. Maria took her hand and walked beside her. No one in the ballroom took any notice of them ... there were so many people in the ballroom, dancing a West Indian foxtrot, men holding the women in the small of the back, some just dancing on their own and some had their heads locked together, with their legs intertwined, very slowly moving to their own ridim ... All they received were lots of 'hellos' and 'what-a-gwan' ... This made Hyacinth feel normal; she was going to the bar for a drink, then she would enjoy the night sitting at one of the tables.

Precious decided she was going to have a damn good time tonight; any man offers her a dance she will take him up. She picked out her best cotton dress with the gold patterns – she always looked good in that – and combed her hair. She took a good look at her face – it looked pale, the sea air and colder weather had her skin drying out; she applied oils to her skin that made it look bright and shiny. 'That West Indian soldier Danville kept looking at me when I met him at the bar,' she thought. He just about said hello; he just keep looking at me, well tonight I'm going to talk to him. Betty has the kids tonight, so it party time.'

'Aunty Betty, is it true that white people's house are joined up together?'

'Yes.'

'Aunty Betty, when do we see the show I read about in the books?' 'Aunty Betty, is all the Father Christmas in Inglan white men?' 'Aunty Betty, will the King be meeting us at the docks?'

'Lord, pickney, you read too many books.'

... *Desmond* ...

The passengers were coming inside from every corner of the ballroom; everyone wanted a good night out, all dressed up and ready to enjoy the music.

A lot of the talk on board was about the shootings and rumours that West Indians were not being welcomed to Inglan and white people were turning the ship back. This hurt we West Indian soldiers the most — just back from the front line fighting for the Mother Country, watching friends and family dying in front of us, then hearing that same Mother Country that West Indians volunteered to fight for does not want us?

A small group of us were talking near the bar.

'Man, we soldiers had to put up with racism from the British troops and the Germans from the first till the last day of the war. They always put us in the front line of attack that sustained the largest casualties.'

'We West Indians always got the shit job, moving the live ammunition to the front lines ... every dangerous job that need to be done, we West Indians were put there,' I said to the crowd of men who were nodding in agreement. 'Remember how we had to tell the white boys who was getting "fresh" with us about how we help them win the war?? Hear him ...'

'We English could have beaten the Germans without your help,' a white soldier nearby said loudly, which got the West Indian soldiers mad – we were all shouting loud, standing face to face. The MPs had to step in to cool things down ...

'But guess what?' I thought, looking on. 'Den a tell we West Indian soldiers fe-cool down but never say anything to the white soldiers.'

'Boy, you see what we get?' I said aloud.

Norma sat down beside Roy and held his hand. He was sleeping. 'Why am I attracted to this man?' she thought. 'From day one he has been nothing but trouble.' Roy slowly opened his eyes and smiled when he saw Norma.

'I'm still here,' he said.

'Yes, the devil looks after his own.'

They both smiled.

'You look very pretty tonight,' he said.

'Thank you, I am going to pop into the ballroom tonight. They have some music and dancing. I would buy you a drink but you have had enough?'

'Cha.' Roy said, 'one more day and we will be in Inglan. I can feel it getting colder.'

'The nurses were talking – you and all the other wounded men are going to the local hospital as soon as we dock,' Norma told him.

Roy looked concerned.

'What's wrong?' Norma asked.

'Because I'm going to hospital they may find out my identity.'

'Man, stop your noise – you are the name in that passport and I'm your cousin. So don't mess up now.'

Doris came into the ballroom with Devon, who was very nervous and still suffering shock.

'Come, let's have a drink at the bar. You need to get back to life.'

The hall was heaving with bodies as one by one the tunes were dropping that sound that made man and woman, black or white, get up and dance. As they stood at the bar Doris noted the men in their cream shirts with kipper ties, double-breasted suits and trilby hats were dancing with women in every colour dress you could think of with slingback shoes. Most women had a cardigan on that matched their outfits.

The song 'Inna Mi Yard' was playing. Doris looked at Devon smiling for the first time since the shooting. They sang along to the song 'Inna mi yard mi enjoy the sun, Inna mi yard mi cook ...' Doris did not seem to notice anyone in the ballroom, just Devon. 'He needs some loving and more God in his life,' she thought. 'I will ...' Then came a tap on her shoulder.

'Are you going to introduce me to your friend?' Doris turned to see Precious standing there, looking somehow different in her look and face.

'Precious, this is Devon, my new friend.'

'Pleased to meet you. They playing some good songs tonight, must dance now –' And off she went right onto the dance floor, dancing with any man who asked her.

'I don't know that woman, I really don't know her,' Doris said to herself. She looked at Precious in amazement. What did that person dancing on the floor do with the old Precious?

'Devon, I just need to pop down to my cabin. I will be five minutes.' She felt she needed to get Betty to see the new Precious dancing, which was something she very rarely did.

Lord Pan was ready to play some calypso songs. He looked over at the DJ, who picked up the mike.

'Brothers and sisters, we have the best pan players in the Caribbean ready to play the night away ... Lord Pan and the Pan Players.'

The Pan Players hit the song 'My Lovely Island' and the people went wild – everyone who was seated got up and everyone on the dance floor moved to this popular West Indian song that was a hit all over the islands.

... Roy ...

The music made its way down the corridor, down the stairs to the infirmary. I was lying on my back staring at the ceiling, then I looked over at Delroy flat out in the next bed. I wished he would wake up.

The sound of 'My Lovely Island' hit my ears; my fingers started to tap on the side of the bed. The song made me think about Selwyn and tears came down my face as I sang softly along. It was the last song I sang together with Selwyn, standing by the bar in the ballroom – we were talking about staying in London for five years, going back home to buy land and start a pig farm! I could hear Selwyn's voice in my head: 'Man, mi and the brothers is setting up a import business in Birmingham. I have a uncle living there, him keep write to mi family to send him things he can't get in Inglan; him tell us you can't get any West Indian food over there. So mi brother back home will handle the export and I will be the import.' I remember him saying, 'Roy, you will need a job – you can't work for the white man all your life. Come and work with us.' Selwyn was a good man, him did have ambition and helped me when I needed help, I hope he's in a better place.

'Is the hat still going around?'

'Yes, we just about have enough to pay the tickets for the two stowaways. If we don't get all the money before we reach Inglan then them is going back to yard.'

Norma and Garfield took the hat back to the table, then counted all the money.

'Yes, Norma, we have all the money. Now mek us tell everyone.'

Garfield got up and walked over to the DJ. As Norma waited at the table she remembered talking to Garfield after one of her morning meetings on the deck. Garfield told her about his life back home, how he could have been one of the stowaways … 'Miss Norma,' he said, 'times is hard in Trinidad and there is little work, so when mi friend said him a go to Inglan I was not going to be left behind. So I sold everything mi have, mi bicycle, mi wire-or-les, mi tools, but mi never get enough so mi was going to stowaway on the ship. It was mi Aunty give mi the rest of the money to get the ticket and to live in Inglan.'

While Garfield was talking Norma remembered what she said to Roy when she found out he was the stowaway, how she run him down. Garfield ended his story by saying, 'Miss Norma, not all the stowaways are bad people … they just like me, wanting a better life for them and their family.'

That's when Norma decided to help the stowaways. 'Garfield,' she said, 'let's start a collection to help free the stowaways.'

Garfield looked at Norma and hugged her. 'Sister,' he said, 'you is a good woman. Let us free the men.'

Norma came back to reality when she heard the announcement. Lord Pan had stopped his song to announce to the full ballroom: 'My people, you have made us proud ... Two of our people are lock up and you have all put your hands in your pockets and we have enough money to pay for their tickets. Thank you, my sisters and brothers!'

Everyone started to clap because all the people on the ship had the same dreams as the two men locked up in the Brig.

Lord Pan took the mike and said, 'This next song is for the two stowaways – you're a part of all of us. Pan Players, you ready?'

The notes to 'Am Going Away, But I Soon Come' sounded out ... a song that had a different meaning to everyone who heard it. To some it was about someone going off to war, to some it was about going on the big ship to Inglan, to some it meant 'I'm going to Kingston Town but I will be back tomorrow.' Everyone knew the words and Lord Pan sang the song. The Pan Players hit that song hard, the whole ballroom was in song – and the two stowaways heard the song from the Brig and sang along with the tune, sitting in the lonely Brig cell, not knowing they would soon be free.

The song took everyone back to their home island ...

'What an atmosphere inside here. You can feel the electricity in the place.' Norma sat at the table knowing she had done a good thing.

Anton said, 'Do you know this song?'

'No,' replied Verndo, 'it one of them calypso island songs. Let's have a drink to our friend Pele – gone but not forgotten.'

Anton put his arm around Verndo's shoulders and together they walked across to the bar.

Doris and Betty were sitting at a table when Precious came over, all hot and sweating.

'Wow, I'm having a good time.'

Betty was ready for Precious to let off on her for leaving the kids alone.

'Are the kids OK?'

'Yes, they're sleeping.'

'Cool. You ladies want a drink?' Doris and Betty looked at each other and thought without saying it, 'Who is this new person?'

'Norma, where you going?'

'I'm just going to look in on Roy. I'm taking him some water.'

'Aaahhhh, so in love,' Lucretia said.

Norma looked at Lucretia. She said, 'Lucretia, I would not have made this trip without you by my side.' Then she kissed her on the cheek.

'Love you back, sister,' Lucretia softly said.

Out of nowhere a familiar voice said, 'May I have this next dance?' It was Chef.

Norma looked at Lucretia, who said, 'A sister ha-fe-do what a sister ha- fe-do ... See you later ...'

'You enjoying the dance?' Maria said over the loud music to Hyacinth.

'Yes, I needed this. Just watching people having a good time makes you feel good — and knowing them two men lock up will have their freedom very soon is a good feeling.'

Maria looked at Hyacinth, who was quietly crying.

'I'm OK, Maria, I'm just happy to be alive and I can't wait to see my man, but I'm feeling a bit dizzy. Can we go back now?'

'Take my hand,' Maria said, 'let's go.'

Knock, knock. 'Please come in.'

Mavis pushed the door of the cabin that was their secret meeting place. Standing there was Edward, just back from his patrol.

'You look so good in your uniform.'

'You look so good — all the time,' he said.

Mavis pressed up to him, put her arms around him and gave him the wettest, hottest, sexist kiss he had ever had. 'Mmmmm, he taste nice,' she thought, then she led him to the sofa and sat him down. 'I really like you and I want to see you when we get to London,' she said.

'So do I,' he said, thinking that did not make sense but he knew what she meant.

Mavis gently pushed him down on his back on the sofa and as they locked lips she knew tonight was the night. 'Lord help this man, as I'm feeling very sinful and unholy tonight.'

'Any of you seen Mavis?'

'No, she was sitting at that table. She may be on the dance floor.' Norma kept walking towards the door thinking, 'She find a man?'

'Baby, I love the way you move.'

'Cha, man, your mouth too sweet ...'

'No, Lucretia, I love the way you move that body of yours ...' Chef's eyes were on her pert breasts and when she spun around, that wonderful African batty came into view. Chef knew this was the woman for him; he thought, 'Mi na let her go.' The music changed to a slower beat, the love song 'Caribbean Women, Mi Love to Love You'. Chef moved in for the slow dance: he gently held her hand and pulled her into him. As he felt the two mountains of breasts that this women had, he knew he had to control his manhood ... Lucretia, never the one to back down from a good slow dance, placed her leg deep between his legs then a hand on each of his shoulders; they were locked, then a very slow wine and grind took place. His head fitted perfectly between her breasts. 'Him little but him talawa,' she thought.

If you were looking at them from the outside it looked as if no one was moving as they danced but if you were in that dance you would know this was a very slow and intimate dance on all levels.

Devon asked Doris for a dance. As they walked onto the dance floor Doris felt very nervous. He held her firmly but gently, his left hand holding her right hand; she had her other hand placed on his back and as they moved as one, he looked her in the eye. Doris drank in his looks and felt his full firm body, then she looked away blushing as a wicked thought went through her mind. 'Jesus, please help me with this man...' Devon was singing along to the song, 'Caribbean Women Mi Love To Love You', looking at Doris when he sang. She sang back, 'Caribbean Man Mi Love to Love You' as she laid her head on his shoulder.

'Captain, all is well tonight. The men in the infirmary are stable and getting better.'

'Thanks, Tom. Let's sit down and have a drink.' The captain poured the whisky.

'One more day to go,' Tom said.

'Yes, Tom, one more day.'

'How is that Dangle doing?'

'He's going mad inside his cabin making all manner of threats and insulting my soldiers.'

'Did you get his statement?'

Stanley pointed at his very neat desk. 'Take a look.'

Tom picked up the sheet of paper with words on one side, just four lines:

To The Captain
I am a guest of your government. I don't have to answer to you about any negro women. That would be beneath me. There was no decent woman who came to my cabin, just a negro woman who wanted sex.

I demand to be released from my cabin arrest.
Mr Dangle

'It's time you told me the full story about this animal.'

Stanley gave Tom the whisky, then sat down. 'Dangle,' he said, 'is a double agent and he has information about Nazi agents who worked inside the British government and Nazi treasures worth thousands of pounds that the British government needs to rebuild our country. That arrogant shit must be delivered in one piece to MI5. But I give my word, Tom, once the government has got what they need I will make sure that bloody Nazi pays for what he did to that woman. It bloody well sticks in my throat to have to protect a Nazi on my ship. I just want to go and kill …'

'OK, Rick, calm down. You're raising your voice.'

'Sorry, Tom. That Nazi animal gets under my skin.'

'Maybe I can help you there?'

Captain Stanley looked at Tom and took a drink.

CHAPTER 23

NIGHT ENCOUNTER ... ANOTHER PASSENGER LOST

'Would you like to go on deck to get some air?'

Precious looked at Danville, a man she had just met in the ballroom. From the moment he laid his eyes on her he had not left her alone; they had been dancing most of the evening and talking about everything and anything funny. He made Precious laugh.

'OK, I am hot – some cool air would be nice.'

As they left the ballroom two pairs of eyes were looking at them that belonged to Betty and Doris. Betty looked on in amusement and Doris put her head back on Devon's shoulder as they danced.

'Nice and cool up here.'

'Yes, Precious, it nice and cool.'

'Do you have a woman or wife in Trinidad?'

As she was saying this, she looked at Danville. He was not the type of man she would normally talk to or be alone with.

He did look good in his tank top, with a shirt and tie that complemented his dark skin and cream trousers that fitted him perfectly.

'No,' Danville said, 'just a mother and grandma and sister.'

'What will you do in London?'

'I is a master craftsman. I can do anything with wood. Them Inglish have to rebuild them yard and I can help ... I will work for the white man till I can mek mi own shop and have mi own business.'

'That's good, Danville. Lots of people on this ship want to open their own business then after five years go back and build up their islands.' As she talked Danville looked at Precious in her close-fitting light blue cotton dress that emphasised her shapely body. He enjoyed talking to her and did not want to let her go.

'It's so exciting ... We will be in England in one day,' Precious said.

'Yes, but when the ship docks you will go your way and I may not see you again.'

Precious turned from leaning on the guard rail looking into the dark sea. 'Danville, I just met you. Why you carrying on like that?'

He looked hurt. 'I just like you from the moment I see you days ago – "me spirit tek to you".'

Precious leant over and gave him a kiss on the cheek. 'You are a nice man, but let's see where this goes?'

He held her gently and gave her a full wet kiss. Precious had not been kissed like that before – it felt good, really good, so good she held him and kissed him back ... this was the longest kiss she ever had; it was sweet, it was wet, she was feeling hot in the cool breezes. He pulled back and said, 'You mek mi hot,

Precious, you just mek mi feel like a man.' Precious just looked at him, this beautiful black man, and went in for another kiss. They both took a deep breath when they unlocked their lips.

'I think we best go back into the dance,' she said.

He was feeling his body harden, 'Yes we best,' he said.

She moved towards the steps that led down to the corridors. It was a steep flight. 'I will go down before you – I don't want you to fall down,' he said. He stood at the bottom of the steps as she came down, a bit wobbly; when she hit the last step she fell forward into his arms. He held her, then kissed her again ... she did not resist. He pulled back and held her hands. And as they walked down the corridor they passed an open door. It was a small room that had boxes and stock inside; the door was open, the light was on. He stopped, still holding her hands, and said, 'No one in here ... come inside?'

Precious did not resist. She felt what he was feeling; he gently pulled her inside and closed the door. She leant against the wall and he started to kiss her. She let out a moan as he kissed her neck and sucked her lower lip. She felt hot, and had her eyes closed as they started to make love.

'Sisters and brothers, we have come to the last song of the night. It be the best dance of the voyage ...'

'Ah you mek it so!'

'Tomorrow we is in cold, cold Inglan ... Drink, dance and be merry ... Good night!' The crowd all cheered then the DJ put on the hit record 'The Windmill'. The floor was heaving, everyone was waving their hands up and down like a windmill, bent over, smiling and moving, left to right. Sweat was visible on everyone: the DJ was toasting over the record, even Cliff and Simon were dancing behind the bar, the ship was rocking and the people rocked with it. As the song faded to the end, the DJ picked up the mike.

'Yes, yes, dance done, gwaan your yard,' the DJ said. Everyone laughed and slowly left the ballroom.

'Me mash-up,' Lucretia said to Chef. 'Man, mi never dance so much.'

'Baby, you was on it.' Chef gave Lucretia a kiss on the cheek.

'Can you see Precious anywhere?'

'No, but she may be in the lower hall.'

'Mmm, let's look in on the way back to the cabin.'

'You ready?'

Betty and Doris made their way downstairs to the lower hall just as a lot of people were coming out. 'Let's stand over here till all the people come out.'

As they stood back in the corridor by the hall Betty happened to look down the corridor and saw Precious coming out of a room – or cabin, she could not make it out.

'Look! There Precious,' Betty said to Doris. They both looked down the corridor between the people moving away. Betty was about to shout out Precious's name when a man came out behind her. Doris grabbed her arm.

'No bother say nothing,' she said.

Precious and the man walked down the corridor out of sight.

'Wow,' Betty said, 'do you think ...?'

'I don't know what to think. Precious has been different over the last few days – maybe this is why.'

'Yes, she find a man,' Betty said, 'and maybe some loving too?' They looked at each other and laughed.

'Come, mek we go to the cabin. mi want to hear what she have fe say.'

'Roy, I'm going now – you need anything?'

'Just you!'

'You too bad,' she said, then she kissed him on the lips quietly for the first time. She said, 'Good night, my dear.'

'Good night, Norma, my sweet guinep.'

Norma looked at him lying there on the hospital bed with tubes in him. 'Get well, see you tomorrow,' she said, as she left the infirmary.

'Betty, I will see you in the cabin – I just want to talk with Devon before I get back.'

Betty gave Doris a 'be careful' look as she walked away. Doris thought how things had changed with her two friends. 'We have grown up from young girls to women,' she thought. 'We will have a new way of living in London; we needed to come out of our young shells.'

'Doris!' a voice said over the crowd of people. 'I'm over here.' As she looked down the corridor there was Devon standing there, looking as good as the first day she saw him. 'Let's get some sea air before we go to our cabins.'

'You're drunk?'

'Yes, my friend – I'm drunk. They killed him – that bloody drugs gang killed him!'

'Keep your voice down, just keep walking – we're nearly at the cabin.'

'Is it because I'm drunk or is the ship rocking?'

Anton put his arm around him to keep him upright. Just as they crossed another corridor Verndo looked up and saw Ada. He let go of Anton and stumbled towards her, with Anton hurrying behind him, trying to stop him from hurting her.

'You bloody killer! You're one of the gang! You're one of them!' he said as he pushed her to the floor and gripped her neck between his two hands. 'You killer, you bloody killer!' Anton got through the crowd to see Verndo sitting on top of Ada, strangling her, with people trying to pull him off. He ran over to Verndo, grabbing him around the neck.

'Get off her!' he yelled. She was turning red and white, gasping for air, then out of nowhere two MPs pushed back the crowd and used the butt of a rifle to knock him out. Anton held his friend as blood was pouring out of his head.

'Get a doctor – get a doctor!' he kept shouting. Two more MPs arrived and picked up Ada who was still trying to catch her breath.

'Wake up, Verndo, wake up, man! Wake up! He not waking up!'

An MP pushed Anton out of the way and checked Verndo's heartbeat. 'Get a doctor!' the soldier said. 'Hold that order, soldier, let's get him to the infirmary now.' The three soldiers and one passenger picked him up and hurried towards the infirmary. The other soldier pulled up the still-gasping Ada.

'Come with me to the infirmary!' He held her up as they made their way through the crowd.

The soldiers burst into the infirmary, placing Verndo's bloody body on the operating table.

Two nurses ran over: 'What happened?'

The MPs calmly briefed them as the nurses looked over his head wound.

'Is there a pulse?'

'Soldier, get the doctor on your radio!'

The soldiers stood back as the nurses went to work on Verndo's bloody body. The ship's doctor burst into the infirmary, followed by the captain.

'Brief me!'

'A wound to the head made with the butt of a rifle ... loss of blood from the left side of the head ... slow heartbeat, high levels of alcohol in the system. We have started infusions and cleaning out the head wound.'

'Thank you, nurse. Pass me the stethoscope.'

'I feel dizzy,' Ada said. 'That mad man tried to kill me.'

'Please keep still,' one of the nurses said. 'I'm trying to take your pulse.'

Across the other side of the infirmary the nurses were working on Verndo.

'We are not getting a heartbeat, doctor.'

'Nurse, we need to pump his chest. Give me some space!'

Ada was across the room with a full view of what was going on.

The doctor looked very concerned. He pumped at the chest, listened on his stethoscope. He tried again, more desperately, listened again.

He exhaled. 'Nurse, please give me the time of death.'

'Death at 12:48 a.m.'

'Please log the head injuries. He must have had underlying illnesses. That blow should not have killed him.'

There was a silence as the doctor's team and the soldiers who hit him looked on.

'Where is the other patient?'

'Over here,' the nurse said.

The doctor took off his gloves and threw them to the floor in frustration. The shooting on the ship ... the rape ... this whole voyage had been the voyage from hell, he thought.

Ada looked at the outline of the dead body under a white sheet lying on the table. 'Two down, one to go,' she thought. 'That will teach them to mess with me and the gang.'

PART VIII

Approaching the Motherland

CHAPTER 24

'WE SOON COME'

6:30 a.m.
Mavis woke everyone up with a 'What a wonderful morning!'
 Norma rolled over; Lucretia was still snoring.
 'The last day on the ship, sisters ...'
 'Mmmmm, easy na.'
 'Mi head not good.'
 'The music was the best him play the whole voyage and mi foot a hot me,' Lucretia said.
 'It's what's you is talking about this time of the morning?!' They looked at Lucretia with her hair in one place and her make-up the other place ... 'Gal, you is a mess.'
 'Cha, mi did dance with Chef all night, he lick mi up on the dance floor, him jitterbug me, spin me, till mi get dizzy, then the rum get mi.'
 'Yes, it get mi too.'

Norma listened, then rolled over in her bed again; all that was in her head was Roy, Inglan and more sleep.

'What time is it?'

'About six thirty.'

'Sister, mi mush up. The drinks lick mi up.'

'We know that!' came the cries from Betty and Doris.

'Gal, it what you was drinking?'

'Mi mash-up.'

'We know that,' Doris said, 'so what happened to you last night? We was looking for you.'

'Well, well,' Precious began hesitantly, 'mi was moving from the bottom hall to the ballroom, yes that was mi throughout the night.'

'You must get a man the way you was moving around!'

Precious looked over at the kids still sleeping, then lay back in her bed.

'Actually, I met a nice man, the kind of man that you want to meet on a dark night ...'

Betty and Doris sat up and gave Precious their full attention.

'He was dark, clean, sexy – and just what I needed.'

Betty and Doris were beside themselves with excitement. 'What happened?' they asked, like little gals.

'We did dance and drink the night away. We took a walk along the deck, then ...' Precious went quiet. She took in a deep breath then said without any embarrassment, 'He took me to heaven and back ... he gave me the loving I needed.'

The two other women in the cabin went quiet, hanging on Precious's every word, feeling her excitement ...

'Was that the room we saw you coming out of?' Betty blurted out.

'You did see me?'

'Yes, we did!'

'You did look mash-up, gal!?'

'Yes, mi was, it was a wonderful experience and you know what?'

'What?' came the joint excited voices of Betty and Doris.

'It was my very first time. I have been deflowered and it feels good.'

'Precious, you is a bad gal.'

'How was it? Did it hurt?'

'Best hold it down, the kids will be waking up.'

'Mmmmm, yes this is big-people talk ... Now I have been honest to you, are you going to finally tell me about your secret men I know you two have been seeing?'

Doris and Betty were lost for words. They looked at each other, then Doris said, 'I have met a man that I would like to get to know. He has God in his heart, I feel this.' She looked at the two women for their reaction.

'Good for you, sister,' they said. 'I hope he is a good man?'

'Your turn, Betty. Well?'

'Give me a minute, na? ... Yes, I met a very cool man. It's fun right now, so let's see what happens when we get to London.'

'So you want to meet up with him in London?'

'Don't you two want to meet up with your men?'

'Let's face it, we are all new to this game – so let's see where it goes.'

'We just have to look out for each other ...'

'Yes, we do.'

'Come here,' Precious said, 'group hug.'

As they hugged, Betty said, 'I like my new gal-friends.'

'Any news from London about the ship docking in London Docks?'

'No, Captain. The orders remain the same: we hold at the mouth of the Thames till we receive further orders.'

'If I don't get my orders within twenty-four hours of us getting into the Thames I will damn well dock the ship myself. For God's sake, we have wounded people on board. They have no right treating these people like this. Hell, this government invited them in the first place,' the captain said in a loud voice.

'Yes, sir.'

CHAPTER 25

DEAR DIARY ...

... Norma ...
What would Mother say? Mi taking up with a stowaway and a man who has just been shot even though the shooting was not his fault ... I must admit I am mixed up about this whole thing with Roy. Part of me likes him, but parts of me does not like his bad-man lifestyle. Lucretia is being Lucretia but ...

... mi still love mi sister. Mavis is a dark horse, I'm just getting to know her as we get to London. It so cold ... I hope London not as cold as this. There are rumours going around about the Inglish people not wanting us in London; this is vexing some people. Well, it was that Inglish king who sent for us. Them is damn fools – they need our help, just like in the war.

I am missing mi family, mi island and mi bed.

... *Mavis* ...

I feel a million dollars. What a morning ... what a night! Lord forgive my sinful ways ... I never thought white men could make love like that – it was better than my first time ... Lord, he was a loving man, and Lord, you know I needed some loving.

We dock in Inglan tomorrow ... I can feel the cold air. I hope I'm not just a 'one-night fling' ... I feel he has respect for me. Well, I hope he does.

Let mi pray ...

... *Hyacinth* ...

I don't write in diaries. I never saw the point of writing down your feelings then hiding it away so no one can see it. But Maria give mi a diary to put down mi feelings if I wanted to. Well, it does help ... I now look forward to writing in mi diary – For My Eyes Only! When I close mi eyes I still see that man on top of mi, I still feel him inside of mi, hurting mi, I can still smell him and that cigar ... but mi ribs feel a lot better and mi swelling has gone down. I have asked the doctor what will happen in London, but I just don't believe him ... I can see the lies in his eyes. I don't know how I'm going to tell Carlton when I get to London. I was so looking forward to seeing him standing there at the docks with mi hat and coat and a big kiss ... How can I tell him? I must not say a word ... Yes, I will say I fell down the stairs and hurt myself. I can't take any more questions. A black woman saying a white man raped her to an English court filled with white people will mean I lose, I lose two times over ... I'm not going to lose everything, not Carlton – I love that man and we are getting married. He doesn't need to know ...

My Lord, I feel sick at this time of the morning!

... Sergeant Davis ...
What the hell was that madman thinking. I've bloody well got a gunshot wound in my leg, and me good mate Colin and some wog is dead ... I went through a war and did not get shot, I had to bloody well get shot by one of my own men! What the hell is going on in this world? When I see that little mad bastard ...

... Doctor Tom ...
I have never lost a man to friendly fire – I still don't know why they call it that. That bullet is not friendly. I have never had to deal with a raped woman. That poor woman. I find it hard to look her in the eye as she keeps asking me questions about what will happen in London. Because I know that animal will not go to prison and will be treated like a bloody king by MI5, I just can't look at her.

There's one thing I do know: Rick Stanley will get that man, one way or another, and I will help him. Rick and I fixed that animal Dangle; we gave him a special rum punch that we put together with some very strong laxatives. He will be on that toilet for days, damned Nazi animal. I know it goes against all my doctor's training, but that animal deserved it and we feel really pleased with ourselves. Ha!

... Chef ...
She round, she nice, she funny, she sexy, she can dance and is golden dark brown, has breasts like the Blue Mountain in Jamaica, she can drink, and listens to mi when I talk. Lucretia, mi na let you go ...

... *Lucretia* ...

Mi did learn that not all men must be tall, dark and handsome ... some of the best men I have met have been shorter then me but bigger in personality. I found a new and better relationship with Norma, she is my sister from another madda. I feel for Roy and the dead men. Just to think that them come all this way from yard to dead in the middle of the sea ... I hope Granny is well and the animals na give her too much trouble. I do miss her good nights ... (in Granny's high voice) 'You na sleep yet? Stop listen to the wire-less.' 'Night, night, Granny.' 'Night, my child.'

PS: It so cold mi have fe wear two pairs of knickers!

... *Garfield* ...

I meet some nice people on the ship. Mi and de man from Brazil is talking about a import business and mi hear that two other people will be opening a shop in the Midlands. We don't come to Inglan to beg, we are a proud people. New friendships, lovers and partners has been formed on this ship, and new business has been worked out. We come to better ourselves, we come to help the Mother Country like we did in the war ... why, oh why do some bad-minded Inglish people don't want we here? Five years, just five years, then mi gwan back a yard.

... *Delbert* ...

Mummy, I did just want to get to Inglan to mek the money to buy our land from Mr Jonson. Daddy pass, you is getting old and Mr Jonson is a mean man. I know I is a country boy but I have sense ... I did leave you de note in your Bible that you read every night. I tried to get the money for the forin ticket but only get $9.00 so I did pack mi grip and went to the ticket office at the docks to see if I could get a cheap ticket. The white man told mi to 'two bad words'. Why him so nasty? I will never forget his steely blue eyes and white skin, no soul behind them eyes. Mi was just sitting on the wall outside looking at the mighty big ship when a white soldier walked over to mi and said: 'You cleaners get on board over there. You're not meant to wait here.' I just look at him then looked over to the line of people getting on the ship to clean it. One minute I was on the wall then I was inside the big ship following the cleaning people down the corridor. I was at the back of the line going into a big room – it look like a dancehall ... I see another corridor and mi walk away from the group. As mi do this the woman in front of mi walked into a room; she did turn her head and put her finger to her mouth to signal mi to huss-up.

Mother, she mus-ee be doing what mi a do. No one was around ... I opened many doors till I was in a store room; mi just move the crates forward then set up mi bed and things behind it. The ship set sail and mi just keep mi head down. In the daytime I get free food and drink, I did mix with everyone, then at night mi go to mi crates. One night this big white soldier push a gun in mi face. I did try to run but them get mi and lock mi up. One other man from Bermuda is in the lockup with me. Mummy, mi is now lock up the whole time mi is on this ship. Them say mi is going back to Trinidad when we get to forin. A nice white soldier-guard told mi, 'Your people are trying to get the money to pay for you and your cellmate ...' Mummy, mi don't know anyone on the ship but them people is giving money for mi and the other man so we can stay in Inglan. Daddy spirit is guiding mi on my eighteenth birthday today.

Mummy, God is good.

Amen.

Delbert L. Comberbatch

PS: Mother I did wonder what happen to the woman stowaway?

... *Lord Pan* ...

Mi did write this tune for when we reach Inglan, it go so:

L-o-n-don we soon come

L-o-n-don mi say mi soon come

King you did invite us to the Mother-land

And we did come with friendly hands

L-o-n-don we soon come.

Yes, man, I will play this tune on the pans when we come up the Thames into the docks.

PS: Man, it cold like ice here!

CHAPTER 26

'LET MI TEK A PHOTO'

'Are we still meeting after breakfast on the deck?'

'Yes,' said Norma. 'This will be our last meeting before we get to Inglan.'

Norma sat down with Lucretia, who was there in body but nothing else. She just kept rubbing her head.

'Why you bothering with the meeting? We soon in Inglan.'

'Lucretia, this will be the last time we can talk, give out numbers and addresses and say goodbye. It will be nice.'

'OK, sister.'

The breakfast room was full of tired, sad, spaced-out faces. This was the quietest breakfast they had ever had; there was a strange mood, perhaps due to the anticipation of being in England. Maybe everyone was suddenly homesick; the mood was different, very different.

'I will meet you on the deck,' Garfield said.

'Yes, see you up there.'

As Norma put her plates back and made her way to the upper-deck meeting, she realised she was late and as she popped her head out on to the deck all she could see was people, a great crowd of people. She had not realised how much the morning meeting meant to the people on the ship. Everyone was talking about where they are going, helping others who had nowhere to stay, talking about the Inglish people who did not want us to come to Inglan ... Norma felt very proud of what she had started as she walked towards the crowds in her blue cotton dress with every hair in place. Two men shouted out, 'See, she deh!" Everyone looked over to Norma and smiled and clapped. Norma was embarrassed, but felt special.

'Come let mi take a photo of us,' said the men standing by the stairs.

Everyone was looking good, the men in their suits and ties, the ladies in their cotton dresses, hats, twin-set tops and ankle socks.

'Hold it!' Everyone in the photo posed – some on the stairs, some standing by the stairs, some kneeling down, everyone looking suited and booted. 'Say mi yard,' the photographer said. 'Mi Yard!'

'You must send mi a copy of that photo,' Norma said.

There were so many people at the meeting they had to put Norma on a box so everyone could see her. The men helped her onto the box. All Norma could see was a sea of fresh young faces.

She took a deep breath.

'It so nice to see so many people. This is the last morning meeting before we get to England. I am very happy to say that we have raised all the ticket money for our brothers locked up on this ship ... We will give the money to the captain today.

Our ancestors were taken to England in bondage. We do not want anyone on this ship arriving in bondage.

'There has been talk about the Inglish people not wanting us to go to Inglan; this may be true but not all the Inglish people think and feel that way. We come from strong people and we can take anything that Inglan want to fling at us. Each and every one of us knows why we're coming to Inglan. Let's not forget why we're coming here. Five years ... we can all do this.

'The news of the brothers who got shot is good. They are all doing well and getting on their feet. Please send your prayers to the brother who died. We are all brothers and sisters and we must look out for each other ... Remember when you get to Inglan you must sign on at the government building to get your government money. I hear that some of us will be placed in wartime accommodation, but hopefully it will not be for too long.

'Let's everyone here give their address to everyone else, so if you need a friend you know where to go. Later tonight we will dock in Inglan ... we must not forget the new friends we have made on this ship; we must all meet in the ballroom and the lower hall for a last drink when we get to the Thames River.

'I hope you all realise your dreams. May your Lord be with all of you.'

As Norma stepped down from the box she thought, 'From ten people we ended with more than a hundred people.'

Lucretia looked at her. 'Sister,' she said, 'you made mi and your family proud.'

As she hugged Lucretia, Norma said, 'I don't know where that came from, it just come out mi mouth.'

'Well, it was very good!' Lucretia said, with a smile.

'Captain, we will be off the coast of England in ten hours, sir. We will hold the ship at the mouth of the Thames. I will make a ship announcement about the docking times,' the vice-captain said.

There was unease in the captain's cockpit. The word had got out about the ship being held in the Thames; some of the soldiers wanted to get the wounded off the ship as soon as possible. Some felt the passengers might get upset and start to become unruly, and some soldiers thought, 'I'm not taking all them wogs back to the West Indies.'

... *Captain Stanley* ...
The Tannoy crackled.

'This is your captain speaking. Please pay attention. The ship will be entering the Thames estuary in ten hours. Due to the heavy number of ships at the docks we will be holding our position in the Thames until we get the all clear from the Port Authority. All passengers must have your bags packed and be ready to disembark within the next twenty-four hours.

'There will be soldiers at all the corridor exits giving you direction when we dock. Over and out.'

'Aunty Doris, it so cold ... can I put on two vests?'

'Aunty Precious, will it be snowing in London?'

'All of you pack up your things and leave out the jackets and the jumpers we gave you.'

'Yes, Aunty Precious.'

'Let's go on the ship decks. I will give a prize to the first person to see Inglan ...'

'You said I can see Gladstone at two p.m. Am I too early? Is he all right? Did he get sick again?'

'No, he's just in the toilet. Please wait here.'

Norma took a seat by Roy's empty bed. As she sat down, she looked at the empty bed, wondering how she got mixed up with this troublesome man.

Roy hobbled in on sticks with a big grin on his face. 'You was worried about me?' he said, and smiled with his well-shaped lips and eyes. Norma blushed.

'Cha, you is a bad man,' she said, with a twinkle in her eye. As Roy tried to lower himself onto the bed, Norma jumped up to help him.

'Aaaahh, that's better.' He tried to settle himself in the bed. Norma took his pillows and puffed them up behind him.

'So, we get to Inglan tonight?'

'Yes, can't you feel the cold?'

'Not in here. It's always warm. Any news about the rest of the men?'

'No one dead, so that's good news. Roy, where are you staying when you get to Inglan?'

'Selwyn was going to set mi up with someone he knew, but mi boy not here,' he said with a sad look. 'Well, I'm going to be in a hospital for a week or two, so that's a roof over mi head at least.'

Norma gave him one of her disapproving looks.

'The captain came to see mi last night,' he went on. 'He said I will be taken care of when I get to London. He said as this shooting happened on the King's ship there will be some compensation for my injuries ...'

'Well, I hope they send money to Selwyn's family,' Norma said in a stern voice.

'Yes, you're right. I will ask the captain about that. I get the feeling they want to hush this up ... He did look embarrassed about the whole thing.'

'You could be right, Roy, but don't push your luck.' She lowered her voice. 'Just you remember who you're meant to be. You don't need too many people looking into your history, do you?' she added, giving him the look that said 'don't be a fool'.

Roy lay back on his bed and slowly exhaled.

CHAPTER 27

POINT OF ORDER!

The House of Commons was in uproar.

'Order, Order! The Bill has been discussed and the House has voted. The passengers of this ship and other ships will be allowed to dock and work in London.'

An MP rose to speak. He was in league with Lord Mosley – leader of the 1930s British Union of Fascists, whose members carried out brutal acts of anti-Semitic violence in the streets. Mosley had recently founded the Union Movement, with the aim of establishing a single nation-state in Europe.

'My learned MPs ...'

He was very pale and slender-looking in his dark grey suit with crisp white shirt and old school tie.

'... This country will soon be invaded by the immigrants from all over the Empire and we must protect the English people, their jobs, their way of life ... Living with these immigrants will change the way the English people see themselves as the leaders of the world ... We cannot let the West Indian man get the upper hand, we cannot let him come to England to rule us. Taking in these reprobates will be a stain on this country that will never wash off.'

Some MPs leapt to their feet. 'Point of order!' Again the House was in uproar.

'Order! Order! Take your seats ... Order! Order!' came from the Speaker's Chair.

'I have a statement from the prime minister, Mr Clement Attlee, who is in France:

'The first of many ships will be arriving from the West Indies and India. England has been battered. We need workers to rebuild this wonderful country. I am aware that there will be members that disapprove of the immigrants ...

'You have my full sympathy.

'But we must put our personal views aside. Many of the immigrants will be on a five-year contract that will see them returned to their country and islands. The King has sent out the invitation and we as MPs must honour the wishes of our King and the needs of our country.

'This land we love needs to be rebuilt, and we need help to do this. England will take back her place as the leaders of the free world.'

'Members of this House, this debate is now closed,' came the voice from the Speaker's Chair. Eight MPs rose and walked out of the House in disgust.

Knock, knock.

'Come in.'

The soldier saluted the captain. 'We just received orders from London. We dock tomorrow at 1800 hours.'

'Thank you. Please assemble the head officers. I want a team meeting at 1500 hours in the ballroom.'

CHAPTER 28

'INGLAN IS THE PLACE FOR MI'

'Captain, there are some passengers who wish to see you about the stowaways.'

'Send them in.'

Norma, Lucretia and Garfield walked into Captain Stanley's office.

'Please take a seat.'

'Thank you,' Norma said, sitting down in a very ladylike fashion, pressing out her white cotton dress with the orange border. 'We represent the West Indian people on this ship.'

The captain sat behind his desk with his arms folded, looking at this group of people.

Norma looked the captain in the eye. 'We have raised the ticket money for the two stowaways you have locked up on the ship. We wish to free them before we dock in London.'

Captain Stanley leant forward, looking at Norma. 'The rule of the King's ships,' he said, 'is that any stowaways should be locked up and deported when we dock. It is a criminal offence to stowaway on the King's ship,' he said in a stern voice.

Norma was about to say something. Then she looked to Garfield, who was sitting next to her. Norma knew he was vex with the army before they walked into the office. She had not wanted to take him with her as she knew he was a hothead, but he'd helped to collect the money. And now he going to BLOW, she thought.

'What de rassclaat you a chat bout! We have the money so why you want to deport them?'

Norma touched him on his shoulder, which had a calming effect.

'I did not say I wanted to deport the men. I said this is what the King's rules are ... They are the King's rules, not mine.'

Garfield's language was not friendly. He was still in his army uniform.

'Now if we can all calm down,' the captain went on, 'the men who are locked up have committed an offence.' The captain paused. There was a silence – almost a standoff. 'But I do feel in this instance we can overlook the criminal offence since I'm sure your collection will cover the cost of the tickets.'

The captain got to his feet. Norma had never noted that he was tall – and quite handsome.

'As the captain of this ship I hereby free the men being held in the Brig. They will receive all the privileges of the rest of the passengers,' he said out loud to all the group in his cabin. 'Please place the ticket funds on my desk ... I know there's no need to count it.'

Norma gave the captain an approving smile and he nodded his head to her and the people in his office.

'Soldier!' he shouted in a loud but firm voice that made Lucretia jump. The captain gave her an apologetic smile. 'Take the passengers to the Brig, then release the two men being held there. Take the men to …' He looked down to his papers. 'Yes, take them to cabin 456, so they can freshen up. Also have some food and drinks sent to their cabin.'

'Yes, sir.'

The captain looked around the room at everyone and said, 'I think our business is now over.'

Norma and the others got to their feet and moved to the door. 'Thank you, Captain, for your kindness and respect,' Norma said.

Garfield looked at the captain, then gave him a salute. Then he extended his hand for a handshake … and the captain extended his hand in return. It was a meeting of mutual respect.

... Desmond ...

On the deck you could see a group of men sitting in a huddle talking.

'You hear that the ship will dock in Inglan in the morning then we can get off this rass ship the next day.'

'I can't wait to get off this rass ship and it bad-minded soldiers,' I said.

'You see how them kill one of us …'

'You see how them put guards everywhere we go on the ship – even in the dance hall …'

'Them don't want I and I. Them just want cheap labour then them will dash us out the country so fast your head will spin …'

We were a group of former West Indian soldiers. We'd all fought on the front line. Most people had gone back inside because it was cold, but we were having a deep conversation. We didn't notice the cold or we were used to it after the war. Some of us were standing, some sitting on deckchairs, others just leaning against the metal walls.

'You see how them devils never let us off the ship when it dock on the islands!'

'You see how we never get the better cabins on the ship!'

'Yes, man, there five men in mi cabin,' I said.

'No good food till the yard chef come on board ...'

'You see how dem white boys talk to us like we is shit.'

'But when dem did need us on the battlefield them come running behind us.'

'Yes, man.'

'They always want to put us in the front line so we dead first.'

'Amen,' a soldier said.

'We black soldiers always get the shitty job, like driving live ammo to the front line, loading the cannon that always blow up in your face, recovering the dead from the battlefield ...'

'Mi say them is the enemies ... them is the ones killing us and we like fools volunteer to help them kill the Nazi.'

'Well, mi na see any Nazi in Kingston Town.'

'No Nazi ...!' came the echo from the boys.

'No Nazi called mi a wog, nigger or coon. It a white people tribal war and we get caught up in it. We is the fools.'

'Man, you a talk rubbish,' I said. 'If we never stop the Nazi them would come to the Caribbean and kill us all off. Look what them do in Poland and Africa.'

'Cha, man.'

'You carry on defending them devils ...'

'Mi hear say from mi uncle who did come on the *Producer* ship that did come before this *Windrush* ship that them white people put up signs outside them house saying "NO BLACKS, NO IRISH, NO DOGS". This is the devil you want to defend?'

'Brother, man, it's a white people war, that's all mi a say.'

Norma was leaning up by the stairs listening to the soldiers. They had put their lives on the line and had come back bitter. As she started to walk away from the group she thought about what they were saying and how it would impact on all West Indians in England. She just knew it going to be a long, hard winter ...

'LAND!'

'I can see land, Aunty Precious!'

'Pass mi the binoculars ... You're right, that's land out there.'

The kids were jumping up and down with excitement. A white soldier walking by stopped and said in Precious's ear, 'That's Ireland over there. You West Indians will not be going there. We got you wogs in London.' Then he walked off.

'You wogs?! You wogs?! Who the hell him a talk to?' Precious was hot with anger. Doris and Betty had to calm her down as the kids were looking on and they did not want to upset them. They were so happy to see land.

'Ssshhhmmm ...' Precious sucked her teeth – she was fuming. Betty gave the soldier a 'cut-eye' look as she turned her head away.

'Aunty, what is a wog?'

As this was happening more people saw land and one by one they all came over to the side of the ship where you could see the land. Some were very excited, others just kept complaining about the cold; some just looked out to sea, quietly lost in their thoughts about London and what lay ahead.

As Norma walked by Precious's group she heard the kids shouting and noticed people moving over to their side of the ship. She looked for herself and saw land, then went back to the soldiers on the other side of the ship and told them, 'There is land over there ...' Everyone stopped talking and walked over to the other side of the ship. As they got up Norma noticed Lucretia coming up the stairs with Chef.

'Sister, come here!' Lucretia looked up. 'There land over there ...' Lucretia moved so fast she nearly knocked Chef over and collided with some soldiers. Norma tried to keep up with her, but she was off – with Chef in tow. By now you could not see anything as there were so many people; some were hanging from the upper decks, others were standing on any box or part of the ship to get a better view.

'Inglan ...'

'Na Inglan dat,' said Chef,

'No,' Norma said, 'it's ENGLAND not INGLAN. And that's Ireland not England. It is further away.'

No one was listening to her. As far as they were concerned that was England.

'Captain, the fast tide has put us ahead of schedule by three hours, sir.'

'Go to slow and hold at the English Channel. They will not be ready for us, so let's take this very slowly ... I don't want any more trouble on the ship.'

'Yes, sir.'

'I will be in my quarters.'

'Yes, sir.'

... *Captain Stanley* ...

I sat down wearily, and alone, and a little sad, in my cabin, took off my captain's hat and gave it a good look.

I have worn this captain's hat for many years but had not had a good long look at it for so long. I was so proud to receive it, but it's now looking a little worn, just like me. It brings back vivid memories of the war in Europe, of my first command ... capturing and refitting the MV *Monte Rosa* into the *Windrush* ship. Going to the West Indies for the first time and seeing the fine-looking coloured people from many islands. I often wondered what it would be like to be a coloured person.

Seeing the West Indian soldiers fighting and dying on the battlefield and the way the government has treated them since the war ended, it seems to me that white people want what the coloured people have but do not want the people themselves ... That's a hell of a trick to pull off.

Let me pour a drink and raise a glass to those who haven't made it this far. 'To the dead ... To you, my brave men, I toast you.'

It went down in one go. I leant back in my chair, poured another and thought about what was waiting for me in England, about what I'll do with my life in retirement ... I wonder if that special person at home is still there? Is he still alive?

At the start of the war I made a promise to myself that when I got home, when I finally made it, my first stop would be at his house, to tell him how I feel. I always knew I would make it back. To him.

I know the risks involved. Our kind are unwanted, our love illegal. Prison waits for both of us if we are caught.

I always knew ... Well, from the age of fourteen I knew without doubt that I was more interested in men than women –

but I did nothing to make myself happy, though I had a special, an intense, if a non-sexual relationship with my friend at home for years before the war. Now it's time for that to change ...

'Hyacinth, I hear you can see the land from the deck. Come up to the deck?'

'OK. I can't wait to see Inglan.'

'Put on some warm clothes. It cold out there.' As she put on a jumper Maria asked, 'Did the doctor come this morning?'

'Yes, he gave me some pills, and the usual talk about "when you get to London" ...'

Maria looked at her, but said nothing.

'They think I'm some damn West Indian from the jungle,' she thought. 'They think I'm going to go away quietly. Well, they wrong. I want that man in prison. It may cost me my relationship, but ... I keep changing my mind about pressing this matter. I don't want to lose Carlton.'

Just then there was a knock on the door. Maria opened it. Standing there was a soldier.

'Miss Hyacinth?' he said.

'No, she over there.'

He looked around the cabin. 'Miss Hyacinth, I have a message from the captain. Can you meet him in his quarters at 1800 hours?'

Hyacinth looked at the young man. 'Tell the captain I will be there,' she said.

As the soldier turned to leave Maria said, 'Do you want me to come with you?'

There was a silent 'No'. 'I need to do this myself. I need to tell that captain about himself and that dutty man who rape me.'

Maria saw the hot look in her eyes. 'OK,' she said. 'Let's go and see Inglan from the deck.'

The Tannoy started up: 'There will be a farewell party at 1600 hours in the ballroom and the lower hall. All are welcome. The drinks will be free until we dock.'

'Free drinks,' Anton thought. 'I need to get drunk. I need to forget this ship and all the people on it ... I just want my friends back.'

'Hey, Devon, can we meet in the ballroom later today? I want to have a farewell drink with the ladies and you?'
'I would love to see you later.'

'What you wearing tonight, Mavis, and where you been? I can't see you any more?'
Mavis thought about what she was going to say ... 'I met someone. He so nice and a gentleman.'
'What's his name?'
Mavis hesitated.
'He a soldier on the ship.'
'You meet one of them nice West Indians soldiers? I must say they do look good in their uniforms ... What island him from?'
Lucretia sat on her bed, combing her hair, looking into the mirror.
'He from Inglan!'
Norma and Lucretia both gave out a 'WHAT?!' at the same time. They both stopped what they were doing and looked Mavis dead in the eye. 'A Englishman?'
'You seeing a England man?'

'A what the hell you a say?' Lucretia gazed at her.

'Mavis is a big woman who can choose who she loves,' Norma said.

'Tell me, have you kissed him? How does he taste? Does he smell different?'

Norma was giving Lucretia a bad look.

'Have you done the ting? Is it true what they say about white boys? You know! Please do tell.'

Mavis looked at Lucretia and stood up. 'I should have never said a word ... I knew you would be like this. Just forget everything!'

'Mavis, come and sit down. We not pointing fingers at you. You do what you want to do. We're just curious, that's all.'

'Yes, yes,' Lucretia said. 'Mavis, my sister, don't get vex. I'm just talking. I don't mean any harm.'

'Now sister, do tell ...'

... Hyacinth ...

Knock, knock.

'Enter.'

I walked into the captain's office.

'Please take a seat.' He pointed to the sofa. I just looked at the sofa, which was the same type that Dangle had in his cabin. Bad memories came back to me.

'I will sit in this chair if you don't mind,' I said.

'Of course ... wherever you wish. Would you like a drink of water or wine?'

'No, thank you.'

'OK, well. It's my duty to let you know what will be happening to Mr Dangle when we get to London. He is on this ship as a guest of the English government. He is helping them with war information ... that's all I can say about that.'

I shifted in my chair. 'Will he face charges of rape and assault? When will that be?' I asked.

'He will be held in a government facility, then the government will be interviewing him. Once they are through with him he will face the courts.'

I sucked my teeth, then said, 'So what you're saying to me is you don't know how long it will be before he goes to court as your government is more important than my rape?'

The captain took a deep breath. 'Let me be frank with you. I am outraged by this sad affair. This man will face British justice, I promise you ... I will not let this animal get away with the outrageous thing he has done to you. I assure you I myself, with the support of the doctor, will make sure he has his day in court. It may not be a public court, but he will suffer for what he has done.'

'Will I get to testify?'

'Yes, you will. But, as I said, it will be a closed court. He will be going to jail for a long time. And I myself and the doctor will keep in contact with you until the court case. Please leave me the address at which you will be staying in England.'

I looked at this white man, who did not know me but was obviously ashamed of what had happened. I could feel and see the raw emotion in his face; I believed what he was saying.

'I'm very sorry I lost my composure talking to you about this animal. He will not get away with it.'

I almost felt like I should comfort him.

'Would you like a drink?' he asked.

I looked at this shaken man.

'Yes,' I said, 'let us have a drink together.'

'It six thirty, you're still not ready. What the hell you doing?'
'It mi brassiere, it don't look good with this dress.'

'Then change the dress ...'

'Cha, mi a wear this dress ... I soon come.'

'Let mi help you,' Mavis said. 'Just tuck this into there ... that looks good.'

Lucretia looked in the mirror. 'Yes, now I look good. Thank you, sis.'

'Right, now the drama is over from the drama queen, can we go?'

'Guys, you all ready?'

'Yes, man.'

'Then let's light up the place!'

Lord Pan put up his stick. All the Pan Players had their eyes on that stick as he hit it down on the tin-pan. The full steel band burst out with 'My Lovely Island in the Sun'. The ballroom was half-full, but the people hit that dance floor when they heard the song. Lord Pan looked up at the band and gave them the winning smile. All was well with the world.

'It cold on the deck. Let's go downstairs where it warm.'

Doris looked at Devon. 'I have really enjoyed meeting you,' she said.

Devon looked at Doris, at this woman who had comforted him when he needed someone. He gently pulled her towards him and kissed her long and hard. She melted in his arms; her mind went blank; her body went very warm ... his taste was wonderful ... he pulled back, then they just hugged.

CHAPTER 29

SAVE THE LAST DANCE FOR ...

As Sir Noxson walked into the lower hall where the equipment had been set up ready for the last dance on the ship, the bar staff were filling up the bar with drinks and someone had found Christmas lights and had put them up all around the hall, giving it a merry feel. The lights were dim and the mood was right.

Sir Noxson had all his record boxes lined up. He was adjusting the speaker boxes he had put together on the ship from bits of wood he had found. Tonight he was going to blow up the dance hall with back-a-yard tunes.

'Noxson, the speaker boxes ready to try out ...' his box man said.

'OK, let mi fire up this bloodclaat ting.'

Sir Noxson put on a record. The sound that came out of the speaker boxes made the barman jump, the glasses vibrate and a passing soldier look into the hall to find out what the hell was making that noise.

'Yes, man. Now we have the right sound for tonight's blues party ... yes, man.'

The soldier walked over. 'Can you turn that bloody noise down? Bloody' 'ell, my ears are hurting me!'

Sir Noxson turned down the music. 'Soldier-man,' he said, 'what is the problem? It just music.'

'Well, it's too bloody loud!'

'Yes, man, yes, man – I will keep it down ...'

As the soldier walked over to the barmen the box man said, 'Noxson, how you let soldier-man tell you that after all the work we did making the boxes?'

'Don't worry, my youth ... Sometime you have to "play fool fi ketch wise".'

The ballroom was filling up as Mavis, Norma and Lucretia made their way through the crowds.

'Mavis, Mavis – over here!' said a woman's voice. As Mavis went across to the big round table she saw Olga from Bermuda – a woman she had met on the ship. 'Come and sit over here with us.' There were three women already sitting at the table. 'Mavis,' Olga said, 'this is Betty, Precious and Doris.'

'Hello,' they said.

'This is my friends Lucretia and Norma and as you and the whole of the ballroom heard, I'm Mavis!' Everyone started to laugh.

'Is what you saying I have a big mouth?' Olga asked.

'If the cap fits!'

More laughter ensued as Mavis and the ladies sat down.

'Is what you drinking?'

'I must get a dance with one of them women in this dance hall tonight,' Elroy said. 'What a way them look good.'

'Well, you can do it after we don play for the people,' Lord Pan said.

'Pan Players, you ready? Then it's dancing time!' Lord Pan raised his hand and the Pan Players were off again. The music filled the ballroom and the corridors leading to the infirmary, where Roy was sitting on his bed as the steel-pan music hit him. He thought of Norma dancing with them wutless men ... it got into Roy's head all he could see was Norma rubbing up against a man. 'Nurse Sharon, can I attend the last dance?'

'Mr Carman, you know you're meant to rest!'

'Nurse, I feel good ... Can I just sit in the dance hall with mi cousin and watch the people dancing?'

'Let me find out. Doctor?' she shouted.

Over came Doctor Tom. 'Yes, nurse?'

'Mr Carman wishes to go to the last dance tonight.'

'Doctor,' Roy interrupted, 'mi friends is in there and it will make mi feel better.' He said this with that killer smile on his face.

Doctor Tom looked at him and said, 'You can go for one hour but you must be seated ... Nurse Sharon will go with you – one hour, that's it.' Then off he went into the next room.

... *Norma* ...

'Let's make a toast to the lost souls, the injured – and to us beautiful Caribbean women!' Olga said. All of us women around the table held up our glasses.

'To us.' Clink went the glasses.

I was looking at the dancers on the full dance floor. Some were doing the Windmill, some were doing the Step, some were dancing hand-in-hand. I noted the men standing by the bar, appraising the women while holding their beers, laughing and pointing. Smoke filled the hall alongside the pan music.

'You not dancing, ladies?' Olga asked. As she said this the song 'Sweet, Sweet, Sweet Caribbean' started up, and everyone wanted to dance.

'Cha, move ...'

'Norma, mi is going to dance,' Lucretia said.

'Me too,' I said, as we made our way onto the dance floor.

Precious looked at Betty and Doris. 'It's the last night. Let's have some fun ...'

One by one the men converged on the group of women as the Pan Players segued in to 'My Lovely Island'. The hall went mad, the dance floor full of bodies dancing to the back-a-yard sound.

Below in the hall Sir Noxson was firing up the place with his loud tunes, the domino and card tables were full of players and the barmen could not keep up with the orders.

'Yes, man we a lick it up tonight!'

'Gwan, Sir Noxson!'

'What a tune! Rewind! Rewind!'

Sir Noxson lifted up the needle to put it back at the beginning. As he was doing this he said, 'I want everyone on their feet ...!' As he put back on the record, the hall went crazy with movement.

... Norma ...

'Lord, I need to sit down ...' I said. 'That's three songs and mi foot a hot me.'

Olga moved over to let me sit down at the table.

'The Pan Players are hot tonight.'

'Yes, Olga! Them na ramp tonight!'

I took up my drink and looked at all the dancers. Suddenly there was some sort of disturbance on the dance floor – people were stopping and moving out the way of something coming across the dance floor. As the two people got nearer, I saw the figure of a man holding a walking stick, and as more people made way for him, a white smile hit me, a smile I knew very well, a smile I adored ... The crowds parted like the sea for Moses.

There he was standing in front of the table.

'Roy!' I shouted out.

Roy looked at me. He said, 'Woman, you look good!'

'Is your friend?' Olga said. 'Mek him sit down.'

I jumped up to greet Roy, then saw the nurse standing behind him.

'Mr Carman is not drinking,' she said as he sat down. 'I will be back in one hour. Ladies,' the nurse said to the table, 'if he gets dizzy please come and find me.' With that, she placed one hand on Roy's shoulder and said close to his ear, 'I know she's not your cousin,' then winked at him as she disappeared into the crowd.

'Is how you get them to let you out?' I asked.

Before he could answer, Betty and Doris – who were sitting at the table – asked, 'Don't we get introduced to this fine young man?'

Roy turned and said to the table, 'Forgive my bad manners, sisters. I am Roy. I did get shoot by the mad soldier ...'

Everyone looked at him with sympathy. I wondered why he used his real name, but 'To hell with it,' I thought, 'he here and he alive.'

'What's a man got to do to get a drink around here?' he said and everyone laughed.

Just then, Lucretia emerged from out of the mass of dancing bodies.

'My Lord, is you dat?'

Roy looked up. 'Yes, it me. God noh tek mi yet ...'

Lucretia gave him a big kiss. 'Is what you a drink?'

'It like them a starve mi tonight,' Roy answered.

I looked at Roy smiling with his big smile, and the women fussing over him. Olga appeared with a drink that she placed in front of Roy.

'Thank you, he took a drink, but them forget something?' Olga looked at the orange drink he was holding. 'Them forget to put in some Jamaican rum?'

'Cha, you is a madman,' Olga said.

'Maybe, but I'm here ... if soldier-man can't kill I, the rum na kill me ...' Everyone held up their glasses to toast him.

'To Roy.'

'Thank you all, but where the rum deh?'

A voice came over the PA saying that the Pan Players would be taking a rest '... your DJ will keep you dancing.'

'Mi see one hot woman on that dance floor ... I soon come,' Elroy said as he put down his pan sticks, took a drink, wiped his face with his hankie then made his way over to Lucretia who was standing by the table talking to Siphiweh and the other women.

'I hope you and your ladies enjoyed our music?'

Lucretia looked around at this dapper-looking man, whom she recognised from the Pan Players. As she did this, all the women around the table were now looking at Elroy because he was in the pan band and he was a good-looking man.

'Yes, your band played so well.'

'May I get you a drink?'

'Yes, I will have a Cherry B. But who is you?'

'Sorry. I am Elroy – and you are?'

'I'm Lucretia.' He smiled, then turned to walk towards the bar.

'Na mek Chef see you with that Casanova man,' Norma said.

'Is what? Mi just a talk ...'

'Gwan,' Norma said as she sat down with Roy who was talking to all the people around him.

'Man a you that?' said a voice. Roy looked around and standing there was Devon. He had not seen him since the shooting. Devon leant down to give Roy a big hug. 'Man, mi so glad to see you ...'

Roy looked at Devon. 'Pull up a chair, mek we talk.'

'Roy, we is lucky to be alive today.'

'How is the rest of the men?'

'The soldier-man never tell mi anything about the shooting – dem ask is who had the gun like it's mi...'

Roy saw the hurt in Devon's eyes. 'Come, man,' he said. As Devon sat down he looked fondly at Doris across the table. And Betty looked at both of them with that knowing expresssion.

Precious came back from the dance floor with a man in tow. 'This is my table and my friends ...'

Betty thought she looked a bit drunk. Doris just kept looking at Devon.

'You want another drink?' Garfield said to his group of friends standing by the bar.

'Mi want one of them women inna this place. Sir Noxson is dropping some bad tunes and mi a go dance with that lovely sister over there ... Mi gaan.'

Garfield looked at his friend as he walked off into the crowd. 'Him na get a rass tonight.' All the man laughed out loud.

As two women walked past, Garfield looked at them. 'Cha man, mi gaan,' he said and followed them across the dance floor.

'Soldier-man, come mek we dance?'

Edward looked up to see a tall, smiling woman standing in front of him.

'I'm on duty, madam,' he said.

'I'm too young to be a madam,' she said, 'and you're too fine to be a soldier.'

Edward blushed and moved gently out of her way.

'Wanker!' came the voice of Private Paul standing behind them. 'Just take that black savage around the back and give her one,' he laughingly said.

Edward looked him dead in the eye. 'Do you really think they are animals? I believe they look at us, the white man, as the savage,' he said as he walked off, shaking his head.

The ballroom was buzzing. Everyone who could get on the dance floor was on the dance floor; lavender filled the hall, followed by cigarette smoke.

Anton was sitting on a table with people he didn't know – but they were friendly.

'Man, you want a drink?'

'Yes, I will have a big rum,' Anton said.

'Jamaican or Trinidad rum?'

'Let me walk over to the bar with you.'

As he got up he thought he saw Pele through the crowd of dancers ... he was looking at him and smiling ... Just then a man passed him making him take his eyes off Pele for just a second – and when Anton looked back Pele was gone. Anton kept looking as he made his way over to where he had seen Pele standing on the dance floor, but he was not there. Anton kept looking around and around and around, but Pele was not there. He felt a cold chill up his spine.

'Man, you coming to the bar?'

Anton looked dazed.

'You all right, my brother?'

Anton just walked off the dance floor, out of the hall and the deck to get some air and get himself together. 'Was that a ghost or was that ... no, what the hell am I thinking? Am I losing my damn mind?' he thought as he leant on the guard rail of the ship looking into the swirling blackness of the sea that now and again showed the white of the waves when they hit the ship. Just then a gentle woman's voice hit his ears.

'Let me buy you a drink ...'

Anton thought the voice was in his head.

'Well, are you going to let a woman stand out here and freeze?'

Anton looked around, and standing there was a Mexican-looking woman whom he kind of knew. 'Yes, I remember her,' he thought. 'The night we got pissed she came over and asked if we needed any help ... all this time I thought she was not real, just a drunk illusion.'

'Well,' Anton stepped away from the guard rail and smiled. Let's get out of the cold,' he said.

'Let's take a walk, Tom.'

'Where are we going, Captain?'

'Into the ballroom dance.'

As the captain and Tom made their way down the corridor into the ballroom the MPs stood to attention. They were about to follow the captain into the ballroom, when he said, 'Stand down, soldiers, we are fine.'

'Yes, sir.'

As they entered the hall Captain Stanley and Doctor Tom took in the sight of West Indian people and some soldiers dancing and waving their hands … then the captain noticed the slow dances in the corner.

'Tom, is that legal?' he said as he watched bodies interweave.

Tom burst out laughing. 'I don't know, but it looks like fun. Let's have a drink, Rick.'

As they made their way to the bar a West Indian woman took hold of the captain's arm.

'Captain, you not going to dance with me?'

By now most of the people on the dance floor had noticed that the captain was in the hall and were staring at him.

'Madam, I'm not a dancer,' he said, releasing his arm from her grasp. But she would not take No for an answer. She started to dance up against the captain, which made Tom laugh.

'Get out of that!' he said to Captain Stanley.

The captain touched his hat at the woman and made a quick exit to the bar.

'Look over there, it's the captain of the ship a ramp up with that woman,' Lucretia said to the group of women she was dancing with. 'Mek him come over to me, I will give him a good rub up!'

The women laughed.

'You're too bad, Lucretia,' one said. 'But the man does look fine in his uniform.'

Edward was taking in the action on the dance floor as he looked at Mavis dancing with her friends. Mavis knew he was looking at her, which made her dance more sexily.

'That woman will be the death of me,' he thought.

There was an air of enjoyment, wild dancing and drinking ... At the back of their minds, everyone was a little nervous about the new life that would begin tomorrow in England.

'Mr Carman, it's time to go back to the infirmary.'

Norma looked up at Nurse Sharon. 'Can he stay for just ten minutes more? Then *I* will take him back to the infirmary?'

Nurse Sharon replied to Norma. 'Ten minutes,' she said, 'or I will be back to get him.'

Roy looked at the nurse. 'Thank you,' he said over the sound of the music. Just then Garfield appeared out of the crowd.

'Nurse Sharon,' he said, 'how you do?'

'Garfield, nice to see you again,' she said, with a big smile on her face. Norma and Roy looked at Garfield and the nurse.

'Roy, you good?' they asked.

'Yes, man, just a enjoy the dance, but the nurse want to take mi back.'

'Cha, Sharon mek mi buy you a drink. Come, sister.'

'I am on duty.'

'Well, mi na say nothing to dem. We soon come ...' He had one hand in the middle of her back, guiding the nurse towards the bar.

She turned and said, 'I will be back,' as she walked off with Garfield, who looked back, giving Roy a wink.

Just then the captain was walking by and saw Roy sitting at the table. 'Mr Carman, why are you not in the infirmary?'

The whole table looked up at the impressive captain in his white uniform and the doctor standing behind him. Just then the doctor intervened. 'I said he could join his people. This is good for his recovery.'

The captain looked at Roy. 'No dancing for you tonight!' he said, with a smile that made Roy, Norma and Tom laugh along with him.

'Don't stay too long, Mr Carman,' the doctor said as they made their way out of the ballroom.

'Ladies and gentlemen, Lord Pan and the Pan Players will take you back to the Caribbean with some old-time tunes that will have you on your feet.' By now the ballroom was hot and everyone was dancing, sweating and singing along.

'Garfield, I need to take Mr Carman back.'

'Woman, we just a get comfortable ... I will pass by the infirmary later tonight. Is what time you done tonight?'

'About one thirty,' she said before she walked off.

Garfield knew this woman liked him from the time they met as he was walking along the deck of the ship and she was looking out to sea ... 'Good morning,' Garfield said. Sharon looked around at this tall, fit-looking man with lovely black hair, dark brown skin and a thin moustache: 'Good morning,' she replied, 'the sea feels calm today.' 'Yes, it does ... I am Garfield – and you are?' 'I am Sharon ...' From that instant there had been a spark between them; they knew it and enjoyed the private moments they snatched in different places around the ship. One time they kissed and told each other how they felt. 'We can meet in London ...' 'I can take you to some nightclubs where they play American music and that West Indian music I have heard on the ship.'

Sharon knew that her family didn't like anyone who was not English – let alone a black man. This romance would have to be kept away from them once she was back home. This would be their secret.

'Lucretia, where you been?' Chef was standing by the table with Roy and the group.

'Mi was having fun ...'

'Well, you save the last dance for me,' he said as he made his way back to the kitchen.

'What away him a-gawn like him own mi,' she thought. 'We will see,' she said as Chef was walking away. She knew he was vex that she was dancing with other men.

'Roy, I will see you tomorrow.' Norma kissed him on the cheek as she left the infirmary.

'Good night, Nurse Sharon.'

'Good night, Norma.'

At that moment there was a look between the two women that held so many stories and secrets.

'Last song!' Sir Noxson said, as he placed the needle on the record. The opening notes sounded of 'Leaving Portland Parish', a beautiful instrumental tune that is a Caribbean classic ... the crowd in the lower hall were dancing and swaying, even the MP guards were tapping their feet to this rich violin-led instrumental tune.

Chef was looking for Lucretia in the ballroom. 'Where that woman da?'

'May I have this last dance?' Devon said to Doris, extending his hand.

'Olga, mek we dance,' a well-dressed man said in a way that left her no choice. The whole table were on their feet, dancing and feeling good. Chef saw Lucretia slow-dancing very intimately with a man ... he was more than vex with the way she was going on with him. He walked up to them dancing and just looked at them, but they didn't see him as they were in the moment of the dance.

'I think this last dance is mine,' he said over the music. Lucretia looked at his vex face. 'Sorry, man,' she said to her dancing partner, 'but mi did say I would save that last dance for mi friend Chef.'

'Is what the rass a gwaan here the man dancing with? You no see mi a dance with the woman.'

'Cha, man go find yourself a woman!' said the man.

As he was saying this Lucretia was trying to move away from the man but he held her tightly. Chef looked at his arm around Lucretia's waist and his blood was boiling. 'Lego de woman before mi thump you down!' he said.

'Is who you a talk to like that?'

'Don't mek mi lick you down in here!'

The voices were getting higher; the men were standing face to face cussing; people were beginning to look at what was potentially a fight. But before anyone could say a word Norma came between the men out of nowhere.

'Come, come, brother, mek mi and you have the last dance.'

The man recognised Norma from the morning meeting and liked what he saw ... Lucretia moved Chef away from the other man.

'Come mek we dance over here, and stop your fool-es-ness.'

Norma took the man's hand and started to dance with him, talking to him to calm him down. Just then the MPs appeared from the doorway.

'Everything cool,' Olga said. 'Let us done the dance in peace.'

The MPs looked around and moved back to the doorway.

'I can't leave you men for five minutes and you're a carry on bad.'

'Sorry, Norma. You know my name? Of course mi come to your morning meeting.'

'Why you men can't behave yourself,' Lucretia said.

Chef looked at her, then rolled his eyes. 'Only you could say that when it's you a cause it.'

The DJ's voice came over the speakers. 'The dance done … Inglan tomorrow. Gwan your bed,' he said, to loud laughter from the dance floor. This man always sent you to bed with a smile.

'Sisters, you ready?'

'Soon come …'

Most of the women were talking to men. Norma just looked on, happy that the night was just about trouble free and her friends were being loved up. 'I'm going to miss this ship,' she thought. 'I'm going to miss this group of people.'

PART IX

Journey's End … A Rough Reception

CHAPTER 30

BLACK STICK AND DEAD FRIENDS ...

0600H
'Good morning, crew.'

'Good morning, sir.'

'What's the latest report?'

'Sir, the orders are that we still hold at the mouth of the Thames until we get docking orders.'

'Then let's follow HQ orders.'

'Where is the rest of the kitchen staff?'

Chef was busy getting the breakfast ready.

'Chef, I think they had too much to drink last night!' said Junior.

'Well, go and wake them up! We can't do all this food with two men ...' Chef banged down his pot.

'Are we in England?' the kids wanted to know. They were prodding Precious and Betty, who were in their beds a little worn out from last night.

'What? What? Pickney, is what you want?'

'We want to go and see Buckingham Palace. What time can we go?'

Betty wiped her eyes and sat up.

'Good morning, children.'

'Good morning, Aunty Betty.'

'Now leave Aunty Precious and Doris alone. Let's get you all washed up so you're all clean to visit the King at Buckingham Palace.'

'Morning, Lucretia.'

'Morning, Norma,' Lucretia answered, with her eyes closed and the covers over her head.

'Morning, Mavis ....' There was silence. 'Morning, Mavis?'

Norma focused her eyes on Mavis's bed, which had not been slept in.

'Lucretia, Mavis not here?' She slowly moved the covers and looked over at her bed.

'Yes, that nasty gal a sleep-out ... she mus-ee find a man.'

They looked at each other, then lay back down to sleep for five more minutes.

'What de ... I must of fell asleep ...'

'No, we fell asleep.'

Mavis looked down to see she was fully clothed, lying on the long sofa with Edward.

'Good morning, my dear,' he said. She gave him a warm hug. 'Thank you for a wonderful night,' he went on. 'I have never talked for so long, I guess we better get up as I'm on duty at 0800 hours.'

'I now have to face them women in my cabin ... Thank the Lord we get off this ship today.'

0800H

'Doctor, we have all the paperwork ready for the dead bodies.'

'The wounded will be in a wheelchair or on stretchers. I have radioed London, who will have two ambulances on the docks when we arrive. Did the sergeant pack all the deceaseds' belongings? They must go with the bodies.'

'Yes, doctor, they came late last night.'

'Then let's start the clean-up and get the other men some breakfast.'

'Man, it feel so good to sleep in a real bed. Them prison beds mush up your back.'

'Yes, man ...'

Delbert and Alphonse – the other stowaway – were in a passenger cabin. They had celebrated so hard last night they could not get up.

'Is what time them have the breakfast? Cha, mi need some sleep, mi mush-up.'

... *Tannoy* ...

'Good morning, passengers. Today we dock in the Port of London. This is the timetable of the day ...'

As the voice went through the day timetable, some passengers were hungover and were not in the mood to listen to the loud Tannoy that you could not turn off. 'Shut up, man,' someone shouted. Some were covering their heads with the pillows, some slept right through it, some just thought, 'We reach a forin.'

'... and at 1700 hours all passengers must be back in their cabins. We will move you floor by floor. Please listen out for your orders.

'As this is the last day, breakfast will be from 0900 to 1100 hours.'

MI5 HQ London Telegram to the Prime Minister. TOP SECRET.

WE HAVE RECEIVED INTELLIGENCE THAT RACIST AGITATORS AND SUPPORTERS OF OSWALD MOSLEYS UNION MOVEMENT WILL BE AT THE PORT OF LONDON STOP THERE MAY BE CIVIL DISORDER STOP WE ESTIMATE ABOUT 100–200 MEN STOP DIVERT THE SHIP TO TILBURY DOCKS END

Navy Command HQ to the captain, HMT *Empire Windrush*. TOP SECRET TELEGRAM.

MORSE CODE CAPTAIN DO NOT DOCK THE SHIP AT THE PORT OF LONDON STOP DIVERT TO TILBURY DOCKS STOP MI5 AND THE POLICE EXPECT CIVIL DISTURBANCE STOP FURTHER ORDERS WILL BE SENT ESTIMATED DOCKING TIME 1900H END

'What the hell is going on in London? What do I now say to the passengers who may have people waiting at the Port of London docks?'

The captain banged his black stick on his desk, then bellowed, 'Vice-captain Hobbes. The latest new orders from HQ are to dock at Tilbury ...'

'Sir, should I inform the passengers?'

'No. Not yet. I think we should leave it till 1700 hours when we are outside Tilbury Docks. I feel there will be a lot of upset passengers. We don't want any more problems.'

0900H
In the breakfast hall: 'Just put the food on the table,' shouted Chef. 'If you never drink so much rum you would not feel so bad!'

... Mavis ...
'Is what time you call dis?' Lucretia said in a voice her grandmother used on her.

I had just opened the door to the cabin.

'You think you is a big woman?' Norma joined in with the voice her mother used on her when she was not happy.

'Lord, what a pickney mi have,' Lucretia said, throwing up her hands.

Then all the women fell about laughing at my reaction ... the made-up voices they were using and the funny noises I made when I laughed – it always sounded like a hiccough.

'You're sure you have the energy to walk over to your bed?' Norma added.

'You best give her a walking stick ... she don't look so good!' By now tears were coming down, all the women were rolling about laughing. A part of my laughter was relief – I didn't know why, as the women in my cabin were not my mother.

'You're out of order,' I said, wiping tears from my eyes.

'Gal, go and tidy – you nasty gal!' Lucretia said, as I made my way across the cabin floor to the bathroom laughing, wiggling my hips and waving my hands as if to say, 'I surrender!'

... *Devon* ...

Mi was packing mi grip. It did not take long ... all mi had fitted in a handheld grip. Mi looked in the mirror; mi was looking good, in a V-neck jumper, shirt and neat tie with baggy, high-waisted trousers. Mi looked down at mi black shoes, so clean mi could almost see mi face in them.

Mi sat down and exhaled. Mi friend is dead. 'Selwyn, man, mi miss you, my brother.'

Mi remembered Selwyn walking up the hill to mi family land in Spanish Town, Selwyn talking to mi father about mi coming to Inglan ... Dad was not happy to let mi go, but Selwyn reasoned with the old man, telling him of the benefits of going to Inglan. Dad was a country man ... all he knew was animals and country life. Selwyn made him see the bigger picture – he was good at that. Mi brother Selwyn, you had the sweetest mouth I will ever hear ... Mi put mi head in mi hands, tears came down hard, very hard. Mi had not mourned mi friend, it was all flooding out from somewhere so deep – mi never thought there was so much emotion in mi. As mi wiped mi wet face mi thought, 'How the hell am I going to tell Selwyn family him is dead?'

Rosemarie, George and Carmel were in their nice new English clothes, the gals in light pink dresses, ankle socks with white matching twinset and gloves, George in his V-neck jumper, white shirt and blue tie with black trousers. Precious, Betty and Doris looked them up and down as if they were in the army.

'You look so nice, my lovely family.'

The kids looked a bit baffled.

'You do look wonderful ... your families would be so happy to see you looking so good,' Betty said. 'Have you packed all your things?'

'Yes, Aunty Betty.'

'Good, let's go and have breakfast. And don't you mess up your new clothes!'

... *Anton* ...

This whole mess is down to me. We should not have went back for the drugs ... We could have got away. Now Pele and Verndo is dead and just me and that bloody woman on this ship. I will get her in London – I will not rest till she meets my dead friends.

'Good morning, Garfield.'

'Good morning, Hyacinth. I never see you last night? I was looking out for you.'

'I was there, but mi head was hot so I went and rest.'

'You feeling better now?'

'Yes, man, much better.'

Maria listened to the conversation as they lined up for their breakfast. Garfield looked at Hyacinth as she walked away and thought, 'That is one woman who got away from me ...'

'Let's sit over here, Hyacinth.'

'OK.'

'Garfield, you want to join us?'

'Captain, I will undertake the morning round with the soldiers.'

'Good idea, Vice-captain Trevor Hobbes.'

Hobbes turned and smiled as he knew that Stanley only used his full name when he was having a joke at his expense.

Hobbes had served with the captain for two years. This was his last mission – and it was the hardest.

As Hobbes walked out of the ship's HQ he thought about the last two months and the journeys in Europe and the Caribbean.

It had been an education meeting more West Indians than he had met in the army. This ship was full of them. Because he was half-Welsh he thought he knew what discrimination was – until he met the blacks. He heard the nasty and hateful remarks of some of the other soldiers. 'I so look forward to getting back to Wales and my family,' he thought. 'I will be glad to see the back of them English army men. They were never welcoming of a Welshman.'

CHAPTER 31

BLACKSHIRTS

1300H
London. In a church hall in London five miles away from the Port of London Alfred John Williams was addressing a meeting. He was notorious throughout England as one of the right-hand men of Sir Oswald Mosley.

'Englishmen and women!' he shouted. 'We stand in the very heart of England ... We have a mission today once again to defend the pure English people of this land.'

Williams was addressing the crowd dressed in his famous black polo-neck jumper with black trousers and a thick black belt with a silver buckle. Standing about 5ft 5in tall, he was a pale-looking, well-built man with a thin black moustache and black hair combed fully over to the left like a black wave on top of his head, and closely cropped hair just over his ears.

He held up the front page of two copies of The *Daily Express* with both hands. The headlines read, **Black Man to Show**

English Woman How to Move the West Indies Way and **Black Babies with White Women.** He moved the papers from left to right just looking at the crowd who were booing, shouting and swearing at the headlines.

'We will march on the Port of London ... We will defend our land. We will not let the blacks set one foot in our land, this proud land of the white people.'

Some in the crowd of about one hundred and eighty men and some women were wearing the Blackshirt uniform they wore when they were followers of Mosley before the war. They roared their approval of Williams' words, some even raising their right arm in a Nazi-style salute. Williams took a seat at the side of the stage. A supporting speaker, Reg Jones, came forward to speak. He was short, sweaty, with pasty white skin and a thick head of red hair.

'We will fight any aliens who think they can come and take our jobs!' Jones shouted. Some in the crowd made the Nazi salute again. 'Take our white women ...' the arms went up again, 'our houses ...'

'Kill the black bastards!' came a shout from the crowd.

'The government is going to give away our land, give it to slaves who should be on the plantations or back in the jungle!'

Jones walked up and down the stage, a man possessed. As he passed the lectern he banged his fist.

'At seven p.m. today we meet at the Port of London, my brothers and sisters. Arm yourselves. Don't let the black man get the upper hand. We are doing God's work, we are doing the white man's work; we will never rest, we will never give the blacks a place to rest. We will put them back on the banana boat, put them back in the jungle. We, the white people of this land, will put those animals back in slavery.

'We did not fight against the Jews and Communism to give our land away to those inhuman bastards. Always remember ... England first!

'God bless the white people of this great land and God bless England!'

The hall erupted with terrible cries. 'Kill the niggers!' 'Destroy Communism!' 'Death to the Jews!'

CHAPTER 32

'A WHAT A COME OF WE?'

The ship's deck was crowded with people looking at the coastline of England. They were pointing at the land ... there was excitement and curiosity. Everyone was wrapped up in anything they could find to keep warm. Many of the passengers had never felt cold like this. They had never seen the mist and fog of England.

'Have you got anyone meeting you at the dock?'

'No,' said Garfield. 'The army will have coaches for the ex-West Indian soldiers. I hear that they will take anyone who has no transport to a place called Clapham South, where we will live until we find housing.'

'Yes, mi hear them a give out jobs to people when we get to forin.'

There was a lull in the conversation. It hit the group of men once again that they were heading into the unknown and they had no friends and family.

1400H

'Captain, we will be holding the ship at the Thames in two hours.'

Captain Stanley looked though his binoculars at the English coastline as the ship glided across the Channel.

'Make an announcement to the passengers that they must be packed and ready and in their cabins for 1900 hours when we will be docking. Let them know that we will be making a special announcement at 1700 hours.'

'Yes, sir.'

'Have you put the four MPs on Mr Dangle's cabin?'

'Yes, sir,' the sergeant replied. 'He will be escorted off the ship and handed over to MI5.'

'Good. Don't you take your eyes off the bastard until you hand him over.'

'Yes, sir.'

Knock, knock.

'Come in.'

'Hello, it's the ship's doctor. I am just checking that you still do not wish to visit the hospital when we dock?'

'No, thank you,' Hyacinth responded.

'Do I have the address you will be staying at?'

'I gave it to the captain.'

'I will make an appointment for you to visit the local nurse for a check-up. This will help your court case if we can present your medical records and the injuries you sustained in the attack.'

Hyacinth looked at the doctor and agreed.

'I do hope your stay in England will be a pleasant one and I will be in contact with you.'

'Thank you, doctor, for your kindness.' Just as the doctor turned to walk out the door he stopped, looked around at Hyacinth and Maria and said, with a very angry look, 'We will not let that animal get away with what he did to you ... You have my word on that.' Then he coolly closed the door.

Some of the passengers were already packed and were sitting on the deck ready to get off the ship. The soldiers kept telling them to return to their cabins and await further orders, but they continued to come out on deck. It was pure excitement that was sweeping the ship. The average age of the passengers was twenty-three years old ... many had never seen another country. The excitement was immense, their dreams were big.

'I would like to walk off this ship. I beg you, please don't put me in a wheelchair.'

Doctor Tom and Nurse Sharon were standing by Roy's bed. The doctor looked at Nurse Sharon and asked, 'What do you think, nurse? How was he at the dance last night?'

'Doctor, he was fine on his feet ... and there were no dizzy spells.'

'OK, Mr Carman,' he said, 'you can walk off the ship with the nurse into the ambulance.'

'Thank you, doctor. Thank you, Nurse Sharon.'

... *Norma* ...
1500H.
'There a rumour going around that the ship is going to dock at Tilbury Docks.'

'Where the hell is Tilbury Docks?'

'Is it in London?' I asked, and, 'How you know this?'

'Chef did tell me. Him overheard it when him take in the food into the control room,' Lucretia said, with a 'I know it all' tone.

'Them can't do that ... Many people on the ship have people waiting for them in the Port of London!'

'Well, mi just a say,' Lucretia said, leaning back on her chair on the deck of the ship.

I felt confused as Mavis sat down beside me. 'Mavis, you know about the ship not going to the Port of London?'

'No. Is this true or just some gossip? You know how this ship love a gossip.'

'Well, Chef get it from the control room ... them must know!'

'Look there, Garfield over there – he may know something.'

'Sheeee sheeee!' Lucretia made a back-a-yard sound.

'Stop that! You're not back-a-yard now, Cha ...'

'Mavis,' I said, 'can't you ask your new friend?'

'No, I can't and no, I will not,' she said in an annoyed tone.

'Hum.' I made a sound of disapproval. 'Mek mi go asks Garfield.' I got up from the deckchair and walked over to Garfield's group of men. The boys were smoking and running jokes.

'Is wha happen, Norma? You look upset.'

'Garfield, you hear that the ship will not be docking at the Port of London?'

'No, mi never hear that one ... is who tell you so?'

'Someone hear the conversation in the control room.'

'Is what the backside a gwan here?'

The group of West Indian soldiers were not happy. Some had people waiting for them at the dock.

'Norma, you is sure the person did hear this from the control room?'

'Yes, Garfield, he was giving them food when him hear them a chat.'

'A what de rass-a-gwan here? Them rass white men a mess with us ...'

The former soldiers were in no mood to hear this. They were pissed off with the way the army had treated them, pissed off with the way the white men dealt with them and pissed off with this latest news.

The mood became dark. More and more people overheard the conversation, which was getting very loud. There was a jump in the temperature despite the coldness of the air and the more people joined the conversation the more the temperature went up, until now there was a crowd of people all cussing and praying.

'Lord mi God, na let them white people tek mi to the Nazi people.'

'A what a come of we?'

'Them is a rass.'

'Just like in the war you can't trust them.'

As this was going on I took Garfield to one side. 'This could get out of hand,' I said. 'Let's calm this down. Mi and you go and see the captain. I feel he will be honest with us.'

'You tink?' Garfield said in a very untrusting way. 'You really tink?'

1530H

'That's the vice-captain over there.'

Garfield and Norma made their way over to him on the deck of the ship. 'Vice-captain, can we have a word with you?'

'How can I help?' said Hobbes.

'Is it true that the ship will be docking at Tilbury Docks not the Port of London?'

Hobbes looked stunned. He thought, 'How the hell did she find out about that?' He knew the announcement was being made at 1700H. 'Madam,' he said, 'I don't know what you are talking about.'

'Is the ship going to London?' she said again.

'Yes, the ship is going to London.' He stopped himself from saying any more. Hobbes was depending on the fact that the West Indians did not know the layout of London. Technically, he was not lying; the ship was going to London, just not the Port of London. He turned on his heel and made his way back to the captain's HQ. Norma and Garfield just looked at each other.

'You believe him?' Garfield said.

Norma replied, 'I believe he telling a half-truth.'

'Something a gwan,' Garfield said as the vice-captain made his way to the captain's HQ to let him know that the cat was out of the bag. He kept thinking as he walked down the corridor, 'How the hell did they know?'

1545H

'WHAT?'

'Who the hell told the passengers!? If I get my hands on that loudmouth! England can win a war but this ship can't keep a secret for twenty-four bloody hours! God help us!'

Captain Stanley walked out of the HQ in disgust.

The rumour went around the ship like lightning. People were stopping soldiers all over the ship, but they really did not know what was going on ...

'Just listen for the announcement at 1700 hours,' they said.

'Trevor,' shouted the captain. 'Go on the Tannoy and let the passengers know there will be an announcement at 1700 hours shipwide.'

The captain was furious. He knew this could get out of hand. He went back to his office, looked over his notes then prepared for his big speech at 1700H.

1630H
The atmosphere on the ship was getting rowdier and rowdier.

Many of the passengers were on the top deck gossiping, talking, looking at the coastline ... The former West Indian soldiers were the most vocal about the treatment 'we West Indians are receiving'; some of the passengers were just eighteen years old, and really upset by the rumour that they would not be seeing the people they knew at the docks.

'What if them kidnap me?'

'What if the white man sell me into slavery?'

'I will be left alone in London.'

A prayer group was praying about anything and anyone: 'Lord, we come to this strange land; take our hands and lead us safely home, Amen.'

Norma made her way down to the infirmary so she could hear the announcement with Roy.

Everyone on board was ready ...

The ship had a stillness about it. You could hear the throbbing of the engine; everyone stopped what they were doing ... in the kitchen, the HQ, the infirmary, the engine room, the bar. The ship became a ghost ship, just silent. But Precious's cabin was noisy. The kids wanted to get out and look at the English coastline.

'When can we go upstairs?'

'I want to look at Inglan.'

'First, it's England, not Inglan. Now you all just sit down for five minutes or you're not going on the deck till we get off the ship.'

The two youngest kids sat down, but George disobeyed Precious; he wanted to see the coastline and kept on nagging.

'SIT your backside down,' Betty said, 'before I give you a box.' He sat down and did not make a sound.

1700H

'This is your captain.

'We will be docking at 1900 hours in London. Because of the heavy use of the Port of London, the British government has ordered this ship to dock at Tilbury Docks in East London. We are fully aware that some of you may have relatives waiting for you at the Port of London docks. We will be informing your relatives that coaches will be laid on and they will be transported to the Tilbury Docks to arrive at 2100 hours.

'The British government and I myself apologise for the inconvenience ... When we dock, there will be government officials, press, film crews and the BBC taking photos as you disembark from the ship. This will be seen all over the world.

'Because of the inconvenience to you I have opened the bars for free drinks until we dock. When you hear the alarm please return to your cabin. The soldiers will help you to disembark floor by floor. It now remains for me to say, "Welcome to England from Captain Stanley and the crew".

'Over and out.'

CHAPTER 33

WE REACH?

1800H

'I will meet you in the bar. I'm going to look for Edward,' Mavis said as she walked out of the cabin with a puzzled look on her face.

The tide was rough going into the Thames Estuary ... the ship was rolling around. 'Maybe this is a warning of things to come,' Mavis thought.

Port of London ...

'KEEP ENGLAND WHITE! No blacks here!'

Mosley's followers, some still wearing the black shirts they had worn when they fought on the streets as the British Union of Fascists in the 1930s, were gathering not far from the Port of London – about 180 of them waving Union Jacks around the place. The police were out in force, also in their black uniforms with white straps on the wrist. Even with their curious 'bobbies' helmets', it was hard to make out who was who?

Some of Mosley's Blackshirt followers set up a line of men by the entry to the port. The Blackshirts could not get into the port as the police had two lines of officers and police vans ready for the protesting men and women.

'Keep the niggers out!'

'Send them back!'

The mood was ugly.

There were West Indian people arriving at the docks to be met by a mob of angry white people. As the Mosley people saw them, they shouted, 'Keep England white!' 'Go back home!' The police went up to any West Indian person walking into the port to escort them inside.

'Is what the hell a gwan here?'

'What them white people a say?'

'Please follow me,' a white police officer said to a group of West Indian people who had just arrived outside the docks.

'Officer, what is going on? We just come to meet our family.'

'Please follow me.' Five officers surrounded the Caribbean group and led them through the Mosley mob, who were shouting, spitting and throwing tins and other objects at them.

The group walked hurriedly into the port building, frightened and bemused by what was going on. As they went inside there were more West Indians sitting in the reception area of the port ... they were talking to each other. They did not know each other but they knew that this was about their black skin.

A white officer who was obviously in charge by the way the policemen reported to him and the way he was giving out orders, walked up to the group of about ninety Caribbean people.

'Can I have your attention?' The talking stopped and everyone looked over at the white policeman. 'My name is Commander Thomas. I am from Scotland Yard. I received information from the British intelligence services that we would have former members of the British Union of Fascists at the port. We have therefore taken steps to avert any situation here today ... We have been ordered to move you to a different place so you can meet your people off the ship. There are coaches waiting for you outside – if you have a car you can leave it where it is or follow us. We will be coming back with your family and friends later tonight.'

The group of West Indians all started talking at the same time.

'Where is the boat?'

'Where are you taking us?'

'Why is them white man in black shirts trying to attack us?'

All the members of the group were talking at once. The officer looked at the group, then banged his truncheon on the table. 'I am not going to answer your questions ... I am here to keep you and the passengers off the ship safe. Now you can follow my orders or you can stay right here! But if you stay here you will not meet your people ... and I will not be responsible for your safety.

'If you wish to come with us, assemble over there where the police and the army are standing.'

With that, he turned on his heel and walked away.

'What a facety man,' a woman said.

'A what the rass is going on here?'

'How you can just tell us what to do but don't tell us why?' another man said.

By this time Commander Thomas was walking towards the group of policemen and soldiers at the other side of the port. A few West Indian men were hurrying along beside him, asking him questions, which he ignored with a contemptuous look on his face. This only made the men feel more enraged. The commander stopped walking and so did the five men around him. 'I have given you the orders from my government. I will not be saying any more. The coaches will be leaving in twenty minutes.'

Then he walked off, leaving the five men even more angry. As the commander walked over to the group of policemen he said, 'I told the wogs that we are leaving in twenty minutes. I don't care who is on the coaches or who gets left behind ...'

One of the West Indian men heard him say that and shot him a cut-eye look, to which he calmly responded with a 'so what are going to do about it?' stare.

'Our last drink on board this ship,' Desmond said.

'Yes, man, we reach Babylon,' one of his fellow-soldiers said, looking around.

'There's not a lot of people at the bar.'

'Is what you expect? Them is packing and worrying, but we soldiers know better — you just pick up your tings and move forward.'

'Man, we reach?' Garfield said to his men, standing on deck of the ship. There was still a big crowd of West Indian passengers on the deck looking at Inglan for the first time. 'It so cold!' and 'It so grey?' was heard all over the ship.

The ship was slowly moving down the Thames Estuary, pulled by the tug boats, almost in slow motion, towards Tilbury Docks

... As it did this all the people on the shore were looking at this big ship full of black people looking back at them thinking the same thing they were thinking: 'Who the hell are you?'

Lord Pan and the Pan Players were playing on deck as the ship moved slowly down to the docks, which made the shipful of West Indians appear even stranger to the people on the docks. Those on shore stopped what they were doing and just stood there gaping at this ship: as far as they were concerned, these new arrivals were aliens from another planet.

The ship moved slowly down the estuary, giving the passengers time to take in the view of dockyards, poor housing, rundown buildings and bombsites from the war. This was not the view the passengers expected.

As Garfield looked at this sad view he wondered, 'What happened to the people in the bombed-out buildings? What do the people on the docks think of this ship full of black people?'

'You pack up all your belongings?'

'Yes, man.'

Just then the alarm went off. It was a pulsating sound that went all over the ship. Time to get back to the cabin.

'Man, we soon in forin.'

'Man, I'm going to pay back everyone who helped us to get out of the prison cell. Just think, we would have been lock up all the way to Inglan then sent back.'

The two men sat for a minute.

'Cha, man, we did try a thing and it never work ...'

'I don't want to stay in this dutty country. I just want to make some money then go home.'

'Look! Look! I can see Buckingham Palace!' the excited children shouted and laughed.

'Look! It over there!'

Betty and Doris looked where they were pointing.

'No, that's not the palace ... it looks like a big church.'

'Captain, we are twenty minutes from Tilbury Docks. I have sounded the alarm two times, sir.'

'Just make sure all the bars are closed and all the passengers are in their cabins.'

'Yes, sir.'

'There is something going on with the blacks on the other side of the port!' a man from the Blackshirt group shouted at Reg Jones.

'What's going on over there?' Jones said.

'I took a short cut to get here and saw coaches with some black people inside them and the army standing by!'

Jones looked around, thinking about the next move. He ran his right hand though his red hair, mulling over the new information. Jones, like his idol Mosley, was razor sharp and could work out tough mathematical problems in minutes ...

'Get me Oliver,' he said.

Off went the white boy ... Jones turned to his second-in-command. 'Find a phone box that works, Fred, and make sure you have enough coins to feed it.'

'Aye, aye.'

'Oliver, over here!'

'Yes, Reg?'

'Oliver, your father works on the docks?'

'Yes, he's worked on most of the docks in London.' 'I want you to go with Fred and phone your dad – ask him if they have a ship coming in today that was not planned? Hurry up, boyo.'

Oliver and Fred like the wind to the phone box.

'Where is the colour in this country?' Lucretia said, looking through the window. 'Why is there smoke coming out of that house? Is it on fire?' Them must have a lot of factory in London – look at all that smoke. Look – the house are joined together!'

Norma kept looking out the window saying nothing. B-o-y, the white people looked so white ...

Lucretia peered at that small boat next to the ship. 'Is what it think it is doing with this big ship? Why them a throw out the ropes to the little boats?'

'Mr Jones,' said an out-of-breath Oliver, 'my dad said there is a ship coming in at Tilbury Docks where he's working in about forty-five minutes. I asked him if it is the banana boat and he thinks it is as there is no name on the docking papers. They only do that when they're trying to keep a ship secret.'

'Right,' Jones said. He jumped up on his soap box. 'Listen, men,' he bawled. 'The government is trying to trick us ... they're moving the wogs over to Tilbury Docks!

'Oliver, take about a hundred men over to Tilbury. I'll meet you there. The rest of you brave lads stay here – and hold the ground. Don't let any wogs into the docks. Do whatever it takes to stop them. We will attack the Tilbury Docks. All the lads over here follow me, the rest stay here. Remember: England first!'

With that, there was a melee of Blackshirts going in different directions, cars starting, men jumping on the backs of lorries, lads getting into small cars, some of them holding the Union Jack: they all lined up at the entry to the Port of London.

Jones leapt into a Wolseley car to lead the way. He stuck his head out the window. 'For England!' he shouted. The rest of the mob looked on as Jones and his posse went on the hunt.

'The tugboats are guiding the ship into Tilbury Docks. Everything is looking good,' the vice-captain said.

'Prepare the soldiers on every deck … I will give the order when we are safely in the docks. All passengers remain in their cabins until further notice.'

'Is this the quickest way to Tilbury Docks?' Jones said to the driver.

'We can cut out the traffic this way and come up by the back of the docks, guvnor.'

Jones looked behind to see a line of cars and trucks following the Wolseley, running red lights, overtaking slower vehicles, screaming 'England for the English!' at passers-by.

1900H

'Sir, the docking has been successful. The ropes are secure and the ramps are now being put in place.'

'Vice-captain Hobbes, start disembarkation from the ship,' the captain said in his commanding way.

Hobbes made the announcement over the ship's Tannoy. 'Attention, attention. The ship has docked. We will be disembarking floor by floor in the next thirty minutes. Please stay in your cabin until the soldiers call you.'

'How far is it from here?'

Jones's driver was getting angry with all the questions. Born and raised in the docklands, he knew every back street.

'Less than ten minutes, guv.'

'Well done, boyo, well done ... We will get there before the wogs, so yourselves,' he told the men in his car. 'We are going to war.'

'Doctor, I just looked on the docks. The ambulances are standing by for the injured men and the deceased.'

Roy heard this and said, 'I can walk out to the ambulance.'

The soldiers came into the infirmary to inform the doctor, 'Your patients will be among the first to be disembarking from the ship. Before them we will be taking off the dead first.'

Knock, knock.

Mr Dangle's door slowly opened. Dangle was seemingly completely at ease, a cravat around his neck, an expensive overcoat resting on the shoulders of his well-tailored suit, holding a crocodile-skin suitcase.

'You will be escorted off the ship by the MPs and handed over to MI5.'

'It's about bloody time. I will be reporting the captain to your government. His treatment of me has been disgusting and your foul food gave me diarrhoea.'

The MPs just looked at him.

'Do you have all your belongings?' a soldier said calmly.

Dangle was about to say something negative when he caught the look on the faces of the four very hefty MPs.

'Let's just go,' Dangle said in his arrogant way.

Norma and Lucretia stepped out of their cabin. They were walking down to the infirmary to say goodbye to Roy. As they got to the end of the corridor a soldier stopped them.

'Please remain in your cabin until we call you.'

'My cousin was in the shooting. I want to say goodbye before he is taken to hospital,' Norma said.

The soldier looked at her with suspicion.

'Please follow me,' he said. 'Only you can come with me. You can meet your friend in the port.'

Lucretia looked at Norma. 'See you on the deck,' she said.

'Captain, the gangway is down and we are ready to disembark the passengers,' Vice-captain Hobbes said.

'Please can you tell the Pan Players to stop playing and to get ready to disembark.'

'I must say, sir, it was a nice way to enter the docks ... it is a very catchy song,' Hobbes said.

'England is the place for me,' he sang. 'England is where...'

Captain Stanley gave his vice-captain a stern look that said 'I just want to get off this ship'.

'Yes, sir, I'm on my way,' Hobbes said, as he hurried off.

'Just around this bend and we will be here,' the driver said.

Jones looked round to see more than fifteen cars and vans still behind them.

'Where should I stop, guvnor?'

Jones saw the big ship coming into view.

'Right over there.'

The car pulled up on the dock. There were policemen and soldiers waiting, but that did not stop Jones and his thugs. All the Mosley supporters' cars and vans stopped together, all the doors opened and all the protestors, including many Blackshirts, fell out of the vehicles with their Union Jack flags.

'England for white people!'

'No blacks!'

'No blacks!'

'Kill the blacks!'

The Blackshirts became a mob walking behind Jones holding a Union Jack and heading towards the ship. There was a barrier where the policemen were standing. The Mosley Blackshirts went up to the police line and shouted their racist slogans. The police stood firm. The Blackshirts were outnumbered five to one, plus soldiers were standing behind the police line.

Jones took in what was happening and turned to his followers, shouting: 'We may be outnumbered but we will make the loudest noise that ALL of England will hear …'

'Keep England white!'

'Keep England white!'

'Keep England white!'

The soldiers entered the infirmary to take the injured off the ship. Roy was fully clothed and sitting on his bed. The rest of the injured were on hospital stretchers.

The loud voices of the protestors could be heard all over the ship. The West Indian passengers looked out of their portholes to see a mass of white men in black uniforms shouting, 'Blacks go home!' and other white men in black uniforms with pointed helmets and white straps on their arms holding back the men dressed all in black. It was a confusing, and terrifying, sight.

'Aunty, why are there white people fighting each other outside?'

Precious heard the noise and looked out. She was not happy with what was happening. At the same time there was a knock at the cabin door. A soldier's voice said, 'Your floor is disembarking. Make your way to the exit.'

'Go to the phone box,' Jones said in a military voice. 'Ring this number.' He handed the phone number to his lieutenant, Ernie Jacks. 'One of our men is standing by the phone box. Tell him to send all the men to Tilbury Docks. NOW.'

'Mr Carman, you sure you can get up the stairs?'
'Yes, woman. Mi is walking off this ship the same way mi come on board.'

As he and the nurse got to the top deck they encountered a small group of passengers standing by the stairs taking photos. Roy stopped by the stairs.

'Can I and my friends take a photo with you all?'
'Man, come over here.'

Norma and Lucretia who had waited for them on deck and Roy stood by the bottom of the stairs. He gave his walking sticks to the nurse and leant on Norma. Behind him was a group of people on the stairs, some kneeling while others were standing around them.

With Roy and Norma in the front of the group the photographer Mr Burton shouted, 'Hold that pose ... We reach what a backside this.'

The members of the group laughed out loud as they were not expecting him to say that and Mr Burton took the photo when everyone was laughing.

'Please send me a copy of this photo,' Norma said. 'Here my address.'

It was a weird moment. With the backdrop of Mosley's followers and their raucous voices floating from the docks – 'Blacks go home!' 'Blacks go home!'– Norma and her group prepared to leave the ship, excitement mixed with fear.

The BBC and Pathé film crews were filming the big ship docking at Tilbury. This film would be used to recruit more people from the West Indies. Just as they started filming, the Mosley Blackshirt mob was rushing towards the police line yelling racist chants. But they were being held well back from the ship.

The demobbed West Indian soldiers were starting to come off the ship with the injured … while the dead were taken off out of sight of the camera. The film crew rushed over to record the confrontation, setting up their cameras. Jones, like Mosley a lover of any type of publicity, made sure his face was in front of the cameras telling the camera crew 'England for the English! We are doing this for the British people … for YOU!' he said as he looked into the camera.

*

What could the MI5 officers be saying to a mysterious man in a brown suit and trilby hat, smoking a cigarette and holding a notepad in his hand?

'When all the West Indians get off the ship and have reported into the Port Authority I want all the film that was taken today that includes the Pathé films and the BBC. If anyone questions you, say it's a matter of national security, and that will get the film back once the government have cleared it for viewing. If they do not give you all the film, then use force. No one is to see this mess.'

Into this mad scene came the five coaches from the Port of London with the relatives and friends of the West Indians on board the ship. Somehow Mosley's men had got there before them. As the coaches pulled up at this hate-filled mob of white people, the Blackshirts saw the black faces looking down from the coaches and went into a frenzy, hitting the coaches, banging, kicking, spitting ... This was not the welcome the people on the coaches were expecting. They were terrified! Men were shielding their women and children. They just did not understand why there was so much hate ...

'Everyone ready? It time to go.' Precious looked around one last time at the cabin that had been home for two weeks. She took the hand of George and thought of the lesson she had learned about herself.

'Aunty Precious, what that noise?'

'I don't know.'

'Look! Look over there!'

As Precious got to the top side of the ship she looked over the side to see the white mob in the distance shouting.

'Aunty? Aunty! There are film people there!'

Precious looked at the film crew.

'Now, everyone listen!' The group stopped. Betty and Doris wondered what was up now? 'There are film people on the docks. The film may be shown back home so I want you to look nice. Keep smiling and say nothing, OK?'

'OK,' everyone said. 'OK.'

... *Mavis* ...

As Lucretia and I came down the gangway from the ship holding our grips and bags, we were wearing our Sunday best. We had thought back in the cabin that we would honour Grandma by wearing her Sunday hats she gave us.

Looking at Lucretia acting like a film star, playing up to the cameramen filming us coming down the gangway, made me love her more. We could feel the bitterly cold English weather going through our clothes ... we were holding onto our hats before the wind swept them away ... It was all too much to take in.

In front of us Lord Pan was being interviewed by that unpleasant man from the *Daily Express* and by the BBC TV. Poor Lord Pan barely had a chance to feel the land beneath his feet before a microphone was shoved in his face. He was snappily dressed in his light blue suit and brown trilby hat ... he looked the part. Lucretia and I stopped to look at the BBC reporter asking him to sing the song they had heard as the ship was docking. Lord Pan could not let this moment go ... he knew all the people back home would be seeing him on the newsreels as a star in England.

'L-o-n-don we soon come
L-o-n-don mi say mi soon come
King you did invite us to the Mother-land
And we did come with friendly hands
L-o-n-don we soon come ...'

'Lord, look Pan him? Him feel say him is a big star now,' Lucretia said as everyone stopped to look at Lord Pan performing at the bottom of the walkway.

'What a way it cold!' Lucretia said. 'Mi need a coat.'

'We have to look good for the cameras,' I said, holding onto my hat. As we stepped across the docks there was a tall white man in a blue uniform taking names and pointing where to go. No smile or eye contact, just orders ... 'You go that way', 'You over there.'

Lucretia sucked her teeth at him. Just then Norma walked over.

'There you are,' I said.

'Roy is on the way to hospital. Did you find our bags?'

'Not yet.'

'OK. Keep looking.'

There were so many people just sitting around with bags; they were all waiting to be moved to the Port of London. Some people just picked up their bags and left. There was a constant refrain of 'Uncle, Aunty, Mother, Father, Brother, Sister' ... voices of people meeting each other. Joyful sounds.

The noise from the Blackshirts mob kept coming. Everyone was looking at the angry white men at the entrance of the docks making a lot of noise and waving the Union Jack.

'Chef, I'm over here.'

Lucretia gave him a hug.

'You get all your things?' he said.

'Mi still looking for one grip and a bag ... Them soldier-man just fling the bags on the dockside. NO RESPECT.'

'You have mi address?'

'Yes, Chef – I will write you once we reach the new place we is staying in.'

'I is getting a lift from one of the white boys from the kitchen. Talk soon.' Chef gave her one last hug then walked out of the docks in his round hat, and beige suit with his kipper tie of many colours.

'This cat and mouse game with those Blackshirts is getting to me,' the Scotland Yard commander said to the army officer.

The army officer replied: 'What time are moving them back to the Port of London?'

'In about an hour. We've got more coaches coming and some of the West Indians are going off with their families. All this trouble for a bunch of bloody wogs!'

The army man looked at the commander and said, 'One of those "wogs" as you called them saved my life on the battlefield.' He gave the commander a nasty look and walked off.

As the commander walked over to the barrier where they were holding back the Blackshirts there was a shout. 'Over there!'

The commander looked across to see about ten Blackshirts who had somehow got past the army and police and were rushing towards a group of West Indian people with children. But just as the Blackshirts were about to attack them, out of nowhere came a group of ex-West Indian soldiers in full uniform. They tackled the Blackshirts to the ground, knocking two of them out and flooring the rest before the police came over to help.

Everyone stopped what they were doing to take in this scene of black soldiers, Blackshirts and black-uniformed policemen all mixed up. The Blackshirts were all arrested and the West Indian soldiers received a round of applause from the crowd.

Garfield looked at his fellow-soldiers and said, 'We didn't fight in a war to let some white boys push us around.' Then he walked over to the men in black shirts, putting his face right up to the white faces. 'Same knife kill sheep, kill goat ... Never you mess with mi people.'

'What a carry on, and we not here two minutes ... Thank the Lord for our West Indians soldiers ... Mi never see any white police or army come to help us.'

'We never come this far to get box down by some man mi don't know,' Betty said out loud to anyone.

'Betty, Betty ... that's our bags over there,' Precious said as she moved over to the mountain of suitcases.

'Precious, Precious!' A voice came from out of the crowd. 'Precious, Precious!'

'Mother!' Precious screamed. 'MOTHER!'

Precious's mother ran up to the group, and embraced her daughter. She gave the kids a long, long hug.

'Come, come, you are in England now ... you're safe with me. You all look so well!'

'Mum, what's going on with them English people over there? Why are they so angry?'

'Don't you worry about them nasty people. Just get all the bags together so we can get on the coaches back to London.'

Captain Stanley was looking down from the top of the ship at all the coming and going below him.

'I must say I will miss these people,' he said to himself. Then he turned to Vice-captain Hobbes. 'Trevor, did the MP and MI5 pick up that animal?'

'Yes, sir.'

'Thank God.'

'All the patients and the dead have been removed, sir.'

'Very good, let's go ... I want to get home.'

'Look over there! It Uncle Winston!' Norma ran over to him. 'Uncle Winston, it's mi, Norma!'

'What a way you grow! You is a big woman now. Your mother did say to meet you at the port, but them move us to here. Where is your bags?'

'Over here. Come, Uncle, come and meet my friends Lucretia and Mavis. This is my Uncle Winston.'

'Is this all your bags?'

'No, Uncle, I can't find mi other grip.'

As Norma went off into the crowd Lucretia asked Mavis, 'So when is you going to meet your white soldier-man?'

'Why you need to know? You is so noseeeey ... We will be meeting in two weeks in London outside Victoria station. We will be spending the weekend together.'

'Well, mi hope you na carrying-belly.'

'Lucretia, you're so out of order,' Mavis said, with a strange look on her face.

'Garfield,' Norma shouted over the noise of people looking for their luggage and the background roar of Mosley Blackshirts outside the docks.

Garfield looked around. 'Norma, mi soon come ...' He kept looking for his grip. 'Found it!' He made his way over to Norma who had just found her own bag.

'Lord, it cold!' she shivered.

'Yes, man ...'

'You never give mi your address,' Norma said.

'Well, I'm not sure where I will end up. I know I'm going to a place called Clapham South to some army air raid shelters ... after that I don't know. The army is letting me know.'

'OK. I'm staying at my Uncle Winston's house in Balham. I don't know how far that is from Clapham South. You just ask anyone for Uncle Winston you will find me.'

'Yes, sister, see you again.'

'Miss Hyacinth,' the soldier said, 'you must go in this car. They are taking you to a hospital for a check-up, then you can go home.'

'Nobody told me about this. I'm meeting my man when I get off the ship. He will be waiting there with my coat, gloves and hat. I'm not going to no hospital and they can't make me. Have you got your bags?' she said to Maria.

'Yes.'

'Then let's go.' Hyacinth walked past the soldier, who just looked at her, then moved away. He was in no mood to stop a West Indian woman who wanted to get off the ship.

As she came down the gangway, standing at the bottom was a man she recognised, a man she had dreamed about, a man she had let down but truly loved, and she was not going to let anything get in the way of that love. A light-skinned, well-dressed man in a sharp dark-blue suit with a yellow and blue tie and the shiniest shoes you had ever seen opened his arms to welcome her onto the docks.

'Carlton!' she shouted.

'Hyacinth, me sweet woman!' he said with a Bajan accent as they hugged. He gave her one big kiss that went on and on and on. When she finally freed her mouth from his, he held open a brown coat with a fox-fur collar so Hyacinth could put it on, then he gave her the white hat with blue flowers woven into it and of course the white gloves. Just the way Hyacinth had dreamt it would be. Maria looked at the love Hyacinth had for this man ... she hoped more than anything that Hyacinth could put what happened behind her and start a new life with this fine-looking man. All the women on the port were looking at Carlton ...

'Now that's how you meet a woman,' Maria said to the other women on the port side looking at this romantic welcome. 'Makes you wish you had someone like that waiting for you.'

'Come, my dear, let's go,' he said.

'Carlton, my friend Maria is coming with us.'

'Yes, my woman.' With that he touched his trilby in the direction of Maria and said, 'This way, ladies.'

People from the ship were meeting their friends and relatives. There was the sound of happy laughter, crying, the sight of people hugging, smiling, just happy to get off that ship and be on dry land at last. Soon the sound of the Mosley Blackshirts was forgotten among the happy faces of West Indian people.

'How was the journey?'

'Mother, so much happened. It was an adventure. Have you heard from Daddy? Is he all right?'

'Yes, he is.'

Betty and Doris asked, 'How are our families?'

'I got a telegram from Father,' she said. 'Airmail letters should be coming to England any day soon for all of you.'

'Can we go now?' the children all said. 'We want to see the King.'

Precious looked at them and said to her mother, 'You see how we had to put up with dem bad, bad pickney ...'

Everyone laughed.

'Welcome to England,' said Precious's mother.

As Norma, Lucretia and Mavis put their grips, boxes and bags into Uncle Winston's blue Austin Cambridge car, Norma looked back at the Tilbury port with its crowds of angry white people and joyful West Indians. The white people's faces were red, angry and sad. Norma stopped hearing their voices … she just saw their ugly faces.

'What have we come to, Uncle?'

He looked at them and hurried them into his car. He had been living in England for many years and knew that look on the white people's faces. He had lived with it and run from it over the years. He just wanted to protect his family. As he looked at the angry white faces of the Mosley supporters he thought, 'Let the women put down them things in mi car before them see the REAL England.'

Norma, Mavis and Lucretia looked out of the car window as they moved out of the Tilbury Docks, at the crowds of people they had met and might never see again. Lucretia, sitting in the back seat with Norma, was mystified by the houses.

'Why them houses link up? Them all have smoke coming out of them and everywhere is all brown.'

Norma looked out of the window on her side of the car, not paying any-mind to Lucretia. 'It's so grey, it's not what I heard about in Jamaica. I don't see no "street paved with gold"?'

'The people look so grey and down,' Mavis said, sitting next to Uncle.

Uncle's car made its way down to New Cross and up to Camberwell. The car's occupants were silent. Norma, Mavis and Lucretia could not take in what they were seeing. It was London after the bombing. Hitler had inflicted serious damage on it. The car went past many bombsites. Camberwell and Brixton – both a bombsite.

'Uncle, is where we is going?' Lucretia asked.

He said, 'The Nazis did do a good job on London, but we did survive. There is a lot of work here, you can better yourself and help your family back home.'

'Uncle, you was here when them drop the bomb?' Lucretia asked.

'Yes, mi child, many of us West Indians were here from the First World War. Them people don't tell you about that, do they? Them want you to think we Caribbean people did not fight in the two wars. Them is damn blasted liard... many of us did dead in them two wars and the same white people want to now kill us in the same country we did fight for, and lots of us dead for what – what a rass something this is.'

Lucretia looked at Uncle who had hurt all over his face. He did not look at her, just at the road in front of him. They all knew not to say anything to this elder, but they all just kept looking at a very grey and wet London.

Norma stared out at the disappointing view. 'This was not the colourful image I had keep in my head when I read the advert about England,' she thought.

'Five years,' she thought as a tear ran down her face.

MY STORY

In 2011 I was at a wake, following the funeral of Mr E Burton – a very old friend of my late father. Sitting in the Burton family's front room, taking in the wonderful colours of the Windrush furniture and ornaments, a black-and-white photo caught my eye. It showed a group of young Caribbean people in their Sunday best on the deck of a ship, some perched on the stairs, others gathered around the foot of the steps. All smiling and laughing, posing for the camera. Examining the faces in the photo I saw a group of very young people, full of hope and wonder.

I asked members of the Burton family whether their dad was in the photo. I couldn't recognise him. His daughter told me: 'He was the one taking the photo. It was on the deck of the *Windrush* ship the day before it landed in England.'

That photo kept pulling me back time and time again. I felt as if I was there on the ship, in the 1940s, with these young people. This was a different era. This was a new beginning for the passengers. It was a time when Caribbean people were called West Indians ... or 'coloured' ... or 'wogs', or even worse. My parents would often tell us kids stories about their experiences in England in the 1940s and '50s. As I got older and 'had sense' the stories became more graphic – and more upsetting.

The best stories about the old days would come tumbling out when the Wray & Nephew rum or Guinness was flowing and they forgot we were in the room. 'Come out, big-people talking,' sounded the loud voice of my father when the worst stories were falling out of all the intoxicated mouths of Dad's friends sitting in the front room at our home in Cavendish Road, South London.

For many years after the funeral I was a visitor to the Burton family house and every time, somehow, I ended up in front of this photo wondering what the young people's stories were, what had become of this youthful group who didn't have Google, satnavs or any modern tools to work out where they were going or what it would be like. They had nothing more than 'hear-say' about the 'streets of London being paved with gold'.

Most West Indians coming to England, 'the Mother Country', just had the address of a relative or family friend in England on a piece of paper and a grip that contained all their worldly possessions. When I look back at that 'Windrush Generation' I see pioneers and adventurers, people who were brave or naïve – or both. The 'welcome' they received in the UK was not warm, like the days they were used to back home. Like the English weather, it was cold and many got 'frost bites' from the people of England.

This novel consists of stories I heard from elders in my family and from the Windrush generation who were passengers on the HMT *Empire Windrush* and the many other ships that came to England from 1948 up into the '60s.

GLOSSARY

£28.10s 0d – old money

A box – slap to the head
A-gwan – happening
A-a wa de bloodclaat a gwan – what is happening here
Almshouse – prison
Backside, battam, batty – your bottom
Backside – about yourself
Bayed – Wash your body
Bear-face-liad – a clear liar
Bloodclaat – (bad word) bloody hard time
Bloodclaat ting – bad word
Boorya – boy
Bosey-man – full of yourself
Briefs – underpants
Bruk – Broke (no money)
Bumboclaat – Caribbean (swear) word
Bust his backside – beat him up
Bwoy – boy
Coo-coo-maker stick – a wooden stick

Coon – black person
Cuss – to say bad words
Cuss-word – bad swear word
Cut him/her eye – to give a very bad look at someone
Cyaan buy puss inna bag! – Look before you buy
Dem – them
de rass out – the hell out
Drop foot – dance
Dutty – dirty
Eff Gad spar mi life – If God spares my life
Enuff – enough
Every bench has a batty – There's someone for everyone
Every hoe have dem stik a bush – There's someone out there for everyone
Faas wid me – you're trying to play with me
Face-tee/facety – cheeky
Fast with me – you're trying to play with me
Forin – aboard
Gaan from yaad – away from the island
Gwan – go away
God spear life – if God spares me
Gon – me going
Gwan a yu yard – go home
Guinep – a (Caribbean) sweet fruit
Gweh – go away
Her eaise too hard – she's not listening
Him eaise haad – he's not listening/you're not listening
Him little but him talawa – small but strong
Hol-eep – a lot of people
Hush yuh mout – Be quiet
Hush-up – be quiet

Ice scrapings from their wooded-cart – a Caribbean drink made from scrapings from a block of ice and juices, sold by the roadside
If God-spar-life – if God will spare my life
If you cyah hear you must feel… – if you don't listen you will feel it
Inglan – England
Inna de morrows – see you later
JA – Jamaica
Liard – lies
Madda – mother
Mawga – skinny
Me foot 'a-hot-mi' – my feet are tired
Mi gaan – am gone, am going
Noh-ramp – not playing
Nine night – for nine nights after someone dies you celebrate their life
Nuff – enough
Noh buy puss inna bag – look before you buy
Not mawga – not skinny
Nr-tek-me-yet – has not taken me
Nuh badda mi – don't bother me
Look pon mi – look at me
Pass – died
Pickney – kids
Play fool fi ketch wise – act like a fool to catch a wise person
Pum Pum – vagina
Rassclaat – very bad swearword
Ruff neck – rough looking
Same knife kill sheep kill goat – I will use this knife on you

See with them – you allow it
Sheeee sheeee – sucking of teeth
Shuffle – a form of dance when you shuffle your feet, sometimes on one leg
Si wid dem – you allow it
Still tongue keep good head – keep your mouth shut
Stout – well built
Teef – thief
Teif – cheating
The pickney dem – the children
The rass out – the hell out
Them will be bruk them – they will be poor
Tin and tin – your belongings
Toasting – talking over the record
Vex – upset
We na ramp – we are not messing around
Wha-gwaan, whaap'm – what's happening
what sweet you so – what made you feel good
Wutless – no good/ useless person
Wha sweet a mout' hat a belly – you talk very well, you get my attention
Wul heap or nuf – a lot

ACKNOWLEDGEMENTS

Firstly thank you to my mother Mrs Olga Fairweather for all the stories you told me over the years... I saw the laughter and pain in your eyes.

My children Narada, Omari, Siphiweh... learn from your elders.
My grandchildren Cam'ron and Laila... your elders have open the door?

My sisters and brothers: George, Doris, Roy, Trover, Debbie, Paul, Sharon... what adventures and fun we had at Cavendish Road.

All my favourite nieces and nephews... love you all.

My Windrush pioneers Uncle Lloyd, Auntie Linda, Auntie Dorothy, Auntie Vie, Mr E Burton and Mr Bell resting with the ancestors... I miss your stories.

To Rosy Burton who put up with me and this novel for a long time and was the first person to read it and till me 'it made me laugh and cry' … that got me to the end of the book.

Naomi & Nyle Burton… you have strong ancestors, enjoy your youth.

A big thank you to my publisher, the wonderful and unstoppable Rosemarie Hudson who never stop believing in my stories… 'you little but you Talawa'.

The HopeRoad marketing and design team… the baddies in the business. Special thank you to James Nunn for your wonderfully designed cover - you sure you're not Jamaican?

Doretha and Nicky who let me write in the sunshine on their veranda at their beautiful home in Tobago… get the rum out 'mi soon come'.

To my cool editor Charles Phillips, who 'Got It' from the start and guided me with patience… I got a bottle of rum waiting for you.

A special thank you to the members of The Balham And Tooting Sports And Social Club (the oldest Caribbean social club owned by its members in the UK) and the Caribbean ex-servicemen and women who told me many funny and sad stories from 'back in the day' over a glass of Guinness punch… Some of the true Windrush pioneers.

Mary Clemmey… Thank you for your friendship, guidance and wise words.

Archbishop Desmond Tutu Resting with the ancestors... When you meet a special person it leaves an echo on your soul... They were wonderful London events.

Yvonne Baillie... Thank you for your support and honest feedback... how is your garden growing?

Rudolph Walker OBE CBE – You always make time for me wherever you are in the world.

Brenda Emmanus OBE – What a journey we have been on... thank you for always being there.

Terry McMillian We worked together when we were both just starting our journeys... What fun we had.

Dr Maya Angelou Resting with the ancestors... you believed in me from the moment we met... we showed them?

Iyanla Vanzant... Neal's Yard, Caribbean food, and laughter lots of laughter... Beloved.

Junior Giscombe... What fun we had living on Cavendish Road and being in Atlantis.

Clive Francis... We have worked together for over 26 years... your artwork still surprises and pleases me.

Patrick Vernon OBE Windrush campaigner, keep going, the sun is coming over the hill... thank you for your support.

Yvonne Wilks-O'Grady You have always believed in me... I will take the Jerk, you get the rum, see you in Jamaica.

Ray Shell, we have come a long way together... now get that *Iced* film made.

Beverley De-Gale OBE and Orin Lewis OBE... I am proud and honoured to have laughed with your wonderful son Daniel... keep the ACLT going, you are saving lives.

To the many authors I have had the privilege to work with and introduced to the world... I now know how it feels to be the front person.

To all my friends (you know who you are), thank you for your friendship over the years... enjoy the book.

To all the young Caribbean and African pioneers who made a new life in a hostile country with just an address on a piece of paper, a grip and hope...lots of hope.

Thank you for reading our story.
TF